Carl Ullmann, Sophia Taylor

The sinlessness of Jesus

An Evidence for Christianity

Carl Ullmann, Sophia Taylor

The sinlessness of Jesus
An Evidence for Christianity

ISBN/EAN: 9783337166502

Printed in Europe, USA, Canada, Australia, Japan

Cover: Foto ©ninafisch / pixelio.de

More available books at **www.hansebooks.com**

THE SINLESSNESS OF JESUS:

AN EVIDENCE FOR CHRISTIANITY.

BY

CARL ULLMANN, D.D.

Translated from the Seventh Altered and Enlarged Edition

BY

SOPHIA TAYLOR.

EDINBURGH:
T. & T. CLARK, 38, GEORGE STREET.
MDCCCLXX.

PRINTED BY MURRAY AND GIBB,

FOR

T. & T. CLARK, EDINBURGH.

LONDON, . . . HAMILTON, ADAMS, AND CO.
DUBLIN, . . JOHN ROBERTSON AND CO.

ADVERTISEMENT.

THE little work now offered to the public has but gradually attained its present form. Its substance first appeared as an essay in the *Studien und Kritiken* for 1828, since which time it has undergone many alterations, and been enlarged by various additions in the successive editions which have been called for.

In his preface to the sixth edition (1853), the author says that he was first led to publish this treatise in a separate form, from the desire of showing to others the way by which he had himself been brought to a living belief in Christianity, hoping thereby to assist his own hearers, and younger theologians in general, in attaining a firmer foundation for their faith. The work, however, finding much acceptance beyond the circle for which it was chiefly intended, and new editions being repeatedly demanded, much new matter was added to meet the requirements made by the theological movements of the period, and several sections were rewritten.

Of the present seventh edition, Dr. Ullmann remarks that he has for some years delayed responding to the call made for it, because he could neither feel satisfied to reprint it with merely unimportant corrections, nor find time for such a thorough recasting of the whole as he felt desirable. This task has now at last been accomplished. In executing it, the author says that it has been his endeavour, first, to give, in a more condensed form, such matter as he has retained from former editions, and then so to combine with this those new portions—of which some have been derived from the works which have appeared during the last ten years, while others are the result of his own more thorough investigation and mature consideration of his subject—that the organic connection of the whole may be everywhere maintained. By this process about two-thirds of the sixth edition have been either rewritten or are entirely new, while the rest has received minor corrections and alterations. The present translation retains such passages of the former (by the Rev. R. C. L. Brown) as have been left unaltered by the author, and embodies his corrections and additions.

'Amidst the various struggles which the Church has to pass through,' says the author, 'I am fully persuaded that, if its health and vigour are to be maintained, the silent labours of theology must not be omitted. And I am as certain—nay, I am more deeply penetrated with the truth—that as in every age, so also in our own, the first and chief concern is to lead souls to Christ, to implant Him and His salvation in the hearts of men. If the work here offered may, in the midst of the turmoils of these times, contribute, in ever so small a degree, to accomplish this most vital duty of theology, it will not have failed in the purpose for which it has been written.'

FROM THE

PREFACE TO THE SIXTH EDITION.

WHEN I first reprinted the present treatise in a separate form from the *theol. Stud. und Krit.*, it was specially designed for the use of my own pupils and of young theologians in general. I desired to point out to them the way in which I had myself been led to a vital interest in Christianity, and hoped thus to contribute to the establishment of their faith, to encourage them in their studies, and to increase their delight in their high and holy calling. Nor have my hopes been disappointed. But besides the circle for which it was at first designed, this little work has passed into the hands of both theological and general readers, and has gained such acceptance that repeated editions have been necessary.

In preparing this new edition, it was impossible to omit noticing, either to refute or to agree with them, the various theories advanced by the theological movements which have meanwhile taken place. And how varied and eventful has been our experience in this respect since 1828! At the same time, it was also necessary to pay due attention to, and to profit by, whatever might have been said on our subject by theological contemporaries. Thus matter has gradually accumulated, till what was at first but an article of moderate compass, has become a complete and sizeable volume.

The demand for a new edition has given me the opportunity of strictly revising the whole. In doing this—I will frankly own — I became so fully, and in some instances painfully, sensible of the incomplete state of the work, that I could not possibly suffer it again to appear before the public in a state which, though altered as to certain details, was, as a whole, the same as heretofore. The friendly reception accorded to it—but, above all, the great importance of the subject treated on—made it incumbent upon me to remodel the work, a labour which I have been enabled to accomplish.

In doing this, I found myself obliged to give an entirely new form to whole sections, and to endeavour, by copious additions and corrections, to improve and complete those parts which I have allowed to remain essentially unaltered.

The parts which have undergone a complete process of recasting are, besides the Introduction, chiefly the following:—the chapters and sections on Sin, on Sinlessness, on the Gospel Portraiture and Self-testimony of Jesus; on the Proofs of the Sinlessness of Jesus furnished by the effects of Christianity; on the narrative of the Temptation; and especially the whole of the Fourth Part, which treats of the inferences to be drawn from the Sinlessness of Jesus. These portions I desire most to commend to the reader's investigation, since it is with respect to them that I cherish the hope of receiving the assistance of either a correction, an expansion, or a refutation of my opinions.

It is not for me to say whether, amidst the present constellation of devotional and theological works, this little book will find the interest formerly accorded to it. The strife of parties, their internal and external contests,—some really necessary, some provoked by violence,—have turned attention to other subjects. Besides, many at the present day, even among my younger contemporaries, have so exclusively surrendered themselves to the forms of a ready-made dogmatism—whether the dogmatism of faith or the dogmatism of unbelief—as to reject at once all argument and investigation, some because they will not admit the need or benefit of furnishing fresh proofs of the faith, others because they will have nothing to do with faith itself.

But if I feel uncertain in this respect, there is another in which I feel no kind of doubt. I am certain that, if in the midst of all this contention the health and vigour of the Christian Church is to be maintained, the silent labours of theology must not be intermitted. And I am as certain—nay, far more deeply penetrated with the certainty—that as in all times, so also in our own, the first and essential thing is to bring souls to Christ, to implant Him and His salvation in the hearts of men. If this treatise may subserve this, the highest object of theology, and contribute to effect it, in ever so small a degree, its aim will not be unaccomplished.

HEIDELBERG, *March* 15, 1853.

PREFACE TO THE SEVENTH EDITION.

A NEW edition of this book has now for some years been required; but, notwithstanding the representations of its publisher, I could neither find time for such a recompilation as I felt necessary, nor consent to a mere reprint, with detached and unimportant corrections. At first, my official engagements forbade such an undertaking; and subsequently, physical ailments interposed to prevent any continuous labour. Thus I have been unable till now to complete such improvements as might allow me to offer this new edition to the public; and I can only wish that the many interruptions amidst which this little work has been brought to its present state, may be as little perceptible as possible in my execution of the task.

In the present edition my efforts have chiefly been directed to give a more concise and distinct form to those portions which I have retained from former editions, and at the same time to combine with this such new matter as seemed desirable, whether from the works of others, or from the results of my own further investigation of the subject during the last ten years. I hope this has been done in such a manner as nowhere to interfere with the organic connection of the whole. It has been my aim that the book, while losing none of its essential contents, should, in spite of the addition of new elements, be at once more brief and more lucid, and, above all, that its fundamental thought should be more clearly developed and more conclusively argued.

How far this may have been attained, it is not for me, but for intelligent readers, to determine.

My wishes for its success naturally accompany the work in its present, as in its former state; yet I do not allow myself to cherish any sanguine hopes with respect to non-theological readers. I am well convinced, indeed, that there are among these many who will not give up the name of Christians, and who will consent to a Christianity which accommodates itself with but very little scruple to the humanitarian notions of the age. But I see, too, that matters take quite a different turn when Christianity appears, not perhaps as a mere dogmatical system, but in the simple and unadulterated form in which it was delivered to the world by its Founder and first confessors, and especially when it advances those great and deep-reaching moral claims which are absolutely inseparable from its very nature. A willingness to receive it in this form involves more than a wish just to maintain an amicable relation thereto; it implies a mind earnestly striving after eternal happiness,—a mind estimating the invisible inheritance above all visible possessions, and therefore capable of the greatest sacrifices, especially the sacrifice of self, for its attainment; in short, it implies the felt need of salvation.

That the number of such earnest seekers is in our days a large, or even an increasing one, I cannot, so far as my acquaintance with the religious and intellectual condition of the age extends, persuade myself. And since this treatise, though based only upon the general principles of morality, has nevertheless no other end in view than the advocacy of that primitive and scriptural Christianity, with its positive creed and its moral demands upon the obedience of the whole human race, I cannot venture to anticipate for it, in this respect, a very favourable reception.

Yet I do not doubt that there are, in the different classes

of society, many in whom the above named predisposition towards Christian truth exists, but who have not yet been able to find a corresponding access thereto. To such, as well as to theologians, I would again address myself by means of this little work; and if it may, by God's blessing, be useful to them, be they few or many, I shall have abundant cause for gratitude.

ULLMANN.

CARLSRUHE, *June* 25, 1863.

CONTENTS.

	PAGE
INTRODUCTION.—IMPORTANCE OF THE SUBJECT,	1–14
PART I. THE IDEA OF SINLESSNESS,	15–38
Chap. I. Of Sin,	15–32
Chap. II. Of Sinlessness,	33–38
PART II. THE SINLESS HOLINESS OF CHRIST,	39–106
Chap. I. Testimony to the Sinlessness of Christ—	
Sec. 1. By Others.—Expressions of a general kind,	40–47
The Gospel Portraiture of Jesus,	47–69
Sec. 2. The Testimony of Jesus to Himself,	69–81
Chap. II. The Sinlessness of Christ proved from the Effects produced by His Manifestation,	81–106
Sec. 1. The New Life of Christianity in its Moral and Religious Aspects,	83–90
Sec. 2. Morality and Religion united in Holiness,	90–93
Sec. 3. These Effects caused not by an Idea, but an actual Person,	94–106
PART III. OBJECTIONS,	107–177
Chap. I. Arguments against the actual Sinlessness of Jesus,	109–159
Sec. 1. The Development of the Person of Jesus,	109–114
Sec. 2. The Development of the Messianic Plan,	114–123
Sec. 3. The Temptation,	123–144
Sec. 4. Other Acts and Expressions of Jesus as Arguments against His Sinlessness,	144–159

	PAGE
Chap. II. Arguments against the Possibility of Sinlessness in general,	160–177
Sec. 1. Arguments drawn from Experience,	160–169
Sec. 2. Arguments drawn from the Nature of the Moral Idea,	169–177

PART IV. INFERENCES FROM THE FOREGOING FACTS AND ARGUMENTS, ... 178–247

Chap. I. Significance of Sinlessness with respect to the Person of Jesus,	180–206
Sec. 1. The Human Nature of Jesus,	182–196
Sec. 2. Inferences in respect to the Divine Nature of Jesus,	196–206
Chap. II. Significance of the Sinlessness of Jesus with respect to His relation to Mankind,	207–247
Sec. 1. The Sinless Jesus as the Personal Revelation of God,	209–219
Sec. 2. The Sinless Jesus as the Mediator between God and Sinful Man,	219–232
Sec. 3. The Holy Jesus as the Founder of the true Fellowship of Men,	232–239
Sec. 4. The Sinless Jesus as the Pledge of Eternal Life,	239–247

CONCLUSION, ... 248–253

SUPPLEMENTS.

I. THE HISTORY AND LITERATURE OF THE SUBJECT,	254–264
II. THE DIFFERENT VIEWS HELD WITH RESPECT TO THE TEMPTATION,	264–291
Chap. I. Explanation of the Details,	265–276
Chap. II. General View of the History of the Temptation,	276–291
Sec. 1. Explanations which represent the whole Narrative as a mere Product of Thought,	277–284
Sec. 2. Explanations which recognise a Historical Basis of the Narrative,	284–291

INTRODUCTION.

THE idea of sinlessness being the starting-point of the following treatise, it is of the first necessity to point out that this word is not used in the merely negative sense of an absence of antagonism to the Divine law, but in its essentially positive meaning of actual conformity to the will of God. Sinlessness, according to our view of it, is a state in which man occupies that position with respect to the order of life appointed by God, nay, rather to the holy God Himself, which alone becomes a being endued with personality, and created in the Divine image. Sinlessness, taken in this sense, is the culminating point of human development. It is a perfection both religious and moral, not merely resulting from complete conformity to a Divine type, but itself inherent; it is perfect and complete holiness. The very notion of such a quality is highly significant, and is at once both elevating and humbling. Elevating, because it brings before the mind the highest attainment it can possibly conceive. For the moral sense of every one will tell him, that if a man were perfectly sinless, he would be in the state to which, as a human being, he is really destined; would need no wealth to be truly rich, no sword to be a hero, no crown to be a king. He would be in possession of that truth which is at the same time the highest wisdom, and of that purity which is of itself both peace and happiness. But not less is the thought a humbling and depressing one; for it is ever directly connected with the conviction that *we* are by no means free from sin, but that rather, if we say we have no sin, we do but deceive ourselves, and the truth is not in us. There is between the goal set before us by our destination, and the actual attainment of our life, a great gulf, which we are forced to confess we are utterly incapable of passing over by any power of our own.

But we are not about to treat of a mere idea, but of a *reality*,—of the appearance, in the midst of the history of the sinful human race, of a genuine and actual personality, of whose perfect and spotless holiness we have most incontestable evidence. It is this fact which gives its full importance to our subject. For freedom from sin, perfect righteousness, or whatever other term may be used to express the notion, was by no means utterly unknown, as a general idea, whether to the præ-Christian or the heathen world. Some notion of the kind is seen to hover over the altitudes reached even by Pagan wisdom, while the prophetic writings of the Old Testament refer to it with far greater distinctness. But as a reality, as filled with vital energy, and especially as bringing forth actual results, it is found only in *Christianity*, nay, even in Christianity only in one *solitary* instance, in the person of the Author and Finisher of the Christian faith—in Christ Jesus.

It is obvious that a quality thus significant in itself, peculiar to Christianity, and realized therein as an actual phenomenon only in one single Person, must be of the highest importance, if we are rightly to appreciate either the character of that Person Himself, or the entire sphere of life called into existence by Him, viz. Christianity in general. No one can dispute that the tenet of the sinlessness of Christ is deeply rooted in the Christian faith, and has grown up as an intrinsic part of it. It forms, whether as a necessary postulate or a self-evident conclusion, so essential a portion of Christian doctrine, and especially of the doctrine of the person and work of the Redeemer, that it is impossible to remove it without the destruction of the entire edifice. Hence the decisive importance of this point of Christian belief has at no time been misconceived, whether in the first ages of the Church, during the medieval era, or in the present days.

Nevertheless it is not—as the reader is requested to observe—from this point of view, viz. the doctrinal, that we propose to treat the subject. It is rather an *apologetic* aim which we exclusively set before us in our treatment of this matter, and that more expressly and entirely than has as yet been done by other writers.[1] The office of Theology is scientifically to arrange and expound, according to their internal connection and perfect organization, those matters of Christian belief which have been previously established and determined. It is that of Apologetics, on the contrary, to maintain the Christian standpoint with regard to what is external thereto, and to justify it in the presence of such objections as may arise, and thus to furnish the means of entrance to those who are without. If this distinction

[1] As it is my intention to deal more completely with the *history* and *literature* of the subject in an appendix, I shall here confine myself to a short statement of its most recent treatment. Among theologians of our own days, it is acknowledged that it was *Schleiermacher* who first effectually asserted the fundamental importance of the sinfulness or sinlessness of Christ. He did this, however, chiefly in a doctrinal point of view; hence an apologetic use of the subject, which necessarily demanded an entirely different treatment, yet remained to be made. I first attempted to supply this need in the year 1828, in an article on the 'Sinlessness of Christ,' in the *Theologischen Studien und Kritiken*. From this article the present work has, by means of a series of alterations and additions, been elaborated. Since that period, this important question has been frequently discussed by other Protestant theologians from the apologetic point of view; and that not merely in Germany, but in other countries where a lively interest is taken in the development of modern theology. Among the works which have been written on this subject, that of Dorner, *On the Sinless Perfection of Christ*, Gotha 1828, occupies a high position. I

between these respective departments be kept in view, our meaning and intentions cannot but be plainly perceived. We would in fact view the sinlessness of Christ, not as a *single doctrine*, which, in its connection with other doctrines, is one of intrinsic and imperative necessity in the entire organism of the Christian faith; but as a *fact*, whose authenticity must in the first place be independently established. When this has been done, we may proceed to show that it is one involving the most important and far-reaching inferences with respect to the person and work of Christ,—nay, with respect to the whole system of the Christian faith. That the sinless perfection of Christ is, however, of fundamental importance, especially in our days, may easily be made apparent in a preliminary and more general sketch, by taking a closer survey of the special aim of Apologetics. This aim is a far higher one than merely to prove that Christianity is in its own nature better and truer than other religions, and has contributed far more than they have done to the progress of mankind. For Christianity professes to be not merely a religion endowed with pre-eminent excellences with respect to, and among other religions, but declares itself *the* religion, the absolutely perfect religion, which

would also direct attention to the following:—*The Moral Character of Christ, or the Perfection of Christ's Humanity a proof of His Divinity*, 1861, by Phil. Schaff, Professor of Theology at the Theological Seminary of Mercersburg; *The Christ of History: An Argument grounded on the Facts of His Life on Earth*, Edinburgh 1856, by John Young, LL.D.; Chaps. x. and xi. of *Nature and the Supernatural*, etc., New York 1858, by Horace Bushnell; *Essai sur la Divinité du Caractère Morale de Jésus Christ*, Genève 1850, by E. Daudiran; *Le Redempteur*, Paris 1854, by E. Pressensé. Fol. Pecaut, a Frenchman, has, on the other hand, come forward as a decided sceptic of the sinlessness of Christ, in his work, *Le Christ et le Conscience*, Paris 1859. The treatise of Keim, too, *On the Human Development of Christ*, Zurich 1861, and Gess's *Lehre von der Person Christi*, Basel 1856, bear also upon the subject. Compare also in general all the works on the life of Christ which have appeared since Strauss; among which I would call special attention to the *Lectures of Riggenbach*, Basel 1858, Lect. x. I shall adduce other works as opportunity may offer.

alone fulfils the conditions, and furnishes the means, by which the whole human race may be saved,—the *exclusively* divine revelation and plan of salvation. To exhibit and prove it to be such, is the goal which the apologist must ever keep in view.

But a religion is not proved to be the absolutely perfect one, by merely showing that it furnishes true doctrine and a faultless code of morals, and that it has produced many beneficial results. The Greeks might have taught a far deeper philosophy than the Platonic or Aristotelian,—the Jews might have had purer doctrines and precepts than those of even Moses and the Prophets; and yet they would not, therefore, have been in possession of the true religion. Nay, even Christianity itself might have furnished, in the Sermon on the Mount, the parables, and other teachings of Christ and His apostles, the sublimest religious material conceivable, and have even brought mighty things to pass thereby; but if this had been all, it would still have been far from satisfying man's deepest need, from filling up the chasm existing between human nature and the holy God, and from exhibiting that culminating point of religious development, which cannot possibly be surpassed.

Religion—as no one in the present day will deny—is not merely a system of doctrine or a code of morality. It must indeed *have* both, and both must be deducible from its inner life; but it cannot be maintained that either one or the other, or even both together, really *is* true religion. It is not in a summary of ideas, doctrines, and moral postulates, floating, as it were, over our life and influencing it from without, that the special and intrinsic nature of true religion consists, but in being a reality born into life itself,—an effectual all-influencing power therein. True religion is the *real* bond of union between God and man; it is that position of the personal creature with respect to the personal Creator by which the whole life of the former, from its inmost centre, is fashioned and determined, and in which that life has its true purpose and existence. It is this true position of man to God which must more especially be brought about wherever true, perfect religion is said to have appeared. And this cannot be effected by merely teaching or commanding it, but only by *living* therein in the presence, as it were, of the whole human race. Hence its original form, its mode of revelation, must naturally and necessarily have been a *personal* one, exhibited in the entire life of a personal Being. There must be a Man who is Himself religious, religion incarnate and impersonate, in whom the true relation between God and man has become an absolute and perceptible reality, and through whom the restoration of this relation is made an actual possibility to the whole fallen and sinful human race.

By what distinctive mark, then, shall we chiefly recognise this personal Being, thus revealing and founding the perfect religion; and by what means will such a Being be most certainly authenticated? Clearly our most trustworthy sign will be the utter absence of that which separates man from God, even of sin,—the leading of a perfectly *pure* and *holy* life, and a consequent abiding in that vital union with God, by means of which, power to eradicate sin and its consequences, and to create in man a new and holy life, may be attained. For only One thus holy and sinless, entering into all the conditions and conflicts of human life, and when suffering, suffering not for His own guilt, but that of His brethren, could be able to reconcile the discord between the holy God and sinful humanity, and in such wise to purify the latter, as forthwith to implant, in the place of sin, a life of true holiness. But if once the true relation between God and man were brought to pass by such a Being, if once access to God were opened to all, and the power of divine renovation bestowed upon the human race, this cannot be repeated,—it would be done once for all; and that culminating point would be attained with regard to religion, to which indeed mankind may, in the process of its development, thenceforth progressively approximate, but which it will be impossible to surpass; in other words, the perfect religion would be for ever existent in living and personal realization.

We say, then, that the perfect revelation and the procuring of salvation can only be effected by means of a Person, and that a Person of sinless holiness. But then, too, on the other hand, we may affirm that if we can find such a Person, one really proved to have been in all respects sinlessly perfect, we have every reason for believing that in Him we actually possess a perfect revelation of the divine means of salvation, and have therefore attained the culminating point of vital religion. Hence all that proceeds from, or is connected with this Person, will bear for us the impress of an authority far surpassing any other.

Now such a Person is presented to us by *Christianity* in its *Founder*. It is not this or that doctrine, though of ever so fundamental importance, not this or that special fact, though of ever so decisive a nature, but *Himself*, the *personal Christ*, that is the vital centre of Christianity, the pulsating heart from which all proceeds, and to which all returns. There is no other religion in which the person of its founder occupies so central, so all-controlling, so all-pervading a position,—none into which it is so inseparably interwoven. Here, as nowhere besides, the divine revelation is a personal one,—the salvation, one wrought by means of a person. It is, however, obvious, that where the divinity of His work and Person is in question, there is *one* special point which must in the last instance be a decisive one, and that is the great subject of *His sinless perfection*.

This question has, under all circumstances, been one of the deepest importance with regard to the stability of the

Christian faith. For even if the sinless perfection of Christ be not itself the very highest fact or central point of Christianity, it is yet most intimately connected with its highest and most central articles of faith, especially with the divine-human person of Jesus Christ and His work of redemption, and forms a foundation not only indispensable to the entire edifice, but also so constituted as to form a point of special illumination, from which those facts which are above and beyond itself may be inferred, and to which, on the other hand, they may, by reason of a vital connection, be referred.

If there were substantial grounds for rejecting His sinless perfection, the Founder of Christianity must descend from that all-surpassing eminence on which Christian faith has from the very first beheld Him, and mingle in the ranks of other mortals, as one perhaps of prominent moral excellence and superior wisdom, yet still as one yielding homage to the power of sin. He would not then be even, in the full meaning of the term, the Son of man, the realized prototype of mankind, and the spiritual progenitor of a renewed race, well-pleasing to God, still less the only-begotten Son of God of the apostolic faith, and, least of all, the Reconciler of sinful man with the Holy God, and the all-sufficient Redeemer from sin and death for all times and generations. Not only would the Church which is built upon Him be standing upon an insecure foundation, but the Christian faith itself would have lost all solid basis.

If, on the other hand, the sinlessness of Jesus is proved by convincing reasons, He is then beheld as the one perfect man, raised to a moral elevation above the whole sinful race. Then there really is in Him a perfect and new moral creation, and the foundation for a similar new creation of the entire race. Then we have in this fact a pledge of the certainty of that whole summary of doctrines which has from the very first made Him the object of Christian faith, especially for His Divine Sonship and work of redemption according to apostolic testimony. Then, too, the ancient faith still rests upon a good foundation, and the Church which has grown out of it has still such a vitality, that all the powers of darkness and unbelief shall not prevail against it.

Of such critical importance is the question of the sinless holiness of Christ. It is a question of the very existence or non-existence of Christianity itself. If there are no certain grounds for affirming the sinlessness of Jesus, the moral basis of Christianity is itself insecure. If, on the contrary, the faith in His sinless perfection is proved to be well founded, it becomes at the same time a firm foundation-stone for the whole edifice of the Christian faith.

We have now, as it seems to us, sufficiently pointed out the chief features of the aim we propose to ourselves. Perhaps, however, we may be permitted to preface the following pages by a few more remarks, which may contribute to the appreciation of their contents.

In making the sinless perfection of Christ our starting-point for a vindication of the Christian faith, we would by no means be understood to regard it as the *only* valid mode of proof, or to esteem all others slight in comparison. There is in Christianity so great an exuberance of life, and so many points at which it comes in contact with minds of every kind, that it cannot but offer many ways of access to its inner sanctuary; and every way must be welcomed which does but really lead to a sound and vital faith. At the same time it will be granted that different ages and different individuals have different needs; and our age, whose tendencies are eminently moral, practical, and historical, has its own special claim, which we believe will be best met in the path upon which we are about to enter.

The evidence derived from *miracles and prophecy*, which has hitherto been that most frequently adduced, must ever maintain its value so long as it occupies its true position, and is surrounded by its fitting adjuncts. It has, moreover, in its favour the example of our Lord Himself and His apostles. But there is an evident difference in this respect between the contemporaries and fellow-countrymen of Christ and us moderns, who are, moreover, the children of an essentially different sphere of culture. The former stood directly and independently upon the platform of faith in the Old Testament, and had either seen miracles themselves, or had received testimony of such occurrences from eye-witnesses. With us, on the contrary, faith in the Old Testament has to be founded upon the appearance and authority of Christ, while, with respect to miracles, the case is, that we are far more likely to accept the miracles of Christ for the sake of His person, than to believe in His person for the sake of His miracles. Miracles and predictions, too, ever refer to the person of Christ, or proceed from it. Hence that which is most essential and decisive is this personality itself, which in the first instance supports, causes, and casts a true light upon, all else. It is to this, in its moral and religious value, that even miracle and prophecy finally refer us; and its peculiar, nay, its utterly unique nature, must, after all, ever remain the firmest support of the Christian faith; for here we have within the sphere of Christianity that which least needs extraneous testimony to its indwelling truth and excellence,—that which is, on the contrary, in the highest degree self-evidencing, and cannot fail of making an impression upon such an age as ours, more powerfully influenced, as it ever is in such cases, by moral views and motives than by any other.

To this must be added the specially *practical* advantage involved in, and connected with, the mode of proof which we are thus adducing for the production of faith, or at least of a disposition and inclination to faith; namely, that it bases belief directly upon the object of faith itself, upon the person of Christ, and that chiefly in its moral aspect.

Christianity, as is universally acknowledged, is of a more thoroughly ethical character than any other religion. It addresses chiefly the heart, the conscience, the will of man. It would beget in him, not merely a correct knowledge of Divine things, but a new life; it would make the whole man, from the very deepest centre of his moral life to the whole circumference of his practice, other than he is by nature. Hence, even the entrance of the individual into the sphere of Christianity is not brought about by a process of reasoning, but by a change of life. There is, as one has well said, indeed an up-breaking, but it is an up-breaking not of the head, but of the heart. The first step in this process is a man's felt conviction of his sinfulness, and of his inability to effect his own salvation; the second, his believing acceptance of the salvation graciously offered him in Christ, and his attainment thereby of the power of leading a new life. Thus the old apostolic way of repentance and faith is the only one in which the eternal salvation given in Christianity can be really acquired. The evidences of Christianity are incapable of making any man truly a Christian; for this, after all, is a work to be effected not by men, but by God. Yet evidences may contribute to it, by clearing away opposing obstacles, by increasing the mind's inclination to accept the grace of God; and they will do this the more effectually, the more they are of such a nature as to make a near approach to that which constitutes the pole upon which the actual entrance into Christianity turns. Of such a nature is especially that kind of evidence of which we here propose to treat.

If we are to be assured of the sinless perfection of the

Lord Jesus, it must be made evident to us that He was faultless during the whole course of His life. Hence, in affirming His sinlessness, we shall need, first of all, to exhibit such a portraiture of the life of Christ, as may present us with a true and lively representation of the chief features of His character. This very portraiture, moreover, bears within it a power quite peculiar of convincing a man of his sinfulness, as well as of leading him to Christ as his Saviour. The image of the pure and holy One touches, as nothing else can do, our moral consciousness. It presents before us a conscience which actually existed uninvolved in intricacies, uncorrupted by temptations; and nothing in the whole world has equal power with this image, when it becomes a living reality in our heart, to cast down all our imaginations of our own virtue or merit, and to humble our inmost nature before God. But this image of Him who was absolutely pure, is at the same time the image of the Only-Begotten, full of grace and truth. Hence it has the power not merely of casting us down, but of raising us up, of inducing us to surrender ourselves in trust and confidence to that fulness of Divine love which is reflected therein as in an unsullied mirror. It is Christ Himself who thus lays hold of us, and begins to attain a form within us, while we, on our part, enter within the radius of His creative operations, and therefore within the sphere of Christian faith and life.

Thus this kind of evidence, while it objectively justifies the Christian faith, is at the same time that which is most adapted—so far as this can by such means be effected—subjectively to excite or cherish it, by preparing a way of entrance into the mind for that holy Personality who is the object of this faith.

It only remains briefly to point out the course we propose to follow in the following pages.

We start, then, from the phenomenon presented by the merely human life of Jesus. In this we have a stable and independent point of Christianity, comprehensible to all, and calculated to gain access to minds of the most opposite constitutions; a point which cannot fail of producing an impression wherever general moral earnestness and a feeling for purity and holiness exist, and which is of equal significance for men of the most exalted, and of the meanest intellectual attainments. We shall not, however, consider this phenomenon as an isolated one; but, while seeking to maintain it, shall be ever keeping in view our further aim,—the establishment of the Christian faith in general. And in this we are justified by the very nature of our subject. For it is this very moral phenomenon, presented by the human life of Jesus, which is so constituted, that it is impossible to stop at accepting it as a bare fact. Starting therefrom, a very little reflection will necessarily drive us to conclusions of the last importance with regard to the deepest and sublimest doctrines of Christianity.

Hence the matter of the present treatise will naturally consist of two main subjects:—*First*, that Jesus was indeed the sinlessly Holy One which Christianity, on scriptural grounds, acknowledges Him to have been. *Secondly*, that this acknowledgment involves most important consequences, justifying our faith in Him as the Son of God, and Redeemer of mankind, and in the fundamental truths of Christianity in general.

We shall not, however, be able to confine ourselves to the simple establishment of the fact of His sinlessness, and to drawing the inferences resulting therefrom. Before entering upon our first subject, it will be desirable to define more exactly what we mean by sinlessness, and thus to enter into some discussion upon this notion; and before passing on to our second, we must not shun the task of defending our assertion of Christ's sinlessness, against the objections by which it has been assailed. Not till this has been done, shall we have obtained a firm foundation for those apologetic inferences which will naturally form the conclusion of the whole.

Thus the first section will treat of the notion of sinlessness in general; the second, of Jesus Christ as actually sinless; the third, of the objections made against His sinlessness; and the fourth, of the conclusions to be drawn therefrom.

PART FIRST.

THE IDEA OF SINLESSNESS.

WE must not omit to define more exactly than we have done in the Introduction, what we understand by the word sinlessness when we apply it to the Lord Jesus. It is evident, however, that the full signification of this expression can only be arrived at by the definition of its opposite,—viz. sin. Nor can its real importance be appreciated, till the nature of sin, and its power over mankind, are perceived. Hence this section will treat upon two subjects,—first, upon the nature and power of sin, then upon what is to be understood by the term sinlessness.

CHAPTER I.

OF SIN.

THE idea of sin[1] can only exist where a *Divine rule of life*, and a highest aim of human existence resulting therefrom, are recognised. The recognition of both, however, is part of the very nature of reason, which ever requires, in the last in-

---

[1] Only the leading features of the notion of sin can be here given. For a more extensive treatment of this subject I refer especially to the much esteemed work of J. Müller, *Die christliche Lehre von der Sünde;* especially the first book, 'On the Reality of Sin,' pp. 32–366, ed. 3.

stance, connection, conformity to law, and eternal constancy; and must deny itself by seeing, in the whole sphere of existence, only the aimless, unmeaning sport of accident or caprice.

We cannot conceive of the order of the world otherwise than as an all-including unity. There cannot be two different orders of the world,—there can be but one; nor can this have different ends,—it must have one supreme end. But this one world-order unfolds itself in different spheres: it unfolds itself as the order of nature, in which force reigns, and as the order of moral life, where liberty rules.

In the domain of nature, everything that takes place is accomplished by a necessity in the things themselves; and even in those cases where we discover something resembling freedom, as in the actions of animals, it must be borne in mind that even their impulses spring from a mere unconscious natural desire, that is, instinct. Now we call that which thus operates in the domain of natural life a law of nature. This law of nature is not, however, a power acting from without, but it is the nature and constitution of the things themselves making itself irresistibly felt. Therefore, here the law is immediately one with its fulfilment; nor can there ever be a contradiction between the two. Hence, also, when apparent deviations from the ordinary course occur, when dangerous and destructive agencies enter in, we cannot speak of imputation or of guilt in this province, because nature does only what she cannot help doing, and therefore remains guiltless.

The marvels of this course of nature, with its connection and consistency in all its parts, from the scarcely perceptible atom to the sun-systems in their unchanging paths, are innumerable. But, in the midst of these miracles of nature, there arises a miracle greater still. It is the miracle of a will which interrupts the course of nature; it is free personality making her subject to mind. On the basis of the life of nature there rises up a moral life,—an ethical kingdom within the kingdom of nature. Of necessity an order must reign within this kingdom too. It were folly, indeed, to suppose that this most wondrous cosmical arrangement existed for no other purpose than to furnish a theatre on which the rule of caprice might be displayed; that preparations so pregnant with design should issue in results void of reason or purpose. But the order to be established here will undoubtedly differ radically from the order of nature. Thus, moral personality (even although situated in the midst of the course of nature) still possesses a full consciousness that it is not ruled thereby, nor can be, but that it has in it a principle which is determined by a power beyond and above nature. And this principle is free-will. The order which rules in this domain is free, like that will itself; it is not established by force. The law is not summarily enforced: it must be acknowledged and received by the will of him who is subject to it. But the law may not be thus accepted,—a contrary line of action may be chosen: hence the possibility of coming into collision with the law, and of a consequent disturbance of order, not now an apparent disturbance merely (as in nature), but a real one. And this disturbance, although it may, by the hand of the Almighty Disposer, be converted into a means of good, and thus be ultimately made serviceable to the cause of order, does nevertheless carry along with it, to him who commits it, the character of responsibility and guilt, because it is the act of his free choice.

In the order of nature, law does not appear as duty, because it is directly self-fulfilling. In the moral order, on the contrary, it becomes, under certain conditions, duty, because here the law, and the will which performs that law, may be separate. When the law commands—when it is obliged to take the form of 'Thou shalt!'—this argues an unsatisfactory moral condition; for where the moral condition is what it should be, law does not come as a power from without enforcing obedience, but is the indwelling principle of action. Not that this state involves actual opposition to the moral order; for it is possible that due obedience may be rendered to law even when it comes from without, and assumes an authoritative attitude. Real opposition arises only when the personal will refuses obedience to law, which it yet clearly understands, and performs the very reverse of what it enjoins.[1] This is what we call *transgression, disobedience to law*, when relating to others, *unrighteousness* and—to express the notion generally—*sin*.[2] But this definition is entirely formal and external: we must therefore look for other particulars, which regard not merely the form of action, but its substance, and which relate to action not merely as such, but in its inward and abiding source.

In the first place, it is evident that sin, being a deviation from the true order of life, is also a falling short and a failure of the end which that order has in view, of the true *destination* of man.[3] It is a want of goodness; and since goodness in itself has a blessing and ennobling effect upon life, without it there is no true life; that is, sin divests life of its completeness and its blessedness. But it would be false to conclude from this, that sin is nothing more than limitation, restriction, negation. The negation that is in sin turns naturally into something positive, something positively wrong; and indeed it implies this. Even sins of omission are not merely negative, much less are actual sins. Only in one case could sin be regarded as something merely negative, that is, if the Will that would not choose the good could at once suspend its activity altogether, and will nothing at all. But

---

[1] Rom. iii. 20, v. 13.

[2] 1 John iii. 4. Sin as ἀνομία, παράβασις, ἀδικία.

[3] The ordinary N. T. expression ἁμαρτία points this out, as do also the Hebrew and Latin words by which sin is designated.

the Will can never will absolutely nothing: when it shuts itself against the good, it inevitably chooses its opposite; when it contemns order, it surrenders itself to caprice; when it thrusts from it the true principle of life, it admits a false one in its place. Thus sin is not only a coming-short of the true goal, but a tendency towards a wrong one; not merely an interruption, but a perversion; not merely a pause in the advance towards goodness, but an apostasy from goodness.[1] Are lying and cheating, gluttony and debauchery, envy and hatred, to be regarded as the mere absence of truth and uprightness, of moderation and chastity, of benevolence and brotherly love, or perhaps even as but very important stages in the development of these virtues, and not, on the contrary, as their most positive contrasts? In fact there must be an utter absence of all perception of the actual presence of sin in mankind,—of sin rising, as it does in many instances, to obdurate antagonism to all that is good and holy,—where its positive character is denied.

But it is not merely those actions which meet the eye that we must here bring under notice: the important matter is the inward source from which they proceed. It is only by fixing our attention upon that, that we can attain a clear idea of the nature of sin. Too often does it happen that details hide from our view the whole: content to contemplate the phenomena, we forget the substance. So, too, in the case before us. We own the existence of sins,—that no man would deny; but of sin we will hear nothing. And yet sin is the root from which all acts of sin shoot forth; and the man who will not go beyond the latter, but stops short at faults and failings, transgressions and crimes, without penetrating to their source, —the perverted will, which is the source of all the evil,—

---

[1] Sin is a ψεῦδος; it proceeds from the πνεῦμα τῆς πλάνης (1 John i. 8, iv. 6); it shows itself as a departure from God, and a perversion of man in both mind and conduct (Rom. i. and ii.).

must come to a conclusion as destitute of wisdom and insight, as that of a physician whose diagnosis goes no further than the symptoms of the disease, and leaves its hidden causes unexplored. All the external actions of a man are the result of an internal antecedent; and that which is, in a moral point of view, alone decisive of the character of an action, is the inward motive from which it proceeds. Moral order does indeed furnish us also with an objective standard; but whenever the question is one of the relation of the individual to moral order, everything depends upon the disposition ot the mind; and it is not that which is palpable, that which may be the subject of human measurement, which is of primary importance. It is not the quantity of deeds done that imparts to them a character of merit or demerit: much more is it the quality and worth of those actions, as estimated by the spirit which they embody and reflect. And as this is true of goodness, so is it also of evil. The degree of heinousness of even outward acts of sin is determined by that which constitutes their inward motive. There may be sinful frames and dispositions which are scarcely perceptible in the external life, and which are yet the results of the deepest moral depravity;[1] and a murder might, under certain circumstances, entail less guilt than the slanderous word which slays a reputation.

But if we fix our earnest attention upon the real inner source of sin, we shall not run the risk of adopting that false method of viewing it, which looks no further than its isolated external manifestations. The whole of life, and of moral life in particular, developes itself systematically; its several parts are intimately bound up together, and form one whole. Only the most thoughtless folly could for a moment entertain the opinion that a human being can, in virtue of his moral liberty, perpetrate in wanton caprice, first an action truly good, and then immediately thereafter an evil action. This

[1] Matt. xv. 18, and v. 28.

may indeed appear at times to occur: we sometimes see an action that we should pronounce generous and noble in the midst of a course of conduct undoubtedly bad; sometimes, again, we mark an unexpected fall in the midst of an honourable life. But though such occurrences may appear to us abrupt and isolated, it does not follow that there is this absence of connection with the rest of the life, because we fail to perceive it. In truth, everything that a man does, comes from his whole nature: his actions are nothing else but the occasional expressions of that nature,—intimations to the world without of what is going on within. And this is especially the case in the matter of sin. Every sin has its antecedents, as well as its consequents. Every sin springs from spiritual blindness, and works spiritual blindness in its turn: it is a daughter of lust, and it becomes in its turn the mother of still more powerful lust.[1] If sin have once entered into the sphere of mortal life, it is all over with its purity; and the state of perfect innocence can never be restored. It produces a shadow upon the moral consciousness, and an inclination to continue such a course of action. Sin is born from sin, and sin punishes itself by sin. Sin, even when cured, leaves its *scars*, and can never be so obliterated from the consciousness as though it had never existed. That, however, which connects together separate and single sins, is just the sinful *nature*, or sin considered as the principle from which all sinful actions flow.[2]

These definitions of sin are in close connection with the *nature of the moral law*. The fact that we cannot rightly estimate the moral character, except in so far as we have respect to its internal nature, and regard it as a whole, has its explanation in this, that the law is itself the expression of an inner life, and that a consistent and connected life.

---

[1] 'Then, when lust hath conceived, it bringeth forth sin' (Jas. i. 15).
[2] Rom. vii. 7-39.

Nor can appearances be allowed to deceive us here either. It is true that the law, especially the revealed law, may come to us, in the first instance, as a demand from without. Not the less on that account has it really taken its rise from a source within, from a spiritual life; and it is that life which impresses upon the law that proceeds from it the character of righteousness and holiness, for the purpose of producing a similar life in those to whom it is given. It is true the law may come in the form of a number of separate injunctions and commands; but these have their true significance only as members of a complete organic whole, as component parts of the *one* commandment of perfect love towards God and our neighbour, in which the law is summed up, which demands not so much the observance of details, as obedience to the whole, and regards the transgression of a single command as a violation of the entire law, as a renunciation of its spirit and principle.[1] Now, since the law seeks to mould and fashion the whole nature of the inward life, and since it does so as an indivisible whole, everything depends on the relation of man to the law and its principle,—on the one hand in his inmost affections, and on the other, in the sum-total of those outward actions which result therefrom. And the relation can, in reality, be only one of two kinds: either it is a relation of self-renunciation and obedience, or it is a relation of resistance and disobedience. All good springs from the former,—all evil from the latter.[2] But the one as well as the other is a *fundamental fact* of the moral life, which must exist before the separate acts of will and separate deeds of good can in either case take place. In this connection, sin is defined as disobedience.[3] The disobedience is not, however, merely in the external action, and against the external precept,—it is disobedience in the heart and

---

[1] Jas. ii. 8-12; Matt. v. 19.   [2] Rom. viii. 5.
[3] It is called παρακοή in Rom. v. 19 and Heb. ii. 2.

against the whole law, and it is a *spirit* of disobedience by virtue of an internal opposition to the principle expressed by the moral law.

But if we would understand the true nature of sin, we must not stop at mere law. We must first of all inquire *what is the origin of law, and the end it has in view;* for law does not appoint itself, but must be appointed. Behind every law there is a life of which it is the expression, and a power of which it is the command. In the case of the moral law, the life it expresses cannot be merely the life of nature, nor the power by which it is enforced merely the power of nature. The moral, from its very nature, transcends the merely natural; the unity of the law has for its foundation the unity of a consciousness from which it proceeded; and only a personal will can address itself to our will with the command, Thou shalt! There must, then, be a *personal, conscious,* absolutely moral life, exalted above nature, from which the law springs.

Will it perhaps be asserted that it is man *himself* who gives himself the law, and that he bears to himself first the relation of lawgiver, and then of law-obeyer? The natural moral law (as it is called), the law of *conscience*, has been indeed brought forward in this sense, and a system built up, according to which man is his own moral governor and lawgiver. But the moral law cannot be derived from such a source, nor even the so-called natural law. Conscience is not the source of moral principles, but the regulator of moral action. Besides, the material of which it is composed is not absolutely and under all circumstances the same, nor derived from its own resources, but rather furnished from a source external to itself, and hence differing according to the measure of religious development. The conscience of the true Christian is not merely more cultivated, but may be said to be of more intrinsic value than that of a heathen or a Jew. Hence it is not the primary function of conscience to lay down a moral law, but to bear its emphatic testimony thereto in special cases, by urgent exhortation to that which is lawful, by stern warning against its opposite, and by direct reaction against all infraction.[1] Moreover, it is *essential* to conscience, that its commands and prohibitions should be absolute; that its voice should assert its authority as a *voice of God*, as a revelation of the Divine righteousness and holiness within us; and that all opposition thereto should be perceived to be not merely man's opposition to his own better nature, not merely an injury done to himself, but a violation of the Divine order, and a resistance to God Himself. Thus does conscience—far from corroborating the notion of human autonomy—refer us rather to a far higher source of law than a merely human one.

A similar result ensues from the very nature of the subject. For wherever in the sphere of life we find an all-powerful and universal law enforcing itself, we are compelled to acknowledge that it has sprung from the very same source from which that life itself is derived. It follows that the source of both the law and the life must be something higher than either, and lie beyond the sphere of that life. It is the power which determined the conditions under which that life is intended to unfold itself and fulfil its destiny, and under which alone it can do so. The plant, the animal, or the star, did not choose for itself its law of life, but received it from that creative Power which gave it being; and it is because that Power is Omnipotence that the laws it has implanted work with undeviating certainty. The same holds true of man and his order of life; only with this difference, that in his case that order is one of liberty, because it is a moral order. If man had been his own creator, he might

---

[1] Compare Güder, *Die Lehre von Gewissen in den theol. Stud. und Krit.*, 1857, pp. 246, etc.

have been his own lawgiver. But this not being the case, the law of his life must have its origin in that creative power in which his existence is rooted and grounded.[1] It is, moreover, on this fact alone that the authority and majesty, the eternal validity, and the sacred inviolability of the law, depends. Further, it is only under this condition that man can possibly entertain that faith in the absolute, final victory of the good over the evil, which is indispensable to all moral life. For, in order to have that faith, it is not enough to know that the good has a certain authority and supreme right given it by man. No; we must possess a much higher assurance; we must be convinced that the final triumph of goodness is a part of the grand world-plan; that the great design of creation, the reason for which the world exists, is, that goodness may come to its full realization. And this certainty can be gained only from the conviction that the moral law of human life has its source in the very same power which called the whole economy of the world into existence, and which is conducting it to its goal. If, then, the moral law be necessarily derived from a personal Being, even from Him who created and governs the universe, then is the source of the moral law none other than the *living, the personal God*. And if this be true of the natural law, it is still more indisputably true of the revealed law; for that is so thoroughly the expression of the will of a holy personal Being, that it must indeed either be received as such, or else rejected altogether.

It follows, that what we have to do with in the order of human life, ethically considered, is not the law as such, but much rather, in the law and beyond the law, its holy Originator.[2] It is He who personally addresses to us the command, Be ye holy, for I am holy. Viewed in this light,

---

[1] J. Müller, *Lehre von der Sünde*, pp. 108-117.
[2] Jas. iv. 12.

the law attains a religious significance; it is no longer a mere *order of life*, but a *link of life*, the bond of union between man and God. And this gives a deep and wide significance to sin, because it thus appears not merely as disobedience against God, but as a severing of the bond which connects man with God,[1] and therefore as *separation, departure, alienation from God*, nay, as an antagonism to God, which at length rises to open enmity.[2] It is not till this is taken into consideration, that the essential characteristics of sin are fully manifest.

The will of God concerning us, which finds expression in the law, is the will of holy love. In it God gives Himself to us, in order to make us holy and blessed in His fellowship. And the only fitting relation that man can occupy with reference to this holy, loving will of God, is that of absolute, trustful submission, and thankful love; and this state of mind is called *faith*. Where this, and the love that flows from it, are found, the law is fulfilled as a natural consequence. To faith and love, in their inseparable union, the law no longer imposes commands from without, the *spirit* of the law being by them implanted in the human will, as an all-governing principle. He in whom this has taken place has found the centre and nucleus of his life in God, and has therefore attained true liberty, perfect contentment, perfect blessedness.

But if the only real fulfilling of the law proceeds from a personal self-surrender to God in faith and love, sin, the transgression of the law, must of necessity have its source in the opposite of this,—in the want of personal surrender to God, in the want of faith and of love; in a word, in man's having severed himself from his true and proper centre of life in God. Thus sin, in its inseparable connection with

---

[1] This thought underlies the whole parable of the prodigal son; see especially Luke xv. 13 and 18.
[2] Rom. viii. 7.

unbelief,[1] appears as a criminal violation of our relation to God, and as something requiring *expiation*,—something whose guilt must be done away, if this relation is to be restored.

But when man has once severed himself from the true centre of his life, from God, he cannot stop at this point. His life must of necessity have some object, some aim; and if he forsakes the centre appointed him, he must choose for himself a wrong one. This is the point at which the negative character of sin is naturally converted into something positively evil. The first thing to which the man who has forsaken God will turn, is the creature, the *World*, in the good things of which he deludes himself with the hope of finding satisfaction. But when he surrenders himself to the world, the impulse by which he is really possessed is the desire of making all things conduce to his own profit or advantage. It is self that he really seeks in everything,— even in those relations which have the appearance of love.[2]

Thus the *Ego* becomes the real centre of life, and that self-love which in itself is natural and right—nay, which is the basis of the full development of the Divine likeness, of free personality in man—is perverted into the *selfishness* which is alike opposed to nature and to God. It is in this selfishness—in virtue of which a man can know no surrender to anything higher than himself, but subjects everything to his own particular ends, and at length shuts himself up either in dull indifference, or positive hatred and defiance—that we recognise both the essential nature of sin, and at the same

---

[1] As far as Scripture is concerned, we would not so much call attention to special passages, such as John xvi. 9 and Rom. xiv. 23, and least of all to the latter, in which the word πίστις is used in a pre-eminently moral sense; but rather remind our readers that it is one of the leading peculiarities of the Old and New Testaments in general, and of the teaching of John and St. Paul especially, to uphold the indissoluble union of the ethical and the religious, and thus everywhere to insist on the connection of sin with unbelief, and of holiness with faith.

[2] 1 John ii. 16.

time that distinctive feature whereby it becomes directly its own inevitable punishment. For if it be true that in faith and love towards God all goodness is implied, it is not less certain that, in that unbelieving selfishness which severs itself from God, all sin is included: selfishness is thus to be regarded as the radical sin, as the *principle of all sin*. And if true life and perfect peace can only flow forth to man from communion with God as the true centre of life, it follows, as a necessary consequence, that when man, emptying himself of such divine fulness, seeks only himself in everything, he must be consumed by unsatisfied longings, and at last find but death and hell.[1] It is in the full development of this perverted self-seeking, this conversion of the Ego into the central object, that sin *reaches its climax*. On the other hand, as constituting the original impulse of every development of sin, and the essence of sin in general, it may also be regarded as its *commencement*. In the latter case, however, it at first works more secretly, especially in the sensible forms of sin; and it is not till a subsequent period that it openly appears.

The *effects* of sin correspond to its nature.

The proper seat of sin is the will. But the spirit which manifests itself in the will is the very same spirit that is seen at work in the thoughts and feelings, in the imagination and the fancy; and this spirit becomes a living personality only by being united, by means of the soul, with a material body. Now, whatever makes the will go out in a wrong direction, whatever introduces into the region over which the will presides a power which interferes with the development of life, and produces desecrating or destructive effects, must produce like effects in the whole region of the spirit and the soul,—nay, through the soul those evil influences will

[1] Rom. vi. 23.

extend even to the body; and thus the whole person will be affected by them. The moral blindness that has at all times been found to accompany sin,—the perversion, the contamination, the servitude of the will, which sin brings along with it, have, as their inevitable consequence, an increased perversion, likewise, of the moral judgment, an obscuration of knowledge, especially in things moral and divine, the pollution of the imagination, the unbridling of the fancy, the degradation of the entire nature, the enfeebling of the whole soul, and the ruin of the organs and powers of the body.

Man forms a unity, which is, however, only the foundation of that higher unity which is to be brought about in him, as a being made in the Divine image, by means of communion with God. Now sin does not merely obstruct this unity, but sets up in its place that which is its direct opposite. He who has fallen away from God by sin, does, as a necessary consequence, fall out both with himself and with all mankind. True unity in man is possible only when that which is godlike in him—that is, the mind—acquiesces in the divine order of life, and governs the whole being in conformity therewith. But when he has once severed himself from the true centre of his being, that is, from God, then also does that element of his being—his mind—which is akin to God, and which was intended to be the connecting and all-deciding centre of his personal life, lose its central and dominant position; he ceases to be lord of himself, and of his own nature; the various powers which make up his complex nature, begin to carry on, each for itself, an independent existence; the flesh lusteth against the spirit, and the spirit wages a fruitless war with the flesh (Gal. v. 17); sinful desire becomes dominant, and while the man seems to be in the enjoyment of all imaginable liberty, he has lost the only true liberty, and has become a slave to himself; for 'whosoever committeth sin is the servant of sin' (John viii. 34;

Rom. vi. 16–23). He is the dependent of self; and being thus the slave of self, he is also the slave of pleasure, and of all those objects which it requires for its satisfaction. This falling out with himself is, moreover, ever accompanied by a rupture with his fellow-men. When his own personality is destroyed, he can no longer feel any true reverence for the personality of others; where selfishness has taken root in the place of that love which is 'the bond of perfectness,' no fit and lasting relation with others is possible. He degrades others into means of subserving his own selfish ends, or, where this is impossible, into objects of dislike and envy.

Hence no true fellowship, no fellowship worthy of human nature, can exist among those in whom sin prevails. The wicked are never naturally social. The gregarious instinct, however, is indestructible in human nature; and even those who are the servants of sin, mutually need each other's assistance in the pursuit of their various aims. Hence there arises among them, in the place of that moral fellowship, whose prototype is the kingdom of God, a spurious kind of fellowship, an external combination, which being, however, in reality founded only upon mutual spoliation, results in overreaching and violence. Such combination, on a large scale, begets a *kingdom of evil;* a kingdom, indeed, which cannot stand, because it bears within it the germ of discord and destruction, but which is yet so constituted, as to render it fearfully evident that sin is indeed a great and powerful fact.

It is undeniable that sin is a phenomenon absolutely *universal* in human nature; and the saying of Holy Scripture, that the whole world lieth in wickedness, is indisputably confirmed both by history and individual experience. During the whole course of the natural development of mankind, history never brings before us a form of perfect purity, but shows us, on the contrary, that in spite of all the efforts exerted, and all the conflicts waged against it, evil is ever and anon breaking forth again with renewed energy. Antiquity, with all its glorious performances in the provinces of art and science, of legislation and national organization, ended in a tremendous moral dissolution. And ever since the appearance of Christianity in the world, sin has manifested itself to be a power which may indeed be broken, but which, unless it be broken by an arduous struggle, will be a dominant one. It has shown itself to be a power which maintains its position in the midst of all the boasted progress of mankind,—a power which, though in the course of human development it may indeed assume a more refined and polished form, remains unchanged in its essential attributes. Each man's own experience, moreover, convinces him of his personal share in that sin which thus pervades the whole race; and he who would acquit himself of participation therein, would but exhibit either the entire obtuseness of his moral sense, or a boundless self-delusion. Yet it is not the case—as each man's moral consciousness will testify—that sin first shows itself in individuals, in consequence of a fall from a previous state of peace, innocence, and goodness. On the contrary, each man, at the first awakening of the moral sense, finds himself tied and bound with the chain of sin; for he finds that to be present in him which constitutes the general foundation of sin. In other words, he is sensible of an opposition between the flesh and the spirit, of an inclination to act only from motives of self-love, and of an impulse to make self the central object. This sinful disposition is, moreover, deeply rooted, even in the case of those in whom the supremacy of sin is destroyed, and is no longer the dominant principle. Hence its after effects remain, and are ever and anon appearing in the form of incentives to evil, by means of seductive thoughts and inclinations. Hence, too, there is always a dark background to the heart; and so long as man is in the body, he never reaches a stage of progress at which the precept, 'Watch and pray, lest ye enter into temptation,' loses one jot or tittle of its full importance. This absolute universality of sin evidently points to a *cause common to all*, to a tendency of nature contemporary with the birth of man,—for we are here treating of that which is anterior to the conscious activity of the will. The existence of such a sinful tendency in human nature is not taught only by the revelations of the Old and New Testament, but has been abundantly asserted, under every variety of expression, by the deepest and most earnest philosophers of all nations and ages. The origin of this sinful tendency it is beside our purpose to discuss. It will be sufficient for the present to have established the fact of its existence, that we may return hereafter to a more detailed treatment of the subject. We must not omit, however, to bring forward two points which bear upon the notion of sinlessness. *First*, If the supremacy of sin is so universal, and if its cause is a natural tendency in man as he is now born, this must entail upon the whole race, and upon each individual, a still deeper ruin, unless some power exists strong enough to overcome and find a remedy for such a state of things, and so constituted that a new and holy life may originate therefrom. And such a power will be found only in a person in whom sin is shown to be completely conquered. To this must be added, *secondly*, that this person must not only be perfectly free from actual sin during the whole course of his life, but that his inmost life, the basis of his whole development, must be thoroughly pure, and have no kind of sinful taint in it. And this leads us to a nearer consideration of the proper nature of sinlessness.

CHAPTER II.

OF SINLESSNESS.

It is impossible to lay down *à priori* definitions concerning the actions and dispositions of sinless beings. It would be but a perverted manner of treating the subject, to insist upon a series of abstract requirements in all special cases, and then to measure an actual character by such a standard. The right way of proceeding is, on the contrary, to ascertain from an actual character, how sinless perfection, where it really existed, was manifested in the several features of the life. And yet it is both possible and necessary first to state, at least by a few fundamental definitions, what we conceive to be essential under all circumstances to the notion of sinlessness. After what has been already advanced, a short discussion will, however, suffice.

The idea of sinlessness—anamartesia—does not in itself exclude the *possibility* of sinning. On the contrary, it is only where this possibility is in some manner presupposed, that sinlessness, properly so called, can be conceived. Absolute impeccability exists only in Him who is infinitely removed from evil, who never can be tempted with evil,—that is, in God.[1] But wherever there is human nature, and consequent liability to temptation, there is also, by reason of this very nature, the possibility of sin. In this case sinlessness consists in the fact that the basis from which the whole moral life is developed is a pure and energetic one; that in this development, moreover, no deviation from the divine order of life occurs, but that all which approaching from without *would* seduce to sin, is completely overcome by the victorious power within. He, then, of whom it may be said that by

[1] Jas. i. 13.

reason of his nature sin was *possible* to him, and yet by no special condition thereof *necessary*,—that he was, on the contrary, capable of abstaining from sin, and did actually continue to do so,—is a sinless being.[1]

The meaning of the term sinlessness is, first of all, a negative one. But it is not applied in this sense to a single act of the will, or to the outward act. In such cases we employ the expressions 'irreproachability' or 'guiltlessness.' When, on the contrary, the far deeper term sinlessness is used, we always have in view the entire moral condition, and we contemplate this in its inmost nature. It is, however, also evident that here, too,—as in our definition of the nature of sin,—we cannot stop short at a mere negation. Sinlessness is indeed a notion which can be applied only to personal beings, called upon to will and to act as moral agents, and in whom, consequently, the very omission of such willing and acting is a violation of the divine order of life. This, in itself, requires the positive choice and practice of what is good. But this becomes still more decidedly the case, from the fact that sinlessness has to be maintained in a world that lieth in wickedness,—a world in which evil has become a ruling power. At the first commencement of the develop-

[1] In applying to Christ the well-known formula, it is self-evident that sinlessness excludes the *non potuit non peccare*, since any kind of necessity to sin would make the remaining free therefrom *à priori* inconceivable. On the other hand, the fact of sinlessness directly involves not only the *potuit non peccare*, and the *non peccavit*,—the possibility of remaining free from sin, and the actual freedom therefrom,—but also demands, at least as the postulate of the whole moral development, the *potuit peccare*. Without this the temptation of Christ would be devoid of reality, and His example would lose an essential element of its importance. How far, however, when we take into account His office of Redeemer, and other circumstances, together with the *potuit peccare*—the possibility of sin, and the total abstinence therefrom—the *non potuit peccare*, and therefore a higher necessity of not sinning, might be predicated of Him, is a question which, as appertaining to the province of dogmatic theology or speculation, it is beside our purpose to discuss. Compare Steudel, *Glaubenslehre*, p. 241, and J. Müller, *Lehre von der Sünde*, ii. 225 and 226.

ment of the human race, we might indeed conceive of sinlessness as a mere abstinence from sin,—as mere innocence not yet intermeddling with the opposition between good and evil. But after sin has entered and taken possession of human nature, the leading a sinless life becomes inconceivable apart from a most decided *struggle* against evil, even to its most hidden and deepest roots. And this fight for life and death is no matter of mere childlike purity and innocence, but one demanding the most intense activity of the fully matured moral powers, and therefore something supremely *positive*,—the work accomplished by the moral personality; a work everywhere manifested by acts, and in which even endurance must become action.

What this involves in the case of an individual, will be evident if we bear in mind those main features of the nature of sin already stated. We saw that sin was disobedience to the Divine order of life,—a disobedience at first internal, but afterwards appearing in external actions; that it was, moreover, a severance, through lack of faith and love, from the Divine Ruler of the world Himself, from God, the only true centre of life, and at the same time a setting up of the false one Self and the world; which, instead of the satisfaction sought therein, yields only discord, disorder, and ruin, whether to individuals, or to the whole sin-possessed community. In contrast to this, we should regard as sinless, one who should render obedience to the Divine law in the whole extent of its requirements,—an obedience not only maintained under all, even the most difficult, circumstances and conditions, but itself a fundamental fact of the character. Hence the moral life resulting from this obedience is no patched and piecemeal product, but a tissue woven of one material throughout,—an inseparable, undivided whole. Nor will this obedience be rendered merely to the law as such, but through this to its holy Author. The life will consequently be an uninterrupted acquiescence in the Divine will, a walking before God, a walking with God; and the whole constitution of the moral choice and action, together with personal surrender to God, faith, and vital piety, will form an indivisible, harmonious whole.

Such a being is inconceivable, except as perfectly free, peaceful, happy, repelling all defilement and obscurity from the mental and corporeal life, and exercising, under all circumstances, a perfect self-control. From such a one, united by the band of perfect love to both God and man, might be reasonably expected the possession of an incalculable power, both to conquer sin in general in the human race, and, in spite of all the might and authority of evil, to call into existence a moral and religious community, in accordance with the Divine purpose towards the human race.

It is in this its essentially positive as well as in its negative sense, that we apply the epithet sinless to the *Lord Jesus*. We view Him as the sinlessly Perfect, the absolutely Holy One, ever filled with the spirit of obedience, faith, and love, and so constantly and under all circumstances acting up to this spirit, that sin had no place in His life. It is self-evident that such a life could only have been developed from a pure basis: no original sinful tendency, no naturally evil inclination, is here conceivable, but only a fulness of moral power, perfect and inviolable even in its first rudiments. This, however, is not the point from which we start, but the conclusion at which we shall arrive in the course of our discussion. Our starting-point is simply the *historical manifestation of Jesus Christ, the actual facts presented by His human life;* and our task is in the first instance to prove from these His sinless perfection.

In the fulfilment of this task, however, we are conscious of the *limits* imposed upon us by the nature of the subject. Truths of the highest nature, especially those religious and moral truths which afford to our inner life its ultimate repose and inward satisfaction, are neither ascertained by the medium of the senses, nor are they susceptible of a demonstration which, like logical and mathematical axioms, possesses the quality of being utterly incontestable. The very nature of these truths places them beyond such means of proof, and this incapability is to be regarded, not as a defect, but as a mark of superiority. The region of moral and religious truth is a free one, and the supreme blessing which it offers can only be appropriated by free and trusting acquiescence, *i.e.* by faith. Now faith—which, however decidedly it may be referred to a divine operation, must yet at the same time be ever regarded as a moral act—would forfeit its most essential nature if it were compelled by force of demonstration. All that can be shown is, that faith is the more reasonable and moral part, and that it answers to the requirements of human life infinitely more than its opposite.

This, too, is the case with the sinlessness of Christ. As all moral greatness appearing in human form may be denied, or, where its manifestation cannot be contested, may at least have a doubt cast upon its inward motive, so also may the moral dignity and purity of Jesus. Doubt and opposition cannot even here be absolutely excluded or refuted, and, least of all, where there is an absence of all susceptibility for receiving impressions from purity and elevation of character, and of a capacity to appreciate them, unless manifested in a striking and brilliant manner. What is wanted is a willing and joyful confidence in Him who is exhibited to us as so exalted and so unique a Being,—an elevation of our own minds when approaching one so elevated,—a moral soaring towards that height which He occupies. Such a confidence, such an exaltation, may, however, be justified; it can be shown that they are based upon the soundest external and internal evidence, and that their opposites would involve us in a maze of contradictions, and especially in such as are of a moral kind.[1]

In this sense, then, we now proceed to prove, in its special reference to the person of Jesus Christ, the existence of that sinlessness of which we have hitherto spoken only according to its general features.

---

[1] Theologians, says even De Wette, must not, when bringing forward historical proofs, overlook the importance of faith, nor commit themselves to the vain effort of demonstrating, as evident, palpable truth, that which is to be apprehended by the faith which, though it does not see, yet seeing not, believes. Compare my article, '*Polemisches in Betreff der Sundlösigkeit Jesu,*' *Stud. und Kritik.* 1842-3, p. 687, etc.

PART SECOND.

THE SINLESS HOLINESS OF CHRIST.

OUR purpose of treating in an apologetic point of view the sinlessness of Christ, leads us to consider this as manifested by the actual facts of His history. Hence our first task will be to establish these as historical facts in general are wont to be established,—on the one hand by credible *testimony;* on the other, by the undeniable *effects* resulting therefrom. With respect to the first point, we shall not confine ourselves to the testimony of others, but shall adduce that of Jesus Himself. For in this case we need for our full assurance the indissoluble concurrence of the two facts, that Jesus made upon others an inevitable impression that He was sinlessly perfect, and also that He was Himself both conscious of being absolutely free from sin, and ever ready unhesitatingly to affirm the same. With respect to the effects produced, moreover, all will depend upon our being able to exhibit such historical phenomena as can only be satisfactorily explained upon the supposition that the Lord Jesus was sinless; for it is evident, on the one hand, that if one perfectly pure and free from all sin did actually appear in the midst of an otherwise universally sinful race, so unique an occurrence could not fail to produce effects of an utterly peculiar, nay, of a unique kind; and, on the other, that if such historical phenomena actually exist, we are justified in inferring the reality of the cause from that of the effects.

These, then, are the chief points which we have to discuss in the following chapters. We start from the evidence, and draw inferences by referring to effects. With respect to evidence, moreover, we distinguish not merely between the testimony of others and the self-testimony of Christ, but also, as far as the former is concerned, between expressions of a general kind and that portraiture of the Lord Jesus, exhibiting as it does the minutest details of His character, delivered to us by the circle most intimately connected with Him.

CHAPTER I.

TESTIMONY TO THE SINLESSNESS OF CHRIST.

Sec. 1.—*By Others.*

WHEN we cast a searching glance at the *actual events* of our Lord's life, we cannot help wishing that men of the most opposite ranks and dispositions, occupying positions exterior to Christianity, sceptical, or even inimical, had left us express accounts of the impressions produced by His actions and character. Such a wish is, however, but scantily gratified by history. We know, indeed, with unquestionable certainty, from the testimony of heathen authors, that Jesus suffered death by crucifixion in the reign of Tiberius,[1] and that even from the very first, divine honours were paid Him by those who were called Christians after Him, as the Christ.[2] We have also the passage of the Jewish author Josephus in which, so far as it is genuine, Jesus is spoken of in generally

---

[1] Tacitus, *Annals*, xv. 44; Suetonius, *Life of Claudius*, cap. xxiv., and elsewhere.
[2] Pliny, in the well-known epistle to Trajan, *Epist.* x. 97.

favourable terms.[1] And, lastly, we perceive from the various statements of non-Christian authors, that the first importance was from the earliest period attributed to the person of Jesus Christ with respect to the establishment of Christianity.[2] But as far as anything individual or characteristic concerning His person is concerned, we learn absolutely nothing from such sources. Hence we are thrown entirely upon the information furnished us by those who adhered to Him in faith and devoted love,—that is, by the apostles. This information has not, however, been handed down to us in such wise as to give forth, so to speak, only a monotone of approbation and admiration of the moral elevation of Christ. On the contrary, we are thereby presented with a copious, varied, and unique portraiture of the impression He produced. The apostles do indeed also sum up in statements of a doctrinal kind their views of His moral character; but these, bearing as they do the impress not of a standing formula, but of a free expression of conviction, are at the same time accompanied by the Gospel narrative. In this we possess a delineation carried out in a series of most varied pictures, both of the manner in which men of the most opposite dispositions—men indifferent and enthusiastic, devoted and inimical—were affected by the moral conduct manifested by Jesus Christ, and also of this conduct itself in all those conditions and relations of life by which character in general is tested.

We proceed to consider this more closely, and will first review some features and expressions of a more general kind.

It is one leading mark of a strong and sharply defined character, to call forth a decided, and even an inimical re-

---

[1] *Archæol.* xviii. 3, 3. The passage appears to me to be a compound of genuine elements and later additions. At all events, Jesus is mentioned by Josephus as He 'who was called Christ' (*Archæol.* xx. 9, 1).

[2] Compare my work, *Historisch oder Mythisch*, pp. 10-13.

action. And such was the effect produced in the case of Jesus Christ. By a behaviour utterly free from respect of persons, He stirred up irreconcilable enmity. But the vigilant hatred of His foes, though everywhere following His steps, found nothing by which they might impugn the purity of His conduct. On the other hand, even those who observed Him in other respects with indifference, were struck and captivated by the peculiar dignity of His character. His worldly-minded judge,—a man by no means very susceptible of what was noble and exalted, nay, even a hard and cruel man,—felt himself compelled to bear solemn testimony to the *innocence* of the persecuted Jesus.[1] The wife of Pilate, too, who, though undoubtedly of a gentler character, would naturally have but little interest in the fate of a Jewish teacher, was yet so possessed by the certainty of His blameless purity, that the thought that her husband might be stained with the blood of *that just Person*, left her no rest even in sleep.[2] The commander of the Roman guard, at the cross, was so overcome by the impression made by the sufferer, that he gave a testimony to *the righteousness* of Jesus, which displays a reverence far surpassing any ordinary human standard.[3] And even the thief who was crucified with Him was moved by the aspect of the sufferer,—who in this moment of deepest desertion seemed devoid of *aught* calculated to awaken faith, —to the most entire reliance upon His person, and thereby to a joyful hope of a better life.[4]

Nowhere did the conduct of Jesus leave its beholders indifferent,—nowhere did it fail to produce a powerful impression. His Person produced upon all with whom He came in contact, the effect of compelling a moral decision;

---

[1] On the character of Pilate, see especially Philo, in the *Legat. ad Caj.*, t. ii. p. 590, ed. Mang.

[2] Matt. xxvii. 19; especially the words, μηδὶν σοι καὶ τῷ δικαίῳ ἐκείνῳ.

[3] Matt. xxvii. 54; Luke xxiii. 47.   [4] Luke xxiii. 40.

and during the whole course of His life, His mere presence passed a silent but irresistible sentence upon those by whom He was surrounded. This was most powerfully manifested in the case of those who were most intimately connected with Him; and from this circle we will adduce here only two specially striking examples,—viz. the betrayer of Jesus, and that apostle upon whom, as upon one firm as a rock to confess Him, Jesus built His Church. Even *Judas Iscariot* is a witness to the purity and innocence of Christ, and that by an act of the most decided kind,—an act not indeed of faith and love, but of despair. Like the other apostles, he too had, during three years of intimate intercourse, every opportunity of most closely observing the conduct of the Lord Jesus; and if he had detected any flaw in it, he would most certainly have brought this forward, after his treachery was consummated, for the purpose of palliating his deed and quieting his conscience. But finding nothing, he was constrained to confess that he had betrayed the *innocent blood*;[1] and the conviction of this crime was so heavy a burden on his soul, that he went away and killed himself. Thus even in and through the traitor, was the moral dignity and power of Jesus manifested; not, however, as a light unto life, but as a judgment unto death.

A contrast to this picture is exhibited in the case of St. Peter. The same apostle who first made a confession of faith in Jesus as the Son of the living God, makes an equally remarkable, though more indirectly expressed, confession of the moral glory of his Master. We allude, in the first place, to the expressions which broke from his lips after the miraculous draught of fishes: 'Depart from me; for I am a sinful man, O Lord.'[2] Undoubtedly the immediate occasion of these words was that manifestation of the power of Christ which he had just beheld; but it is worthy of remark, that

---

[1] Αἷμα ἀθῶον (Matt. xxvii. 4). [2] Luke v. 8.

Peter does not in the view of it exclaim, 'I am a weak, a perishing,' but 'I am a sinful man.' Hence it is very evident that Peter recognised in Him who had just shown forth such mighty power, pre-eminently One who would be polluted by intercourse with him the sinner, and hence one separate from sinners, the *Holy One.* The sinner and the Holy One of God can, so it seems to him, have nothing in common. We have in this saying the direct utterance of a soul struck with the moral dignity and uniqueness of Christ,—an utterance as strong and definite as can well be imagined, and at the same time an evidence of the light in which the apostle regarded our Lord's miraculous power, viz. as based upon moral reasons, and inseparable from sinless perfection.[1] It shows how intimately connected in his view were the morally and the physically miraculous. With this trait is connected a similar one in the life of St. Peter. We mean the circumstance that, after his denial of his Master, it needed only a look from the latter[2] to produce the deepest conviction of sin, and the bitterest remorse in the heart of the apostle. A mere look could never have had such power, unless the sacred purity and dignity of Him whom he had first denied, had at the same time been irresistibly present to his mind. The holy purity of Jesus and his own sinfulness are, to the apostle's mind, like two opposite poles, which exercise a power of mutual limitation in the effect they produce upon his inward emotions.

The same truth which is in these instances brought before us by facts, is still more definitely and expressly asserted by the apostles in many doctrinal passages; and this is done in a manner which makes it obvious that they are by no means

---

[1] The notion of the incompatibility between the possession of the power of working miracles and a sinful nature is also expressed by others not included in the apostolic circle. See John ix. 16, xxiv. 31, 33.
[2] Luke xxii. 61.

speaking of a moral excellence which might be shared also by others, but of a perfection attributable to the Lord Jesus alone. Neither is this all-surpassing elevation indefinitely and indirectly hinted at, but insisted on in a manner at once most decided and direct. All the apostles and apostolic men, and foremost among them he whose actions we have just mentioned as making a like confession, and St. John, the beloved disciple, recognised in Christ not merely *a* righteous and innocent man, but *the* Righteous and Holy One in a super-eminent way, in an absolutely unique sense.[1] He is in their eyes One who was in all points tempted like as we are, yet without sin;[2] who is our perfect example, because He did no sin, neither was guile found in His mouth;[3] the Lamb without blemish and without spot;[4] the true High Priest, holy, harmless, undefiled, separate from sinners, and made higher than the heavens;[5] who therefore needed not, as other high priests, to offer up sacrifice for His own sins; who, since in Him there was no sin, was for that very reason all the more

---

[1] Acts iii. 14, viii. 25, xxii. 14; 1 Pet. iii. 18; 1 John ii. 1, 29, iii. 7; Heb. iv. 15. Comp. also 1 Tim. iii. 16.

[2] Heb. iv. 15.

[3] 1 Pet. ii. 21. Nitzsch excellently paraphrases the expression ὑπογραμμός by: the living *Reinschrift* and *Vorschrift*—i.e. fair copy for imitation—of a behaviour pleasing to God.

[4] 1 Pet. i. 19.

[5] The expressions 'separate from sinners' and 'higher than the heavens,' used in this passage, must undoubtedly be understood, in the first instance, in a local sense, but they are at the same time as certainly employed to symbolize that inward elevation of an ethical and metaphysical kind, which the writer attributes to Christ. They denote a state of most perfect fellowship with God, far surpassing aught attained by sinful creatures, and proved to be such by the super-mundane glory of its possessor. The entrance upon such a state naturally presupposes the absolute sinlessness and holiness of Him who is raised thereto: hence this, if it had not been most expressly affirmed in the former expression, would be decidedly asserted even by the latter. Compare the full discussion of this subject in Riehm's *Lehrbegriff des Hebräerbriefs*, ii. § 55, p. 400, etc.; and also the same work, sec. i. §§ 37 and 38, pp. 317 and 321, etc., on the doctrine of the sinlessness of Christ in general, as stated in the Epistle to the Hebrews.

able to take away ours.[1] But for this persuasion, moreover, of the sinless holiness of Jesus, the apostles could by no means have recognised in Him, as they actually did, not merely the greatest of all the prophets, but the Messiah, endowed with the fulness of the Divine Spirit,[2] the founder of the kingdom of God, of which He was Himself to be both King and Lawgiver, the Redeemer from sin, the likeness of the alone good and holy God. For it is evident that none but One, the persuasion of whose holy purity had penetrated their inmost hearts, could have been all this, and especially the perfect Redeemer from sin. The traits and expressions hitherto adduced, and especially the latter, are, however, all of a general kind, and destitute of individuality. Hence it might be possible to regard them as the results of doctrinal prepossessions, and to declare that those who believed in Jesus, being persuaded that He was the Messiah and Redeemer, could not fail to attribute to Him the qualities which this character required, and among these was undoubtedly that of sinless perfection. Such a view, indeed, leaves unexplained the fact how faith in Jesus as the Messiah and Redeemer could exist at all, unless He really did produce the impression of a personality entirely pure and sinless. Sinlessness, too, as we shall hereafter see, was by no means so current a notion, that it had but to be applied to some person or other. On the contrary, it was not till the actual appearance of Jesus that it distinctly presented itself to the consciousness; and this being the case, it is but reasonable to infer that its source was this very appearance. It is, moreover, specially worthy of consideration, that the account presented to us of the person of

---

[1] Heb. vii. 27; 2 Cor. v. 21; 1 John iii. 5, with which passage compare Lücke's *Commentary*, pp. 161, 162.

[2] It is not indeed expressly stated in the Old Testament that the Messiah was to be sinless, but His sinlessness is implied by the very nature of the case, and is at least alluded to Isa. liii. 9 (compared with 1 Pet. ii. 22). See Umbreit, *Der Knecht Gottes*, pp. 56–60.

Jesus by His apostles by no means consists of mere general statements, but also places before us a copious and detailed history of His life and character. By this, these more general features and expressions receive concrete completion and living confirmation. And the more so, because the evangelists have handed down to us their portraiture of Christ in a manner which exhibits no trace of forethought or design, but gives abundant indication of that artless simplicity which draws only the actual features,—features, however, which naturally combine to form a perfectly harmonious and utterly unique whole.

The task, then, which we have now to perform, is to gather together into a whole the various features of the *portrait of the Lord Jesus*, as furnished by the Gospels. This is a subject which, as all must allow, can never be exhaustively treated,—a task whose accomplishment can at best be but approximated. It is a theme infinite in its nature, and ever offering new aspects, at various ages of the world, and in successive stages of human development. As such it inevitably meets us in the course of our argument; and we consequently attempt its treatment, though we do so with the fullest conviction of our own insufficiency.

THE GOSPEL PORTRAITURE OF JESUS.

All must agree that the impression produced by the Gospel delineation of the Lord Jesus is one of moral *greatness*,—a greatness which has frequently overcome even the opponents of positive Christianity. It is, however, a greatness utterly *new* in kind. It is not said of Jesus that He was great in the eyes of the world, but 'great in the sight of the Lord.'[1] In heathen antiquity those were regarded as great men who, striving to excel their fellows, raised themselves above their contemporaries, either by mighty deeds, or by brilliant achieve-

[1] Luke i. 15, 22.

ments in the realms of art or science.[1] This greatness, moreover, ever consisted in the fact, that in them the genius of their nation, working in a definite sphere, and with concentrated energy, became, as it were, incorporate. Within the province of the Old Testament it was indeed otherwise; inasmuch as here it was no longer from mere self-reliant human strength that greatness was derived, but from the direct influence of Divine power. Yet even here greatness consisted essentially in those mighty manifestations of the Spirit which, surpassing what was common to man, were displayed in extraordinary and imposing actions, and here, too, all was effected within the closely drawn boundaries of nationality.

Quite otherwise was it with the Lord Jesus. His path was not upwards, but downwards. He was great, not by ascending, but by *condescending:* hence His was not a brilliant, but a *silent* greatness. The aim of His every action was to draw near to the mean and despised, to seek the lost, to minister to others, instead of being ministered to. His dignity was veiled under the form of a servant; and as He ever avoided worldly honour,[2] and never sought His own glory, so did He chiefly manifest the strength of His will, in having no will of His own, but committing all things to God. His soul was silent before God (Ps. lxxii. 1, marg.), and His whole walk—especially when He silently suffered the worst to befall Him—was one uninterrupted expression of perfect acquiescence in the Divine counsels.

This is not a greatness which directly strikes the eye, and makes a powerful external impression, but a greatness of the *inner nature.* Jesus was great in the inner man before He had done anything externally great. And even when He

---

[1] Even Homer expresses in this respect the consciousness of the Grecian world in the pregnant words, 'Ever to lead in the van, and to surpass others.'

[2] John vi. 15; comp. John v. 41.

did perform deeds with which nothing else could be compared, the reason of their super-eminence lay chiefly in the fact that they were done by HIM, by One so unique in His inner nature. His disciples might—as He Himself said[1]—do such works as He did, and even greater; but these works could never be of like significance with His, because in Him the personality whence all originated was of a nature so far more exalted.

But this personality found the roots of its being and the object of its existence, not in anything *special* and limited like national genius, not in any single province of human activity, but in that which concerns all men without exception,—in the manifestation of the true relation to God, and the true relation to man. The whole life of Jesus was spent in realizing this relation in Himself, and from Himself towards all mankind, as at once the Son of God and the Son of man. Hence His was no special calling, but the *calling of callings*, the perfect fulfilment of which was to impart to all individual vocations a sure and eternal foundation.[2] Hence, too, His greatness is not such as is achieved in any special province; it is not the greatness of the hero or the lawgiver, of the profound thinker or the artist, but one which far transcends all these,—that greatness in which is manifested the true and universal Human in its highest relation, its relation to God, and through Him to all mankind; that greatness for which none other can furnish a standard, before which every other which does not unduly exalt itself must be constrained to bow.

It is not enough, however, thus to allude to the greatness of Christ in general outlines,—we must also descend to particulars. Yet we would guard against doing this in such wise as to seem, by presenting a collection of specially striking

---

[1] John xiv. 12.

[2] Compare Martensen, *Christian Dogmatics*, § 142, p. 282 (Clark's Foreign Theological Library); Schöberlein, *Grundlehren des Heils.* p. 62; Dorner, *Jes. sündl. Vollk.* p. 15.

traits, to catalogue the chief and special virtues of the Lord. Jesus did not, in fact, manifest this or that particular virtue; but, according to the very significant expression of St. John, He manifested *the life*. It is His entire life which must be the subject of our contemplation, though, if our view of it is to be a vivid one, details must certainly not be excluded.

The very first thing which strikes us in the Gospel portraiture of Jesus, is the *harmony* which pervaded His whole life, the *peace* which flowed around Him, and which He ever communicated to those about Him. The impression made upon us by His appearance is ever one of repose, self-possession, and self-reliance, combined with deep inexhaustible mental emotion: He was distinguished, neither by the lofty ecstasy of an Isaiah or an Ezekiel, nor by the legislative and mighty energy of a Moses; His nature, on the contrary, was all serenity and gentleness. The sacred flame which glowed in the ancient prophets was in Him transformed into the soft but ever-energizing presence of the creative breath of the Spirit. As it was not the storm which rent the mountains, nor the fear-inspiring earthquake, nor the devouring fire, but 'the still small voice,' which announced to Elijah the presence of the Lord, so was it also with the Lord Jesus.[1] He dwelt without intermission on those heights to which specially favoured individuals have, in isolated moments, been enabled to approximate. Like the sun in a cloudless sky, He quietly pursued with undeviating constancy His appointed path. His words were full of light, and His works of heart and warmth, and yet they were ever free from violent emotion or passion. He did nothing thoughtlessly or without a purpose; whatever He undertook was ever crowned with complete success, and never failed to attain its object. Even when rebuking with severity, nay, denouncing with anger, it was not personal

---

[1] 1 Kings xix. 8-15. See the excellent application of this passage in Joh. von Müller's *Allgem. Gesch.* Book ix. cap. 6.

irritation that moved Him, but the holy wrath of love,—a love which hated sin, while it loved in the sinner the man capable of being redeemed. In such cases, as in all others, even in the most trying circumstances of His life, He ever maintained uniform self-possession and perfect self-control. Thus possessed of inward peace, He was able to address to His disciples the glorious words, 'Peace I leave with you; my peace I give unto you.'

The harmony and peace which prevailed in the character of Jesus did not arise, however, from such a toning down of the various powers and activities as would prevent any of them from attaining its full energy of action. A harmony so attained would be not the harmony of greatness, but of mediocrity. The harmony of greatness can exist only in a *strong* character, where a rich, deep, powerfully stirred life wells up, and where discordant qualities are brought into unison. And this was eminently the case with Jesus,—with Him who came to send a sword as well as to send peace, and is with equal right entitled the Lion of the tribe of Judah, and the Lamb that taketh away the sin of the world. The harmony manifested in His character is based upon the richest fulness of heart and spirit, and proves itself to be the harmony of true greatness, by the fact that the tendencies which in other cases mutually exclude each other,—the powers and activities which are elsewhere found apart,—here work side by side in their full energy, and are blended by supreme power of mind into one glorious whole. In Him the Individual and the universally Human, independence and submission, doing and enduring, sublime majesty and humble condescension, are united, and pervade one another in a manner entirely new, and not even approximated by any who preceded Him. They are so combined that we cannot omit one of them, if we would have His portrait unimpaired and undiminished.

Let us first contemplate the relation of the Individual to the universally Human in the person of Jesus. As a man, Jesus was placed under all the laws of human existence. He lived under the conditions of race and family; He had certain endowments of mind, and a certain mental disposition; He belonged to a certain nation, and lived at a certain historical era; He entered into all these special relations, and did justice to them all. But instead of being limited by them, they served Him as means of realizing and manifesting that which was truly human in and beyond them.

The invincible will which He ever maintained was such, that we must call the Lord Jesus a man in the fullest sense of the word; yet we must not, on this account, make His peculiar characteristic to consist in manliness in so far as this is opposed to womanliness, for He equally manifested all the gentleness, purity, and tenderness of the female character. We find in Him high intellectual endowments; but it would be an error to characterize Him as pre-eminently acute or profound, clever or imaginative, because not any one of these gifts, though they were all seen in rich abundance, was the predominant quality of His mind. Nor less do we perceive in Him varying frames of mind and changes of disposition,—cheerfulness and freedom from anxiety, as well as deep seriousness and depression; quick susceptibility and imperturbable equanimity; painful fear and joyful resignation. And yet we could not but consider it unseemly to attribute to Him a peculiar temperament, in the ordinary acceptation of the term; for all that we know of Him produces the impression of a thoroughly sound and healthy mingling of dispositions, and a constantly natural interchange of emotions.[1]

[1] For admirable remarks on this subject, see Martensen's *Christian Dogmatics*, § 141. Formerly, indeed, even the special temperament of Jesus was spoken of. Winkler, especially, in his *Psychographie Jesu*, Leipzig 1826, p. 122, ascribes to Him the *choleric* as that of great minds. See also Naumann, *De Jesu Chr. ab animi affectibus non immuni*, Lips.

But this interpenetration of the particular and the general, —this repletion of a given individual form with the higher and universal spirit of humanity,—is super-eminently shown in the position which Jesus occupied with regard to His family and nation. He fulfilled all His duties as a member of a family, and especially manifested, even to His dying hour, the tenderest filial affection. But at the same time He subordinated all that occurred in the family circle to the Divine purposes, and made individual interests yield to those which were higher and universal.[1] As the founder of the kingdom of God upon earth, He regarded every one who did the will of God as His mother, and sister, and brother. In this sense, too, He required that every member of that kingdom should be willing to sever even the closest family ties, if they should form an obstacle in the way of his following his only Lord and Master. In like manner, Jesus did not cease to be a member of His nation. He performed with conscientious faithfulness all the Divine appointments which had been prescribed to His people, and submitted Himself even to human customs when praiseworthy and right. In His labours He observed the requirements and the forms of the spirit of His people, and adapted Himself most cordially and entirely to the circumstances of time and place. But while He did this, there was in His demeanour not a shade of those peculiarities which disadvantageously distinguish His peculiar nationality. He rather raised it above its narrowness, and happily exhibited in Himself such of its characteristics as were to be of decided importance to the religious development of the whole human race.

This is one of the principal characteristics by which Jesus

1840; and, on the other side, Thiele, in the *Theol. Lit. Bl.* Feb. 1841, No. 19. In agreement with my views are Dorner, *Jes. sundl. Vollk.* p. 30; and Schaff, *The Moral Character of Christ*, p. 28.

[1] *E.g.* John ii. 4; Mark iii. 32-35; Luke xi. 27, 28.

is distinguished from all the great spirits of antiquity, even the greatest of them. However profound in thought those men may have been, however comprehensive in action, they still bear, all of them, the impress of their own peculiar nationality, they still mirror back the age in which they lived; and this is true, not only of their life in its outward form, but also of their inmost and deepest nature. Even a Socrates knew no higher virtue than a free obedience to the law of his country, and a faithful observance of the customs of the fathers. Their noblest enthusiasm was evoked by the interests of their fatherland, and the highest deed they could achieve was to die for it. They grew out of the spirit of their age and nation: hence their reaction on their age and nation consisted, for the most part, in manifesting the fullest and noblest expression of that spirit.[1]

Jesus Christ was surpassed by no sage or hero of any era, either in power of action, or in readiness for self-sacrifice. But the principle which determined and guided His whole life was not national, but human; not temporal, but eternal. His moral character did not bear the impress of the age to which He belonged, but had 'the ring of eternity' about it. Developed from His own inner nature, He was the first to present an example of a full and perfect *man*, and, though connected with a particular nation, yet, by breaking through and abolishing national restrictions, to realize the idea of

---

[1] Among the ancients, Socrates rises most above national limits, and he himself desired to be regarded as a cosmopolitan (Cicero, *Tusc. Quæst.* v. 37: *Socrates quidem cum rogaretur, cuiatem se esse diceret, Mundanum, inquit, totius enim mundi se incolam et civem arbitrabatur*); nevertheless, his whole nature, not excepting his moral character, had a Greek impress, and stood in immediate relation to the laws and customs of his country (Ritter, *Gesch. der Philos.* ii. 35). The same holds good of his piety, which, in spite of his peculiarities, was based upon the national traditions, and by no means possessed the universal character of Christian piety (*ib.* p. 38).

a *common humanity*.¹ Hence, too, He was the first who, though His labours in their actual order began among His own people, did not confine Himself to their limits, but embraced in holy love the whole human race, and for it dared to live and die. It was thus that He became the portrayer of humanity as a living whole,—as a single body, through which divine energies flowed, the founder of the kingdom of God. And this He could only be, on the one hand, by lovingly recognising the infinite worth of each individual soul, and submitting Himself to all the divinely appointed distinctions in human life; and, on the other, by rising above everything particular, whether in the individual or the family, the race or the nation; by embracing in mind and heart all mankind, and transfiguring, by the new principle which He introduced, that which was special into that which was genuinely human and universally true. Hence it is the universal nature of its morality which specially strikes us in the character of the Lord. Yet this is never a vague generality, a colourless abstraction, but a morality in all respects so replete with rich, vivid, and quite unusual characteristics, that we cannot fail to attribute to Him also the trait of strong and well-defined individuality.²

But not only are the individual and the universal resolved into one beauteous whole in the person of Christ, but other opposing characteristics of human life—self-dependence and resignation, action and suffering—mingle in Him in perfect harmony. It is true, indeed, that in every human development which is not, morally speaking, abnormal, we shall find both self-dependence and submission, power to do and to suffer. In every case, however, it will be manifest that

---

¹ See Hundeshagen *On the Nature and Development of the Idea of Humanity*, Heidelberg 1852; especially pp. 15-21.
² Compare Dorner, *Jes. sundl. Vollk.* pp. 15 and 44; also Schaff *On the Moral Character of Christ*, pp. 26, etc.

one or the other has the preponderance,—that the man distinguished for self-dependence and energy is not equally great in resignation and endurance; or, on the other hand, that he who is in an eminent degree resigned and enduring, is deficient in action and self-reliance. In the person of Jesus these opposites were perfectly reconciled. His self-reliance was maintained in conjunction with absolute resignation, and His resignation was based upon the truest self-reliance. His actions, which ever betrayed a trace of suffering, disclosed at the same time a sublime spirit of endurance; and His sufferings, which were entirely voluntary, manifested at the same time the most untiring energy. Jesus was completely self-reliant, absolutely free and self-possessed. It is true that even He who had not where to lay His head, required, in His outward life, the assistance of others; while, for His inner life, He stood in need of the love of His own. He drew John nearer to His heart than the rest; He rejoiced in the submission of the woman that was a sinner; He desired 'heartily' to eat the passover with His disciples; He wanted them to be near Him, and to sympathize and watch with Him in the last agony of His soul. But this purely human need of sympathy never became in Him dependence upon others. He ever found firmness within Himself, and was ever determined in His outward procedure by inward motives. He could say to the apostles, 'Ye have not chosen me, but I have chosen you. Ye call me Master and Lord; and ye say well, for so I am.' Nor did He merely say this,—He ever acted upon it; for always, in relation to everything that was highest, He appeared not in the character of a receiver, but a giver,—not as one strengthened by others, but as one who imparted both strength and liberty. In His heaviest and most decisive trials, He relied upon Himself alone; and it was in Gethsemane, where the disciples slept,—on the cross, when they forsook Him,—that the independence and dignity of the Shepherd, who remained unmoved when His flock was scattered, were first fully revealed. In order to attain to the dominion which He exercised, He did not, like others, require to make use of means external to Himself: on the contrary, every agency by which He worked was within Himself; and in this sense may the words of the prophet be applied to Him: 'The government is upon His shoulders.'[1] But in this self-reliance in which Jesus, as altogether free from sin, and altogether holy, stood opposed to the world, whose sin He deeply recognised, He never showed Himself exclusive and unsympathizing towards the sinful and the guilty. On the contrary, it was just as one wholly self-dependent that He *gave Himself without reserve to the world;* and it was as He who had life in Himself, that He lived not for Himself, but for others. Nothing that was human was foreign to Him. He wept over Jerusalem; He was grieved for the people; He called to Him the weary and heavy-laden; He preached the gospel to the poor. His practice was to restore the broken reed, and to revive the smoking flax. His whole life, even till His death upon the cross, stands before us as *one* great act of *self-sacrifice.* Self-reliance and resignation both appear in Him in their truly ethical character: the former as the self-reliance of unbounded benevolence, which lives only for others; the latter, as the resignation of an entirely self-reliant, yet at the same time self-abnegating nature. He was capable of entire self-surrender, because of His perfect self-possession; and He was thus perfectly self-possessed, because fulness of self-sacrificing love was His very nature.

Similar to this is the relation between doing and suffering in the life of Christ. Jesus appears, at first sight, to have been essentially a man of action. He was wont, indeed, to

[1] Isa. ix. 6.

withdraw into retirement, for the purposes of recollection and prayer; yet activity, and not contemplation, was the prevailing feature of His life. He went about doing good. He was constantly employed in ministering to the temporal as well as the spiritual wants of men. His very words were deeds, and His whole life 'a work' which the Father had given Him to do, and from which He never rested 'while it was day.' In accomplishing this work, He invariably kept *one* end in view, and manifested, in every circumstance of life, that power of mind which seems peculiar to those who are called to decided action. At the same time, however, He whose life seemed thus dedicated to action, was also super-eminently a sufferer. He was indeed the 'man of sorrows, and acquainted with grief.'[1] He was constantly enduring want and temptation, enmity and indignity. Besides those severe outward sufferings which awaited Him, even till the martyrdom of the cross, He incessantly felt the deepest mental affliction, because all the opposition and enmity which He encountered, arose from the sin of those whose salvation He regarded as His special office. And He bore all this, not with stoical indifference, but with deep and tender human sensibility, without murmuring or bitterness, committing all to God in quiet confidence, and never ceasing, even in the midst of His bitterest sufferings, to love those by whom they were inflicted. Doing and suffering were perfectly blended together in His life; and it is impossible at any juncture to separate the actions of the Lord Jesus from His sufferings, or to think of His sufferings apart from the activities of His existence. The acts of Christ were ever attended by suffering.[2] His very entrance upon His divinely appointed work was caused by *sympathy* for sinful men; how much more, then, must its accomplishment have

---

[1] Isa. liii. 3.
[2] Compare Schöberlein, *Grundlehren des Heils.* p. 64.

entailed continual suffering, as being an unintermitting conflict with sin, which was the original cause of all the sorrows of His soul! At the same time, every suffering of Christ was also an act, for He did not merely allow suffering to come upon Him as something from without, but consciously entered into it, and voluntarily took it upon Himself, as a matter of Divine appointment. On this account, His death and passion must be regarded as the noblest action of His life. He endured the cross, though He might have had pleasure.[1] Thus did He manifest, in equal force and inseparable combination, the spirit both of the hero and the sufferer, and place before our eyes a harmony nowhere else to be found in the wide pages of history; because none but He ever waged such utter war with sin, or carried on this contest after so Divine a fashion.

Again, such a life could not fail to bear the fullest impress both of *humility* and *majesty*,—a majestic humility, and a majesty of a humble nature. Rightly, indeed, could Jesus say of Himself, 'I am meek and lowly of heart.' His whole life was one continuous act of self-sacrifice, and one uninterrupted course of self-abasement. Even at its close, when He knew that He was about to depart to the Father, He gave the most touching example of that condescending love which ministers to others, by washing His disciples' feet;[2] thus bearing testimony that He regarded the service of love as the perfection of life. And yet a kingly spirit was ever shining forth through the veil of humiliation and reproach with which He was covered; and His words as well as His actions expressed a consciousness which we must either not understand at all, or understand as the result of inward dignity of an utterly incomparable nature. Many were the words of majesty which fell from the mouth of Jesus,—from His first utterance in the synagogue of Naza-

[1] Heb. xii. 2 (Luther's version).   [2] John xiii. 2.

reth, 'To-day is this scripture fulfilled in your ears,'[1] to that powerful testimony before His worldly-minded judge, '*I am a King. To this end was I born, and for this cause came I into the world, that I should bear witness unto the truth!*'[2] What an effect, too, did the majesty of His personal appearance produce on all! It struck with the same power, though in such different manners, both the officers who were sent to apprehend Him,[3] and the disciple who had denied Him;[4] both the excited accusers who were ready to stone Him,[5] and the contrite malefactor who recognised in Him a Saviour, even amidst the horrors of crucifixion. And here, as before, these opposite attributes qualify each other. The Lord Jesus was thus full of majesty, just because His high soul bowed in such deep humility before God; and thus perfectly humble, because His was not the humility of the sinner, arising from a deep sense of unworthiness before God, but that of one who had the high consciousness of full communion with God.

Thus is the portrait of our Lord presented to us as full of dignified majesty and holy gentleness; and that in traits so clearly defined, that they cannot fail to strike even the dullest mind. Nowhere do we find aught of show or ostentation,—nowhere a trace of labouring for effect or of imitation: all is truth and simplicity; every act is the product of His inmost soul, and yet every act is sustained by a repose and self-consciousness, whose marvellous composure is never for a moment disturbed. Everywhere is seen the perfect harmony of a strong and noble character,—or, to speak more correctly, of this One character,—which in this its perfectly harmonious blending, both of deepest feeling, and rich, full manifestation, is utterly beyond comparison. What, then, was the *source* of this harmony? It surely

---

[1] Luke iv. 16.   [2] John xviii. 37.
[3] John xviii. 6.   [4] Luke xxii. 61.
[5] John viii. 59, x. 31, compared with Luke iv. 29.

lay in the fact that all the actions of the Lord Jesus proceeded from *one* creative force, that His whole life was regulated by *one* governing principle. It is to this principle, this force, that we must now direct our attention.

And, first of all, the governing principle of the Lord's life was the maxim, *To do the will of God*.[1] This will, knowing it as He did, directly and infallibly, was the only rule of His life. He did what the Father gave Him to do,—what He saw the Father do.[2] To do this was His meat and drink.[3] Without this entire subjection to God, He could not have lived,—could not have been satisfied for a single moment. Hence His life was the manifestation of a perfect *obedience*, —an obedience not merely to Divine law, but to God Himself,—an obedience consisting not merely of a series of individual acts, but forming the one act of His whole life. And this obedience He learned especially by the things which He suffered;[4] being thus made perfect, that He might become to others a source of obedience unto salvation.[5] But this obedience itself arose from a still deeper source,—from the full unreserved surrender of His inmost soul to God, that is, from His *faith*, which, in its very nature, is one with *love*. Jesus dwelt entirely in the faith and love of God: these were the roots of His character, the sources of His life; from these He drew, not to possess them for Himself, but to impart them to others. From His love to God there ever flowed an inexhaustible stream of love to man; and it was this, its source, which gave to the human love of Jesus a character so peculiar and so different from anything that had yet been seen. It was not merely a hearty benevolence, and a general readiness to afford assistance, but a love full of a holy seriousness of purpose, and wholly directed towards *one* end,—to effect

---

[1] John vi. 38, v. 30. [2] John v. 19. [3] John iv. 34.
[4] Phil. ii. 8; Heb. v. 8. [5] Heb. v. 9; Rom. v. 19.

the salvation of all who needed it, *i.e.* of the whole sinful and sin-ruined race of man. Hence it was, by its own inner nature, a love which condescended to those of low degree, which sought out the lost and the reprobate, that it might first make them fitting objects of love; and thus, too, it was a *compassionate*, a *preventing*, a *love-creating* love. It is this which is the fundamental principle of the holy love of God Himself;[1] and since the whole life of the Lord Jesus, till His voluntary self-sacrifice, was passed in the active manifestation of this love, we have in Him, and in His love, not a mere reflex, but an actual and genuine manifestation of *Divine* love.

Finally, it is in this love that we find that unifying power, in virtue of which, varied and seemingly opposite qualities are blended into one harmonious whole in the character of Jesus. This love it was which, entering into all the divinely ordained distinctions of human life, at the same time rose above them to embrace the whole human race; which blissfully resting in God, nevertheless impelled to ceaseless activity for man; which, free and independent in its own nature, gave itself to be a ministering servant to all; which imparted strength both to do and to endure, and was as majestic in its holy earnestness as it was lowly in its condescension. It was this which set upon every act of the Lord Jesus the ineffaceable mark of *religion*, and which elevated what we should else call morality into holiness. Hence it is, that while the piety of Jesus never obtrudes itself as a special, and, as it were, an independent quality, every act becomes in His case one of religion, of worship;[2] and hence, too, His whole manifestation does

---

[1] Compare Rom. v. 8 and 10; 1 John iv. 10.
[2] Everything becomes in His hands, and by the breath of His mouth, a symbol, nay, a typical or prophetic expression of the spiritual and the Divine.—DORNER, *Jesu sundl. Vollk.* pp. 33 and 34.

not give an impression of mere religion or mere morality, but of religion and morality in perfect combination,—in a word, of *holiness*. According, then, to what has been said, we see in the Lord Jesus a character in perfect unison with itself,—equally great in acting as in suffering. In Him we behold a Being whose *one* object was the salvation of sinners, and whose life and death were acts of absolute self-surrender for the sake of accomplishing that object; One whose essential nature was perfect, *i.e.* Divine, love manifested in a purely human form.

In such a Being, *sin*—*i.e.* antagonism to God—could have no place, because selfishness, which is the principle of sin, was utterly abolished by the all-conquering energy of love to God and man. And, in fact, we find the picture of the Lord Jesus which the Gospels furnish, and which all the apostles received, to be such, that even if nothing had been expressly stated on this point, we could never have conceived of sin—of alienation from God—as a feature thereof, without being immediately sensible that we were thus essentially disfiguring, nay, altogether destroying it.

But, it may be asked, is not all this but *fiction?* If it were, we could not but say, with the noble-minded Claudius,[1] 'that one might well let himself be branded, or broken on the wheel, for the *very idea*,—and he who could laugh or mock must certainly be mad.' The portrait of the Lord Jesus, as presented in the Gospels, even if regarded as a mere idea or fiction, is the sublimest and most glorious idea to which the human mind has attained in the sphere of morality and religion,—it infinitely surpasses all other descriptions of character which we possess. Even if not genuine, it has a far greater influence upon our moral and religious life, than a thousand maxims of whose genuine-

[1] See the first of the 'Briefen au Andres' in the *Wandsbecker Boten*.

ness no one entertains a doubt. In short, it is too great, too pure, and too perfect, to be mere invention.

Besides, *who* could have invented it? Is it answered, Many—the whole Apostolic Church? Was such a thing ever heard of in the world, as a whole community combining to invent a portraiture of character so rich in details? How should the Church in general have hit upon such a notion; and how, since the thing could not take place in a dream, could it have set about its execution? And, even admitting the possibility of the attempt being made by the Church, would the portrait produced have exhibited that harmony which is so decidedly found in the Gospel representation of the Lord Jesus? Or is it said that the fiction was the work of an individual? How, then, should the image of One sinlessly pure and holy have entered into the mind of a sinful human being? And, even if this were possible, whence could he, in addition to the idea of sinless perfection, derive all those special features and expressions which give life and substance to the idea? Such traits and such sayings, upon which not only the character of the highest originality is everywhere impressed, but to which, moreover, it must at least be conceded that they are of such a nature as to render it impossible to suppose them to be the mere productions of fancy;—these their inventor must, unless they had really been placed before him by the actual life of Jesus, have derived from himself; and then, as Rousseau strikingly observes, the inventor of such an image would be greater and more astonishing than his subject.[1] And then we must accord to him what we withhold from Christ. Besides, which among such illiterate men as the apostles could have been capable of inventing an image which, even to the present day, is unsurpassed by the performances of the

[1] 'L'inventeur en seroit, plus étonnant que le héros.'

greatest literary geniuses of all ages, nay, is utterly inimitable? If such a fiction, moreover, were conceivable, how could its hero have become an object for which the very persons who had invented him should feel not merely a transitory enthusiasm, but should deliberately and perseveringly endure the loss of all things, and at last even suffer death? Besides, not only must the image of Jesus have been invented, but also the very foundations upon which it is placed; in other words, the whole system of Christian modes of thought;— a system so utterly different from all that preceded it, and one into which the apostles themselves were but gradually and reluctantly initiated. Whence, then, did this arise, if the Jesus of the Gospels were not its author, and Himself but a fiction?

But we will enlarge no further, as we shall subsequently return to this point, especially when treating on the effects produced by the manifestation of Jesus. For the present we confine ourselves to one remark with respect to the *apostolic testimony*. Efforts have been made to depreciate this by such suggestions as the following:—The apostles, it is said, were not so precise in their use of the words in which we find the sinlessness of Jesus testified,[1] and meant to express no more than Xenophon did concerning Socrates, when he said[2] that he had never seen him do an unjust action, or heard him speak an unholy word; in which words no one would find a testimony to the sinlessness of the heathen philosopher. It is also alleged that the testimony of even His most intimate associates to the moral character of Jesus is confined within very narrow limits; they were acquainted with His behaviour only during the three years of their intercourse with Him, and knew nothing of it in the earlier periods of His life. Besides, even during the time they were with Him, they could not see His heart, and were thus capable of judging

---

[1] Strauss, *Glaubenslehre*, ii. p 192. [2] *Memorab.* i. 11.

only of the external lawfulness, and not of the internal motives of His actions. Hence, the utmost to which they could bear witness would be, that they knew of no sin that Jesus had committed, not that there was none in Him.[1] The objections here suggested are, however, but very superficial, ignoring, as they do, the peculiar position which Jesus occupied with respect to His disciples, and failing in a just appreciation of moral development. It is undoubtedly true that the apostles, at the very least, testify as much concerning Christ as Xenophon asserts concerning Socrates, but it is quite as certain that they also go very much further. For Jesus was to them not merely what Socrates was to his school,—a noble, truth-seeking man, one indefatigably striving after wisdom,—He was, in their eyes, Himself the truth, the Son of God, the sole Mediator between God and man; and when, in consequence of the impression they had themselves received, they attributed sinlessness to One whom they viewed in this light, such a statement is undoubtedly one of far deeper and more serious import than that of a disciple of Socrates, when he says that he had never seen him do an unrighteous act, nor heard him speak an unholy word. Nor do the apostles confine themselves to negative assertions; but give us a positive portraiture of Jesus, in which, in spite of its fragmentary nature, that holy love, which entirely

---

[1] These thoughts are further carried out in the programme of Dr. Weber: *Virtutis Jesu integritas neque ex ipsius professionibus neque ex actionibus doceri potest*, Viteb. 1796 (reprinted in his *Opusc. Acad.* pp. 179–192). He is followed, to a certain point, by Bretschneider in his *Dogm.* § 138; and more fully by the elder Fritzsche in his *IV. Commentationes de ἀναμαρτησίᾳ Jesu Christi*, Hal. 1835–37 (reprinted in the *Opusc. Fritzschiorum*, Lips. 1838, pp. 45 seq.): compare especially the last Comment. The objections in question are briefly summed up by Hase in the *Leben Jesu*, § 32, and further developed, in a decidedly inimical sense, by Strauss in his *Glaubenslehre*, ii. 92. The opposite arguments are fully carried out in the article, '*Polemisches in Betr. der Sündlosigkeit Jesu*,' *Stud. und Kritik.* 1842–3, pp. 640, etc., to which I invite attention.

excludes the principle of sin, is reflected with a perfection which none can descry in the description of Socrates, as given by the greatest masters of eloquence.

With respect, however, to the other objections, it must be granted that the apostles in general were acquainted with Jesus only during their three years of intimacy with Him. Is the moral life, then, so to speak, such a piece of patchwork, that during three years of mature manhood its character could be perfection, unless its previous development had been of a similar nature? If not, would not every previous sin, of necessity, have so stunted or obscured the moral character of Christ, that He could not subsequently have produced the impression of sinless perfection? Must not the traces of former sin have been perceived at some one juncture? The indissoluble connection of the entire moral development enables us here, if anywhere, to infer the character of the whole from the part, and the nature of the root from its fruit. But besides this, we have the testimony of one intimately acquainted with Him from His youth upwards,[1] —the testimony of John the Baptist concerning the earlier period of His life. John was himself a man surpassing hi whole nation in moral elevation, and yet he most emphatically acknowledges, both by word and deed, and that in comparison with his own person, the utterly unique eminence of Christ. This he does, not only by designating Him as one whose shoe's latchet he was not worthy to unloose, but also by declaring, at the baptism, that he, a sinner, needed to be baptized of Jesus, and by retiring into the background from thenceforward, because the greater than he was come, who must increase while himself must decrease.

---

[1] I can only understand the expression of John (John i. 32, 33), though it seems to hint at the reverse, as implying his full recognition of the Messiahship of Jesus. See Planck, *Gesch. des Christenthums in der ersten Periode*, Pt. 11, pp. 116-24; and Neander, *Leben Jesu*, pp. 103-8, ed. third.

It is also unquestionably correct to say that the apostles could not look immediately into the heart of their Master, and hence could not judge with the certainty of Him who searcheth the heart and reins, concerning the secret motives of His actions. But does the fact that their knowledge of His moral condition was not Divine, make them forfeit their claim of being able to pass a human judgment concerning His person? This human judgment, when exercised within the province of morals, cannot but infer that where the whole external life is pure and undefiled, the internal source must be pure and undefiled also, and would only be justified in arriving at an opposite conclusion, if reasons existed for supposing a contrariety between the outward course of action and its inward motives. Had the apostles, then, cause for suspecting that the conduct which appeared so irreproachable, could have sprung from any but the purest source? If not, they had every ground for the assurance that His heart was as pure as His conduct; and that because they perceived no sin in it, there was no sin in Him.

Men are not generally *too much* given to the weakness of believing in moral excellence, much less in an entirely spotless virtue. When, then, such a belief strangely enough exists, and exhibits such powers of endurance as it does in the case of the apostles, we are certainly justified in the view that there must exist also a real objective reason, and a moral subjective necessity, for this belief.

Least of all can those who allow the sinless perfection of Christ oppose the possibility of its historical manifestation. If this sinlessness was *actual*, it must also have been *perceptible* by man. For would it not be the most monstrous contradiction, that a moral phenomenon, which must have been of the greatest importance to the whole human race, should actually have occurred, but in such wise that no one was capable of obtaining any certain knowledge and assurance concerning it? This would be a revelation, but one which revealed nothing to any man.[1]

Too much, however, must not be asserted. Apostolic testimony, valuable as it is, does not furnish us with an absolute guarantee. This it could only do, if, referring it to inspiration, we acknowledge its authority to be of directly Divine origin. The whole course of our argument, however, requires us to seek for confirmation and completion in another quarter; and this is furnished to us in *that testimony of Jesus to Himself* which we have now to adduce as a proof of His sinlessness: for though it may indeed be said of the apostles that they were incapable of seeing His heart, the same cannot be affirmed of Himself.

Sec. 2.—*The Testimony of Jesus to Himself.*

The Lord Jesus must best have known what was in Himself. Hence, the manner and nature in which He gave expression to His own moral consciousness, must naturally be of the most decided importance. The impression He produced on others, and their consequent conviction, must not, as is self-evident, be absent. Yet this might be but the echo of what originally proceeded from Jesus Himself; and hence, in the very nature of the thing, His own utterances on the subject must form the final and culminating testimony on which we embrace the persuasion of His sinlessness.

And, first, even the *negative* side of His testimony is in the highest degree remarkable.[2] As might be expected from one so holy, our Lord everywhere stood in most decided antagonism to sin: He drew it forth to light, rebuked, and

---

[1] Further carried out by Dorner, *Sündl. Vollk.* pp. 16–22.

[2] For further confirmation, see my article, '*Polemisches in Betr. Sündl.*,' *Stud. und Kritik.* 1842–3, pp. 661–67. Excellent remarks on this side of the question will also be found in Dorner, Schaff, and Young.

opposed it to the uttermost; nay, His whole life was devoted to maintaining a conflict against it. On the other hand, He was ever merciful to the penitent sinner, and bestowed commendations on those who, in the consciousness of their sinfulness, humbled themselves before God.[1] Now, He who had so keen a perception for the sins of others, must—unless we suppose Him utterly self-deluded—have had as keen a one for sin in Himself. But we nowhere hear from Him—as we do from even the very best of other men—so much as an occasional expression of a consciousness of sin. There is no humbling of Himself before God for sin, no prayer for forgiveness.[2] Does not this most decidedly show that the source from which these feelings proceed—feelings which are found just where the moral character is most eminent—had in Him no existence whatever? It may also be indirectly inferred from what He said at His baptism,[3] that He felt an inward consciousness that He needed for Himself neither repentance nor regeneration.[4] He required from all, without exception, who would enter into the kingdom of God, that they should be born again of water and of the Spirit;[5] while for Himself such a thing is out of the question. A development, a being made perfect, did indeed take place in His case; but a catastrophe in which the old man should die to sin, and the new and Divine man be born in Him, is not only nowhere hinted at, but is, moreover, utterly irreconcilable with the image which the Gospels present of the Lord Jesus. Nay, more; far from manifesting any need of repentance and forgiveness, He claims, on the contrary, with respect to sinners, the high position of One not only able to proclaim the

---

[1] Luke xviii. 9–14.
[2] Compare on this subject, J. G. Steinert, *Dissert. de peculiari indole precum Domini.*
[3] Matt. iii. 13–17.
[4] See Neander, *Leben Jesu*, p. 101, ed. third.
[5] John iii. 5, etc.

forgiveness of sins, but to bestow it.[1] He actually forgives the penitent in virtue of an authority which He evidently regards as one directly inherent in Himself. Could this be the case with a man who found guilt and sin in himself? Would not such an act, if there were no sufficient grounds for it, have been one of unparalleled audacity,—an encroachment upon the prerogative of God Himself?[2] It is obvious that Jesus could only be justified in such an assumption by the felt consciousness of perfect oneness with God,—a consciousness, again, arising from a feeling of perfect freedom from sin. In virtue of such a consciousness, moreover, could He alone have committed to His disciples a power to become the mediums of forgiveness after He had communicated to them the gift of the Holy Ghost.[3]

His *positive* testimony, however, goes much further. And here we have, first of all, to notice that weighty and important saying of Jesus, which we find in St. John's Gospel: 'Which of you convinceth me of sin?'[4] We no sooner hear such words, than we feel they must have proceeded from One whose moral constitution was of the most peculiar kind; and this impression is still further strengthened, when we remember that He who uttered them was a Person whose whole life was a model of truthfulness and humility. Every man, without exception, must immediately feel conscious that he cannot echo the mighty yet simple saying,—that for him, unable as he is to turn a deaf ear to the testimony of conscience, to apply it to himself, would be either empty fanaticism or miserable self-deception. Least of all could this happen within the sphere of Christian life, where the conscience is rendered

[1] Matt. ix. 6; Mark ii. 10; and elsewhere.
[2] Mark ii. 7; Luke v. 21.   [3] John xx. 22, 23.
[4] John viii. 46. Discussions on this and kindred passages will be found in Lutz, *Bibl. Dogm.* p. 294; and Schumann, *Christus*, vol. i. pp. 284, etc. Stier makes also excellent remarks on John viii. 46 in his *Reden Jesu*, Pt. 4, pp. 425, etc.

in so high a degree acute, by a perfect revelation both of the moral law and the Divine holiness, and out of which that same apostle who has preserved this memorable saying of our Lord exclaims, 'If we say we have no sin, we deceive ourselves, and the truth is not in us.'[1] It is in contradistinction to this, that *One* steps forth from the ranks of sinful human nature with the question, 'Which of you convinceth me of sin?'

But the meaning of this question must be somewhat more closely determined. The very word[2] on which most depends has been variously understood. We have translated it simply 'sin,' as Luther and the authorized English version render it; but the word requires a fuller investigation. The Greek expression, which here comes under notice, has, as is well known, the general signification of *failure* (*Verfehlen*). This general idea, again, is specially applied in a twofold sense: it either means a failure in the sphere of mind, and then it is error, mistake, untruth; or it means a failure in the domain of morals, and then it is known as sin, perversion of will, wrong. The word is used in the former sense (though only under a certain assumption) in classical Greek; in the latter sense it is used in Hellenistic, and especially in New Testament Greek. From the earliest times commentators have differed with regard to this twofold use of the word in their exposition of the passage under consideration. Some have maintained that Jesus intended, by this expression, to claim for Himself exemption from error;[3] others have held that He claimed freedom from sin;[4] while some have included the two ideas in one, making the ques-

---

[1] 1 John i. 8. See Lücke, Pt. 3, pp. 98–100.   [2] ἁμαρτία.

[3] This explanation occurs in Origen, in his *Commentary on John* (vol. xx. § 25). Kypke tries to justify it on philological grounds, in his observations on the passage. On the other side see Lücke, *Commentary on St. John*, Pt. 2, pp. 298–301, ed. second; and Meyer's *Commentary*, pp. 243, 244, ed. second.

[4] So many ancient and also the best among modern expositors,—*e.g.* Olshausen, Lücke, De Wette, and Meyer.

tion of Christ imply a reference both to error and to sin— any aberration, whether intellectual or moral, from the true and right way. Others, again, have been of opinion that the word sin is here best rendered *deception*.[1] The two last opinions we may at once set aside, as warranted neither by the use of language nor by the occasion, and as having at best only a probability in their favour; but the two first expositions require a more detailed investigation.

The view according to which Jesus asks, 'Which of you convinceth me of error?' would seem to be favoured by the context. Immediately before, He had designated His Jewish antagonists children of Satan, the man-murderer, the liar from the beginning, implying that theirs was a temper which proved their relationship to Satan, in that they refused to believe on Him who taught the truth of God, and even persecuted Him to the death. Then He asks, 'Which of you convinceth me of error?'[2]—with which is closely connected (for throughout the whole passage the contrast between truth and error, *i.e.* falsehood, is held fast) the further question: 'And if I say (not falsehood, but) the truth, why do ye not believe me?'

Now, supposing this explanation of the passage to be the correct one, even then the passage would be of great importance for our purpose, for it would at least contain an indirect testimony to the religious and moral purity of Jesus. For if He claims exemption from error in the province which here comes under consideration,—viz. that of morality and religion,—does not this imply that He also attributes to Him-

[1] The former is the view of Weber, in his already quoted *Programm*, p. 185, who thinks: Nomen ἁμαρτίας, non solum theoreticam sed etiam practicam aberrationem a vero et recto simul continere. The latter is proposed by Fritzsche, *Commentat.* ii. 2, pp. 7, etc. Comp. my article '*Polemisches*,' etc.

[2] According to one view of the passage,—that, according to Stier, of John v. Müller,—a view in which there seems to be a transition from the sublime to the ridiculous,—the sense of this question is made to be: 'Is there anything *illogical* in my inferences?'

self purity of inward nature and outward conduct in the same province? For freedom from sin presupposes freedom from error, and *vice versâ,*—the two act and react upon each other. Unquestionably the two in the sense of the New Testament, and especially of that Gospel in which this saying of Jesus is found, form one connected whole, just as their opposites, sin and untruth, do.[1]

But this explanation cannot be regarded as correct. In the first place, there attaches to it a verbal difficulty, which it is not easy to set aside. In classical usage, the word (ἁμαρτία) never occurs in the sense of error, without having beside it a modifying and determining clause or word.[2] In the New Testament it is very uncertain whether it can be satisfactorily shown that the word ever does occur in this sense;[3] least of all can this be shown in the use of the word in St. John's writings,—the idea He attaches to it being invariably that of *sin.* But the objections which arise from the passage itself, viewed with reference to the context, are still greater. Were we to adopt this explanation, there would, in the first place, be no progress in the argument; and this verse would not supply the reason or motive of what is said in the preceding verse. For when Jesus in that verse (John viii. 45) said, 'I speak the truth,' He made a statement which required to be proved. Now, if in the 46th verse He asks, 'Which of you convinceth me of error?' this would be a mere repetition, in a negative form, of the statement already made in a positive form, and by no means an argument in proof of it. *Secondly,* such a rendering of the word would destroy the analogy of the contrast which Jesus draws between Satan and the Jews on the one hand,

---

[1] On this connection, compare Frommann, *Doctrine of St. John* (S. 181-309, 550-654, etc.).

[2] See references (*e.g.* Plato, de *Leg.* i. 627, 668; Thucydides, i. 32, ii. 65) in Meyer, *Comment. zu Joh.* p. 243, ed. third.

[3] The passages, 1 Cor. xv. 34, Titus iii. 11, prove nothing conclusively.

and Himself, as the Son of God, on the other. For if, in the first part, regard is had not only to what is intellectually true, but, above all, to the moral condition, this must be the case in the second clause also. *Thirdly*, the notion that because they could convict Him of no error, they must believe on Him, would be one which would be in itself inadmissible;[1] for it would make intellectual demonstration the basis of faith, whereas true faith rests upon a direct attraction of the heart to the salvation revealed in Christ.

If we now take up the second explanation of the passage, 'Which of you convinceth me of *sin*?' we shall find all these difficulties disappear. To this rendering there is no verbal objection; it falls in admirably with the context; it supplies a proof of the statement just made. Jesus had previously maintained, in opposition to the unbelief of His hearers, that He spoke the truth;[2] and, as a pledge that He did so, He appeals to the fact that no one could convince Him of sin,—thus making His moral purity the guarantee of the truth of His doctrine. The idea might be rendered as follows:—Jesus had in his mind the contrast between truth and falsehood[3] already pointed out, and by including falsehood, *i.e.* the special, in sin, *i.e.* the general, He arrives at the conclusion: 'If I am free from sin, I must also be free from falsehood, for falsehood is sinful; and if I do not speak falsehood, then I speak the truth, and ye have no reason to withhold from me your faith.' The entire argument He does not, however, express in words: the middle clause remains unspoken—viz. that He is free also from falsehood; and He goes on at once from the repudiation of sinfulness,

---

[1] So even De Wette (in his *Exeget. Handbuch*) on this passage.

[2] Verse 44: 'Ye are of your father the devil, and the lusts of your father ye will do. He was a murderer from the beginning, and abode not in *the truth*, because there is no *truth* in him. When he speaketh a *lie*, he speaketh of his own; for he is *a liar*, and the father of it.'

[3] ἀλήθεια and ψεῦδος.

to the positive contrary which follows from His sinlessness—viz. His speaking the truth.[1] But there seems to be something artificial in introducing the idea of falsehood, which is in fact unnecessary. The thought is not only clear, but it becomes more forcible when we keep simply to those statements which Jesus has put in immediate connection. Generally speaking, the argument is founded upon the principle that there is an inseparable connection between the moral and the intellectual; and it is from a consciousness of this connection that Jesus says, 'As you, my opponents, reject me, and in me reject the truth, because your temper is sinful—is satanic; so, on the other hand, can I lawfully present myself as one who speaks the truth, because I am free from sin.' The conclusion is at once and immediately drawn—from the fact that He is free from sin, and from the moral purity of His character—to the truth of His words, and to the obligation lying upon His hearers to believe in Him, who was thus accredited: and this is a thought which is so consistent with all that fell from the lips of Christ, according to St. John's Gospel, that it cannot appear in the slightest degree strange to any one acquainted with this document.[2] At all events, it is certain

---

[1] This is also Meyer's view of the train of thought. See *Comment.* S. 244. So, too, Schumann, *Christus*, B. i. p. 287.

[2] Meyer (*Comment.* p. 243) is of opinion, that to maintain either, with Lücke, that 'the Sinless One is the purest and surest organ of knowledge and medium of truth;' or with De Wette, that 'the knowledge of truth rests on the purity of the will,'—would be to presuppose a knowledge of the truth attained by Jesus in a *discursive* manner, or at least in His human state, while His knowledge, especially according to St. John's teaching, was intuitively possessed before His earthly existence, and then maintained only by constant communion with God. But the objection is not to the point. The question is, not how He acquired His perfect knowledge of the truth, but how this was to be proved. For this proof, Christ appeals directly to His sinlessness; for this is, under all circumstances, a condition by which alone a perfect knowledge of religious truth could even intuitively exist and be recognised.

that Jesus in this passage expresses directly, as in previous passages He had indicated indirectly,[1] His consciousness of freedom from sin; and this it is which really concerns us.

But with regard to this testimony of Jesus, two objections have now to be obviated: *first*, it is of a *subjective* character, and, as such, does not of itself afford a complete proof of sinlessness; *secondly*, it is purely *negative*, expressing simply a consciousness of the absence of sin, not a consciousness of positive perfection of life. But neither of these two considerations can at all weaken the validity which we claim for this evidence.

With regard to the former. If *we* are to attain to an assured conviction of the sinlessness of Jesus, this is only possible on the supposition that, above all things, He Himself possessed such a conviction. It was only from Himself that the idea could go forth to those around Him. He Himself knew best what was in Him,[2] and only in the lively expression of His own self-consciousness could the opinion which others formed concerning Him find its stay and strength. There can be no doubt that the self-consciousness of Jesus must at the same time find its objective vindication, and such vindication is abundant; but this would be but unreliable and insecure, were it not that it rests upon the self-testimony of Jesus. And this could not possibly consist of aught else than a simple word of *assertion*. Every assertion concerning one's own state of heart and mind is of a subjective kind; but this circumstance does not in the least degree diminish its value when it is spoken by an intelligent and truthful man, because, from the very nature of the case, it cannot be otherwise. The assertion

---

[1] He did so when in verses 32-36 He called the Jews the slaves of sin, and designated Himself as *the truth* which *maketh free*. This, it is obvious, He could only be, by being free from that sin which enslaved and obscured His adversaries.

[2] 2 Cor. ii. 10.

of Christ that He was free from sin, even though merely subjective, entirely satisfies us whenever we assign to it its proper place, and regard it not as constituting the whole evidence of His sinlessness, but as an indispensable portion of it, which has its full import only when viewed in connection with the rest.[1]

With regard to the second point, it is true that when Jesus in the passage in question pronounces Himself free from sin, He makes only a negative statement. But the positive assertions required to render it complete are also to

---

[1] This is the only correct answer to the objection urged by Fritzsche (*Comment.* i. 21), and by the earliest opponents of Christ (John viii. 13), that a man's testimony concerning himself is not valid. It is true, indeed, that if it stands alone it could not, under all circumstances, and in all relations, be regarded as conclusive; but when it is asserted that in a case like this it is of no value whatever, this is to transfer, in a most illogical way, a principle of law to the domain of morals, and to apply a presumption gathered from the darkest experience of life, and one which is in daily life regarded as an insult among men of honour, to Him who has called Himself the King of Truth, and in 'whose mouth was found no guile' (Hase, *Streitschriften*, iii. 109, 110). It is however, utterly unfitting to maintain, as Fritzsche (*Comment.* ii. 2, pp 4-6), following the precedent of Weber, and laying special emphasis on ἐλέγχω, does, that if it be sin which is really meant in this passage, even then Jesus says nothing more than what any honest man living a life of obedience to law might say as well as He,—viz. that no one was able to *prove* him guilty of any sin! Such an explanation deprives the words of all their importance, and makes them utterly unworthy of the Lord Jesus. For surely it was not possible that He should, with worldly wisdom, thus take refuge in the outward *legality* of His actions, so far as these might happen to be known to those who were then about Him. No; when, conscious that in Himself the external action and the internal motive were in perfect harmony, He asserted the impossibility of convincing Him of sin in general, He assuredly intended to express also the purity of His moral consciousness,—the sinlessness of His inner life. Compare Lücke, *Comment. zu Johann.* p. 299, second ed.; De Wette, *Exeg. Handbuch*, iii. 118; Hase, *Streitschriften*, iii. 109; and especially Stier, *Reden Jesu*, iv. 427. The latter aptly remarks: 'Christ could not have asked the question (John viii. 46), unless He had been conscious that there was in Him no sin in the *sight of God*. If He who so spoke had any secret consciousness of sin before God, He would have *sinned* by the very act of uttering such words.'

be found in rich abundance. Not to dwell on the fact that the sinlessness which Jesus asserted, both in general, and particularly in the midst of the sinful world around Him, could only have been substantiated by a life of most positive holiness, they will be found in a whole series of most emphatic sayings, in which all that could be desired, on this point, is very completely expressed.

Jesus calls Himself the Light of the World, and the King who is come into the world to bear witness to the truth; therefore not merely *a* light among other lights, but *the* light which lighteth every man; and not merely one among many witnesses to truth, but the King of Truth, who can be but One. He designates Himself as the Way, the Truth, and the Life;[1] and would hence be regarded not as one who merely *shows* the way, but as Him who *is* the way, and who, as embracing and manifesting in His own Person the true life and the living truth, leads to the Father. He also says[2] that it is His meat to do the will of Him that sent Him, and to finish His work; He testifies[3] that He does at all times the things which please the Father,—that He never seeks His own will, but always the will of the Father.[4] He holds Himself up as the glorifier of the name of the Father in the world, who sanctifies Himself for His people, who has overcome the world, and who imparts a peace which the world cannot give.[5] He invites all the weary and heavy-laden to come unto Him, because in Him and in His Person they will find rest for their souls.[6] Do we not instinctively feel that these are expressions which cannot proceed from the mouth of a sinful man,—which can only fall from the lips of One whose character and life far surpass all that is sinful and human? What mere man, even though he were the wisest and most exalted that ever lived, could in-

---

[1] John xiv. 6.   [2] John iv. 34.   [3] John viii. 29.   [4] John v. 30.
[5] John xiii. 31, xiv. 27, xvi. 33, xvii. 4, 19.   [6] Matt. xi. 28.

vite *all*, without exception, to come unto *Himself*, with the promise that they should find true rest for their souls?

Two far more important passages, however, must also come under consideration in this respect,—the one, 'I and my Father are one;'[1] the other, 'He that hath seen me hath seen the Father.'[2] If with reference to the former passage it may be disputed whether the words, 'I and my Father are one,' imply a unity of nature, a unity of power, or a moral unity, still it matters little for our purpose which explanation is preferred; for every kind of oneness with God, in that supreme sense in which Christ lays claim to it, must result from that moral union with which alone we are here concerned,—from unity of will. Where the will, the whole moral being, is in any respect turned away from God, there can be no perfect oneness with God in any sense whatever. Where, on the contrary, real union with the will of God exists, there of necessity sin cannot be found, but only that holy love which is the motive power of the Divine will.[3]

There can, then, be no doubt that the Lord Jesus both felt and expressed the consciousness of His own sinlessness. If we are unwilling to admit the validity of this self-testimony, unique as it is,—if we will put no confidence in His sublime words,—there remains no alternative but to regard Him as either a fanatic or a hypocrite. We must *either* declare that, as far as Himself was concerned, He drew no very strict line of demarcation between good and evil, —that He made no searching examination of the secret recesses of His heart,—was not acquainted with every motion of His will,—did not strictly test His words and actions,—and that He exaggerated a consciousness of noble

---

[1] John x. 30.   [2] John xiv. 9.
[3] The objections made by Fritzsche in the third *Programm* with respect to the passages which I have adduced from St. John, are discussed in the article in *Studien und Kritiken*, 1842, No. 3. Compare also Weiss, *Johann. Lehrbegr.* pp. 205 and 208, etc.

aspirations into the overweening notion of being sinlessly perfect; *or* we must admit the still more fearful alternative, that while conscious of transgressing God's commandments in thought, word, and deed, He yet expressly bore testimony to the very opposite. In this case, He who in every other respect gives us the impression only of the most perfect purity and sincerity,—who ever manifested the utmost antagonism to hypocrisy of every kind,—would be branded as a sanctimonious hypocrite, and a contradiction would be introduced into His moral nature, by which it would be utterly destroyed. Who is there that would be willing to undertake the defence of such an assertion?

If, then, the rejection of the self-testimony of the Lord Jesus leads us only to untenable, nay, to unworthy conclusions, *faith* in this testimony, though resting on no demonstrative foundation, yet appears to be perfectly justifiable to reason, and is alone worthy of our moral dignity. Where there are no reasons to the contrary, confidence is far nobler and more dignified than distrust. But when we have a Person whose statements are in all respects corroborated in so unique a manner, as is here the case, it becomes a moral duty not to refuse our confidence to that which He simply yet solemnly asserts concerning Himself.

And this will appear still more in the light of a duty, when we add to His self-testimony that external corroboration to the consideration of which we now proceed.

CHAPTER II.

THE SINLESSNESS OF CHRIST PROVED FROM THE EFFECTS PRODUCED BY HIS MANIFESTATION.

EVERY personality bearing the impress of clearly defined moral and religious qualities, will produce effects proportioned to the degree of force it possesses. The greater and the purer this force, the deeper, the more enduring, and the more wide-spread will be the effects resulting therefrom. If, however, a personality perfectly religious and moral should have existed,—if there ever had been One who was sinlessly holy,—the effects produced would have been of a kind entirely unique. And, on the other hand, if we actually meet with such effects, we have every reason to infer the existence of a proportionate force as their cause. The question, then, is: Do there exist in the special religious and moral constitution of the Christian, as essentially distinguished from the præ-Christian and the extra-Christian world, actual phenomena, which can only be satisfactorily explained on the assumption that the Author of Christianity was a Being of sinless holiness, and which, if this assumption is rejected, remain entirely inexplicable? We answer this question in the affirmative; and shall endeavour, in what follows, to maintain our assertion.

In so doing, while we distinguish between the religious and moral element, we would not, in an argument which must naturally have respect to the very essence of the Christian character, be understood to do so in the sense of regarding either as constituting separate and isolated spheres within the domain of Christian life. On the contrary, it is in the perfect union of these two elements that we recognise not only a leading *feature*, but a leading *excellence* of Christianity. Nor do we only recognise, but shall very decidedly bring forward this property with reference to the sinlessness of its Founder. Nevertheless, the religious and moral elements admit of being distinguished the one from the other, just as man in his inward relation to God, may be distinguished from man in his external operations; and each presents a different aspect to our contemplation. We shall therefore, in the first place, consider them separately; and shall commence our observations by viewing the Christian life from its *moral* side, as that which is most perceptible and prominent.

Sec. 1.—*The New Life of Christianity in its Moral and Religious Aspects.*

The *moral* effects of Christianity are undeniable. It has in all ages produced, in those who have been deservedly called believers, a rich supply of virtues, and, indeed, of virtues which were not previously in existence, or at least not in so pure a form. This applies chiefly to humility, and to compassionate, ministering love. Nor has it exercised a less salutary moral influence upon the social relations of life. In marriage, and in the family, in civil and political life, in the relation of ranks, tribes, and nations to each other,—nay, in the whole condition of the human race,—it was Christianity which first laid the foundation of a state of society truly worthy of man. And these changes it has accomplished, not from without, not by any kind of constraint, but essentially from within, and by mere moral force. But chiefly have they been brought about by the fact, that, through the influence of Christianity, the godlike, free personality of man, and the equality of all men before God have been really recognised as they had never been before. All this irresistibly points to the abundance and depth of the moral forces inherent in Christianity. For the origin of these forces, however, we must necessarily go back to its Author; and this alone is, at all events, strong testimony to the singularly prominent position He occupies in the domain of morals. But when our special subject is the doctrine of His sinlessness, all that has hitherto been touched upon may be considered as essentially comprised in *one* leading point, namely this, that the sum-total of these moral results makes it obvious that Christianity produced something *new* in the moral world, something which is utterly inexplicable, unless it be assumed that the Author of this *creation* was sinless and pure.

The idea of a *new moral creation* is one as peculiar to Christianity as it is indispensable to its completeness. This the Apostle Paul expresses in the most forcible manner when he says, 'If any man be in Christ, he is a new creature: old things are passed away; behold, all things are become new.'[1] The whole aim of Christianity is, that the old man of sin and selfishness may be destroyed, and a new man of righteousness and holiness, of self-denying love, may be born, first in the individual, then in ever increasing circles— in the nations, and in the whole human race. This new birth is not a mere doctrine to be stated, but an actual occurrence to be brought about in the heart, and visibly manifested in the life. The apostle affirms the reality of this occurrence in his case, from his own experience; but to all others who had eyes to see, it was undeniably confirmed by the fact that Saul of Tarsus had become Paul the Apostle, who was not only walking on an entirely different path of life, but was also impelled by an entirely new principle.[2] Paul is, however, in this respect only a type of Christians in general. The same occurrence, though it may be less distinctly marked, is repeated in the case of all who may be called Christians, *in heart* as well as in name. And the more decided Christians they are, the more will they be penetrated by the consciousness that Christianity has begotten in them a new life, and the more clearly will this be manifested in their whole life and conversation.

If, however, we are to define in general terms that new

[1] 2 Cor. v. 17.
[2] An excellent antithetical description of Saul the Jew and Paul the Christian is given by Hug in the Introduction, vol. ii. § 27. A short but brilliant one will be found also in Lange's article 'Paul,' in Herzog's *Real Encycl.* vol. xi. p. 24.

moral principle which distinguishes the Christian from the
præ-Christian world, we should say that it is a principle of
moral perfection surpassing both nature and the law, and
whose ultimate aim is an actual *freedom from all sin*. Before
the entrance of Christianity into the world, we find, on the
one hand, in heathenism a surrender of the individual life
to nature, without any decided consciousness of sin; on the
other hand, in Judaism an overwhelming consciousness of
sin, produced by the revelation of the Divine holiness, and
by the strictness of the law, but unaccompanied by the vital
power and confidence necessary to overcome it. If it be
true that in the heathen world the life of nature was, in the
case of certain nations, ennobled into something supremely
beautiful, and even that certain great prophetic spirits were
able to rise, to a certain degree, above its limits,—if it be
true that in the domain of Judaism there was, beside the
consciousness of sin, a consciousness of grace; yet, on the
whole, the heathen and their gods were under the dominion
of nature, which mind may glorify, but cannot overcome;
while the Jews were in presence of the holy God, under the
curse of sin, which the law could indeed give the knowledge
of, and place under outward restraints, but was utterly unable to eradicate and subdue. When Christianity appeared,
it broke the power of nature, and redeemed it from the
curse of the law. For it is self-evident that a life determined
only by natural motives is not to be thought of within the
sphere of Christianity. By means of Christianity, moreover,
the life will also rise above the essentially legal grade. The
place of the law will be occupied by a morality made free
from within,—a morality for which the law is no longer
written on tables of stone, but on fleshy tables of the heart;
and which, having its origin in Divine grace, and being
conscious of this origin, cherishes also the assurance that, at
some stage of its development, it will become free from *sin*.

Where, then, are we to seek the originating cause of this new creation, which we find in the moral life of the Christian world? Not, as every well-informed person will allow, in the *moral precepts* of Christianity. For it is not in the nature of mere precepts to vitalize: life can only be generated by life, and neither moral law nor moral ideas can produce entirely new characters. To form these, there is needed a character of a typical kind. But, true as this is in general, it especially holds good in Christianity. Here the moral precepts, great as is their excellence, by no means occupy the first place,—they do but spring from a primary source, whence all creative and vitalizing power is derived. This primary source is the *Person* of Christ, to which, in this case also, we are ultimately referred. The same apostle who, both by word and deed, bore such decided testimony to the new creation, says also, when stating the ultimate cause of that new life which was in him, 'I live; yet not I, but Christ liveth in me.'[1] In the important passage, also,[2] from which our argument started, he connects the fact of any one being a new creature, not with his walking according to Christ's doctrine, but with his being 'in Christ,' *i.e.* personally united to Him.[3] And in so doing, he does but express the experience of every true Christian in every age. For all Christians will agree that it is not from ideas, doctrines, or precepts that they derive, and have derived, the regenerating power; but from the personal life, or living personality of Christ, who has been formed, or at least has begun to be formed, in them.

If, then, the primary source of this new life—in which sin is conquered as to its principle, and the pledge of its

---

[1] Gal. ii. 20.   [2] 2 Cor. v. 17.

[3] The formula, εἴ τις ἐν Χριστῷ, must by no means be deprived of its vital significance, by viewing it as an abstract reference to Christian doctrine or Christian truth; but, as the words themselves and their connection require, as a concrete reference to the Person of Christ.

final and complete subjugation bestowed—is inward fellowship with a real personality, what must have been the nature of this personality, that it should have produced such an effect? Evidently it could not have been itself subject to sin, for then it would have differed from others only in degree, and would thus have still partaken of the old nature. It would not have realized in itself a nature entirely new, nor would it have been capable of laying the foundation of a new moral creation, whose ultimate aim should be perfect freedom from sin. On the contrary, it must have been a personality actually withdrawn from all connection with the old nature,—one in which the power of sin was entirely broken,—one which, being itself in the highest sense a new beginning, was thus capable of exercising that deep, far-reaching, creative influence, which nothing but that which was possessed of original perfection could command.

To the objection, that the effect produced by the sinlessness of Christ, if this sinlessness is to be believed, would really have been to produce in those who came under the influence of His life a *like* and immediate freedom from sin, but that neither in the apostles, nor in the Christian world in general, were such results manifested; our reply is as follows:—In the first place, we do actually find in the apostles, and in all true Christians, a something which is here of the greatest importance; we find in them the principle of sin broken, and the assurance of its final and complete overthrow implanted. And this furnishes us with a pledge that a decisive victory has already been achieved over sin. If, however, in spite of its conquest in principle, it is still found operating in their lives, yet with this circumstance is always connected the certainty, that the reason thereof is to be found, not in any inadequacy of the purifying and sanctifying influence exercised upon them by Christ, but in the fact that sin is too deeply rooted in nature to be overcome at once, to be eradicated by any other than an arduous and gradual process. On the other hand, they have a conviction that they can only be more and more, and at last entirely, cleansed from sin, by a complete surrender to the renovating influence of Christ; and such a conviction can be based on nothing but an assurance of the fulness, purity, and infinite efficacy of that holy, sinless life which is found in the Person of Jesus Christ.

It is evident, then, that if we assume the Author of Christianity to have been Himself subject to sin, it is impossible to comprehend how Christian morality, in its purest and most complete form, could have originated from such a being, and how its special nature could be expressed by the words, 'Old things are passed away; all things are become new.' If, on the contrary, we acknowledge that its Founder was without sin, it is but natural that a really new moral creation should take place, within its sphere, through the fact that Christ is formed in the individual believer, and in believers collectively.

In Christianity, however, the moral element entirely depends upon the *religious*. Whenever we meet with a peculiar feature in the province of morals, we shall have to assume a corresponding one in that of religion; and if in Christianity the moral life has been radically renewed, the religious consciousness must also have previously experienced a similar change.

What, then, is it which in this respect characterizes Christians, and makes a marked difference between them and all other religious communities? It is the fact that they regard themselves as *reconciled* to God and *redeemed;* that they cherish the assurance that, in the case of all who truly repent and believe, the guilt of sin is abolished, and a filial relationship to the holy God introduced. It was by means of this consciousness that the Christian Church was called into existence. Possessing this, whatever else she may be deficient in, she does not cease to be Christian; without it, she might still be a religious community of some undefined kind, but could no longer be entitled a Christian one. Least of all could she lay any claim to a new life, in the Christian sense of the term; for this cannot exist apart from a confidence that the guilt of sin is done away with, and a way of access opened to God as a merciful Father.

If, then, we find such a confidence existing in the Christian Church, and perceive, moreover, that by this confidence she either stands or falls, it is but reasonable to inquire whence it originated. The præ-Christian religions also had an abundant supply of means and ordinances for reconciling sinful man to God; and among these, sacrifices played by far the most important part. But if we ask after the result, we find that all they could effect was to allay, for a time, the feeling of guilt, while guilt itself was never radically abolished, nor the certainty that it was *once for all* taken away, begotten. Hence the need of repeated sacrifices was felt; and men were ever moving in the same circle of fresh sacrifices, and ever-recurring consciousness of sin, without attaining the satisfaction of an enduring peace with God. The reason of this was, that in this case sacrifice was nothing more than mere sacrifice, and more or less external to man, and that the assurance of pardon was unaccompanied by the destruction of the power of sin, and the implantation of a new life in its place. There was thus an attempted atonement for sin, but no real redemption from its power. A full and final atonement is only possible when it is *personally* effected, when a person intervenes, who not only by a voluntary self-surrender offers himself as a sacrifice, but also possesses the power of begetting in those who are inwardly united to him a new life,—a life really victorious over sin, by means of that perfect confidence of its pardon which is called forth by an actual revelation and communication of Divine grace. Here the atoning efficacy and the redeeming power coincide. And this coincidence being found only in Christianity, it may readily be perceived what kind of person could alone give to the Christian world the assurance that it was perfectly reconciled and really redeemed by him. Such an assurance could not be grounded upon a sinful man,—it could rest only upon one sinlessly holy; and it is only when we recognise the Author of Christianity to have been such a Being, that we can conceive how the religion which He founded could be pre-eminently the religion of atonement and redemption.

If, then, there is any reality in the consciousness of atonement and redemption possessed by Christians, this reality presupposes the existence of the condition under which alone it could have originated. And that this consciousness is a reality, is founded upon the fact of the experience of each individual believer. The doctrine of the sinless perfection of Jesus is therefore as secure as the experienced fact of His atoning and redeeming agency: they who would deny the former must also deny the latter, and will be either utterly incapable of explaining the phenomenon of Christian piety, in its most characteristic peculiarity, or be constrained to seek for an explanation by which it will be as good as explained away.

Sec. 2.—*Morality and Religion united in Holiness.*

Another circumstance must now be taken into consideration. Not only have morality and religion, individually considered, appeared under new aspects in Christianity, but a blending of the two, such as had never before existed, has been by it introduced into human life. This union of the religious and moral elements, which we call *Holiness*, is the highest quality attainable by man, and furnishes another point whence the sinlessness of Jesus may be inferred.

Undoubtedly a reciprocity of action between religion and morals may be found even beyond the province of Christianity. All vigorous piety manifests itself by moral results, and all deep morality is in some way or other based upon piety. If we conceive of either as existing independently, as entirely severed from the other, we should have, on the one side, a piety either of a sickly and internal character, confining itself to contemplation and emotion, or consisting solely of merely outward observances; on the other, a morality which, keeping closely within the bounds of legality, would exhibit a virtue, strict perhaps, and immoveable, but austere, and lacking all genuine warmth and heartiness. We are not, however, speaking of a greater or less degree of reciprocal action, but of a perfect fusion,—of such a *oneness* of religion and morality, that the one can never be found without the other;—no feeling of piety without moral worth and moral results, and no moral action which does not spring from piety. For *holiness*, as a human quality, exists only where a being, who has either continued free from sin, or, having sinned, has again become free from every stain of guilt, and victorious over every temptation, is ever, both in will and deed, following after good; and this not only from motives of duty, not merely for the sake of good itself, but for the sake of God; impelled, therefore, by *that* love which, like the Divine love itself, finds its objects even in the undeserving and the lost, and is ready to make any sacrifice for their deliverance.

Where, then, do we find even the notion of such a holiness as this?

We cannot seek for it in the *heathen* world. Even here the distinction between the profane and the sacred, between the impure and the consecrated, was understood, and its nobler spirits, at least, conceived that the pure alone could be worthy of fellowship with Divinity. But the Divine itself was not in its view perfectly holy. Heathenism is essentially the religion of nature, and consists either in the deification of nature, or the introduction of the Divine into natural life. This naturally and necessarily excluded from the sphere of the Divine the stricter notion of holiness; and where this was already wanting in the province of religion, it would be vain to seek for its impression in that of morals. In fact, though we do find in the ancient world the ideas of justice, of virtue, and of the good and beautiful, we by no means meet with that of holiness.

The revelation of the *Old Testament* is based on an entirely different foundation. Here the holiness of God, the free Creator and Governor of the world, forms the central-point, and the precept, 'Be ye holy, for I am holy,'[1] is, as it were, the root-word of the ancient covenant, the whole aim of which is to sanctify all to Jehovah, and to hallow all through Him. But, powerfully as this key-note pervades the whole of the Old Testament dispensation, the revelation of the Divine holiness itself is not as yet absolutely perfect. Far greater prominence is given to the unapproachable majesty and glory of God, than to His mercy and condescension: the full impress of His holy love is yet wanting; and hence that which is enjoined with respect to human sanctification and holiness still bears rather a preceptive, legal, and ceremonial character, than one truly spiritual, mental, and moral. It is only where the prototype of holy love is seen in God, and where man has become an image of that love, both in the relation he occupies towards God, and in his desires and external conduct, that holiness, in the full meaning of the term, is possible.

And this we find in *Christianity.* Here first, and here

[1] Lev. xi. 45, xix. 2.

only, do we meet with that perfect idea of holy love in which piety and morality are indivisibly united. Christianity, moreover, does not regard this idea as a standard exalted above ordinary practice, but cherishes the most assured confidence of its realization, even in the sphere of human life. Not till the appearance of Christianity did a community exist whose fundamental characteristic and aim were not any one particular virtue or religious exercise, but *sanctification;* and that a sanctification extending from the inmost heart to every circumstance of life,—an existence wholly in God and from God, as religious in its motives as it is moral in its activity. Whence, then, arose so deep-reaching, so wondrous a change? Was it effected merely in the way of reasoning and instructing? Such an issue would be contrary to all analogy. It could only have been brought about with the results which actually accompanied it in the way of life; in other words, by the appearance of a person who should make a profound impression that he possessed such holiness in unmistakeable perfection, and should thus set up an entirely new standard of excellence within this sphere of life. It was precisely in this manner also that the type of truly classic excellence was introduced into the province of art. This was not effected by devising beforehand some theory of beauty, but by its actual exhibition in the creations of some more than usually gifted artist.

We have now, however, reached a point which will give rise to a special discussion. For it might be said: Granting that what has been hitherto advanced is correct, is it certain that the *reality* of a sinless life is needful to account for it? Might not the mere idea, the mere belief in such a life, produce the like effects? To this subject, then, we shall now devote a few words.

Sec. 3.—These Effects caused not by an Idea, but by an Actual Person.

The objection just hinted at is founded upon a spiritualism which everywhere flees from reality to dwell apart in a world of ideas, and seeks to resolve all life into mere intellectual conceptions. In fact, however, mere ideas have not the power of creating new life; reality can only arise from reality; and unless we are willing to regard the whole moral and religious life of the Christian world as a collection of mere ideas, instead of acknowledging it to be a reality, confirmed as such by our own experience, we must admit a corresponding reality as its starting-point, since there can be nothing in the effect whose germ was not previously in the cause.

But here *the* question specially arises: Whence came, then, the representation, or, if the term be preferred, the *idea* of sinless perfection? In all other cases, being and life are primitive, representation and conception derived. Yet here a notion is supposed to precede, which would not only have no foundation in an originating life, but to which there would nowhere exist a corresponding reality. And how is it to be accounted for that this thought should have appeared, with so marked a character and so powerful an energy, just at this point of the world's history, while we find nothing similar or equal to it at any other period, nor at the same period in any other instance?

We have already alluded to the fact that the notion of sinlessness had by no means attained so definite a form that nothing else remained to be done but to apply it to Jesus Christ, but that, on the contrary, the idea itself was first developed with and by the appearance of Jesus Himself. We have now arrived at the place where it will be needful to investigate this more closely. It is a fact of no slight significance. For if, on the one hand, we find that, previous to the appearance of Christ, and beyond the circle of Christian influences, the notion of sinlessness was either utterly indefinite, or, where it did occur, was inseparably connected with the certainty that its realization was impossible; while, on the other hand, we see that within the province of Christianity not only is the notion itself fully defined, but also accompanied by a firm faith in its actual realization in the life of a certain individual,—the conclusion forced upon us is, that between the former and latter state of things there must lie something by which this mighty change has been effected. Thus, again, the only natural explanation is offered by the supposition that the idea of sinlessness was realized in the Person of Jesus Christ.

But it is not enough to have made this general statement. It must be historically proved; and for this purpose it will be needful to enter somewhat into particulars.

The reason why the idea of pure holiness was impossible to the whole *heathen world*, lay, as has been already hinted, not only in the fact that polytheism was deficient in a spirit of thoroughly decided morality, but also in the positively immoral elements by which it was disfigured. For where the Divine models themselves were not regarded as pure, there could be no place for the notion of a virtue, spotless and in all respects perfect, within the province of human life. Nevertheless, even the heathen world possessed, in the form of philosophy and poetry, an extensive range of thought, which rose far above the limits of the popular religion; and in these departments we undoubtedly meet with very exalted views of morality. The tragic poets, especially Sophocles, present us with pictures of a virtue as sublime as it is pious and attractive; and those philosophers whose systems are borne up by a spirit of morality, naturally approach somewhat to the idea of a perfection of moral life in holiness,—because it is scarcely possible to go at all deep into the philosophy of moral subjects, without at least verging upon this idea. None of the sages of antiquity is more noteworthy in this respect than Plato. In the second book of his *Republic* he draws a sketch of a righteous man, in which he represents perfect integrity as necessarily conjoined with suffering. This must remind every thoughtful reader of the noblest instance of suffering virtue that we know of, and be regarded as one of the most remarkable anticipations of Christianity to be found among the deep utterances of that prophetic spirit.[1] In opposition to the unrighteous man, who, however, disguises himself in the garb of integrity, in order the better to carry out his ill designs, Plato places the simple and truly upright man,—the man who desires not to appear, but to be good, and who, in order that righteousness, and the love of righteousness, may appear in full purity, does not even appear as a righteous man, but is made to suffer as an evil-doer. This righteous man is thus described:[2] 'Without having done any unrighteousness, he still wears the appearance of being unrighteous, in order that he may be thoroughly proved to be righteous, inasmuch as he is not shaken in his integrity by the slander and other ills that thence arise, but remains stedfast' and constant even to death, having all his life been regarded as unrighteous, though in truth righteous.' Then with regard to his end he receives the following prediction: 'That he will be bound, scourged, tortured, and blinded, and that after he has endured all possible evils, he will at last be hanged.' Now it is very certain that we have here presented to us the picture of a

[1] Plato's *Works*, edited by Schleiermacher, third edition, vol. i.; Notes, p. 535.

[2] Plato, *de Republica*, L. ii. P. iii. vol. i. pp. 65 and 66 of Bekker's edition; in Schleiermacher's edition, as above, pp. 128 and 129. Compare on the passage, Baur in his *Apollonius von Tyana u. Christus*, S. 163-166.

high and noble virtue; and, what is especially worthy of note, it is virtue unobtrusive and suffering, virtue in the form of a servant. But, seen from the Christian point of view, two things are wanting. In the first place, the idea of virtue given here is entirely restricted to uprightness; no reference is made to that inward religiousness by which virtue rises into holiness. Secondly,—and this is the main point,—all this is only a creation of the mind, while, on the other hand, we have no certainty that a righteousness, thus perfect in every respect, was ever actually realized in human life.

It is remarkable that one who lived at a period when he could survey the whole development of the ancient world, should expressly declare, as Cicero does, that 'he at least had never found a perfectly wise man:' on the contrary, he says the philosophers are all at variance as to 'what kind of a man such a one would be, *if ever he might be expected to exist.*'[1] Cicero had a sufficient knowledge both of ethics and history to qualify him for passing such a sentence, and we may well regard his opinion as expressing the consciousness of the educated portion of the ancient world. In fact there did not exist in the sphere of heathenism an individual with whom the idea of moral faultlessness could be associated. If in any case we could conceive this possible, it would be in that of *Socrates.* But though we possess truly glorious descrip-

[1] In the well-known passage of the Second Book of the *Tusculan Disputations*, where he speaks of triumphing over pain, and says that the *pars inferior*, the *molle, demissum, humile* in man, should be governed by the *domina omnium et regina ratio.* Here he says, ii. 22: *In quo erit perfecta sapientia—quem adhuc nos quidem vidimus nominem: sed philosophorum sententiis, qualis futuris sit, si modo aliquando fuerit exponitur—is igitur, sive ea ratio quæ erit in eo perfecta et absoluta, sic illi parti imperabit inferiori, ut justus parens probis filiis.* Here, indeed, only *one* aspect of morality, the victory over pain, is spoken of; but if even in this one respect, which was the very point in which antiquity, and especially heroic Rome, excelled, Cicero doubted whether a perfectly wise man had ever appeared, how much more would he have done so if the realization of a virtue absolutely pure in every respect had been in question!

tions of this great man by two revering disciples, yet neither have they, nor has any one else, asserted that he was absolutely free from moral failings, and in all respects perfect.[1] On the contrary, we find that, strictly speaking, the prevalent conviction of the heathen world was, that moral perfection and faultlessness were impossible to man. This is most expressly asserted in the words of one who, equally with Cicero, may be regarded as fitted to be the spokesman of heathen antiquity, and whose high moral culture is acknowledged: we mean Epictetus. In his writings decided prominence is given

---

[1] The only passage which could be brought forward in support of an opposite assertion is in Xenophon's *Memorabilia*, lib. i. cap. i. § 11: Οὐδεὶς δὲ πώποτε Σωκράτους οὐδὲν ἀσεβὲς οὐδὲ ἀνόσιον οὔτε πράττοντος εἶδεν, οὔτε λέγοντος ἤκουσεν. It is evident, however, from the whole tenor of this defence, and especially from the immediately preceding context, that it is more legality, and especially the legality of his public dealings and discourses, which is here intended, than morality in its higher signification. But granting that the words are to be understood as applied to morality in the widest sense, even then the main point is wanting, viz. *the testimony of Socrates himself.* This, however, is indispensable, since he alone was capable of a thorough survey of himself. We shall, however, do no injustice to Socrates by assuming that he would not have applied to himself that great saying of the Redeemer, 'Which of you convinceth me of sin?' In the very fact that the demons of Socrates chiefly *warned* him against things which he was *not* to do, while Christ *positively* acted in all things from a pure consciousness of God within, from that Divine Spirit by which He was impelled, lies a most important distinction between the philosopher and the Saviour. It is not to be denied that the picture of a perfectly wise man, not merely as an idea, but as a reality, is presented to us even within the sphere of heathenism by Philostratus, in his *Life of Apollonius of Tyana;* but in this case there is a reference to Christianity, and the whole life is but an imitation of that of Christ, translated into Platonism and Pythagoreanism. This is convincingly proved by Baur, in his work, *Apollonius of Tyana and Christ, or the Relation of Pythagoreanism to Christianity*, Tübingen 1832, in which (p. 162) the result of his researches, as far as our present subject is concerned, is thus expressed: 'In the place of Him whom Christianity sets before us as the actually manifested Redeemer of the world, we have here a sage acting only by precept and example; he is, moreover—and this must be the main point—*no living form*, but an image wanting independent reality and actual existence,—a faint and shadowy reflection of a living original, but for whom it is evident that even the creative idea which called it forth would be absent.'

to the notion of moral faultlessness; but to the question, Is it possible to be faultless? he unhesitatingly answers, 'No, it is impossible; the only thing possible is to be ever striving to be faultless.'[1]

Such is the state of affairs with regard to the question which now occupies us, in the intellectual high places of the heathen world.[2] With more probability might we assume the presence of the idea of sinless holiness in the monotheistic religions than in paganism. For here, in virtue of the unity and spiritual nature of God, there naturally exists a clearer impression of the idea of holiness. The Old Testament contains even the hope—at least in pro-

---

[1] The words of Epictetus, iv. 12, 19th ed. Schweigh., are: Τί οὖν; δυνατὸν ἀναμάρτητον εἶναι ἤδη; 'Ἀμήχανον· ἀλλ' ἐκεῖνο δυνατὸν πρὸς τὸ μὴ ἁμαρτάνειν τιτάσθα διηνεκῶς. In an epigram in Demosthenes, de Corona, p. 322, the quality of doing all that is right is attributed to the gods alone.

[2] Since the notion, and the word which defines it, assume each the other, it may not be amiss to offer a few remarks upon the expressions ἀναμαρτησία and ἀναμάρτητος. These undoubtedly occur at a very early period in the language of classical antiquity, but at first they are for the most part applied only to external relations; and even when in later times used with reference to moral actions, they lack that full significance which Christian thought attributes to them. In Herodotus ἀναμάρτητος is applied, v. 39, to a woman who had not sinned against her husband, and, i. 55, to a city which had incurred no debts. In Xenophon and Plato ἀναμάρτητος is sometimes one who cannot err, sometimes one who has not actually erred; but in both instances it is used in no higher sense than as referring to the external affairs of life. In the first of these two meanings, Plato says, de Repub. lib. 1, Πότερον δὲ ἀναμάρτητοί εἰσιν οἱ ἄρχοντες, ἢ οἷοί τε καὶ ἁμαρτάνειν; in the other, Xenophon, Ὁρᾷ γὰρ τῶν ἀνθρώπων ὠδῖνα ἀναμάρτητον διατιλοῦντα. Longinus, de Sublim. xxxi. 8, uses the word in the same sense as καθαρός and ἀσφαλής, to denote the pure and the classical in style, and distinguishes in this respect between that which is merely free from faults, and that which is the work of genius (de Sublim. xxxiii. 2). It is in Diogenes Laertius (vii. 122) and Epictetus that it occurs with the most decided moral meaning. In the latter are found a whole series of passages in which the word occurs:—e.g. i. 4, 11: Ἐν ὁρμαῖς καὶ ἀφορμαῖς ἀναμάρτητος; iv. 8, 6: ἡ τοῦ φιλοσόφου πρόληψις καὶ ἐπαγγελία, ἀναμάρτητον εἶναι; and especially the above-mentioned remarkable passage, iv. 12, 19. Ἀμαρτησία also occurs, though less frequently, with the same various meanings. Compare Stephan. Thesaur. Ling. Gr. vol. ii. p. 1920, ed. Lond.

phetic allusion—that the Messiah was to be a perfectly holy servant of Jehovah.[1] Yet neither of the monotheistic law-religions,—neither the Mosaic preparatory to Christianity, nor the Mohammedan, which, in spite of its partial imitation of the Christian religion, was but an apostasy therefrom,—offers anything like a full representation of the idea of sinless holiness: much less is there implied in either of them a belief in the realization of that idea in any human being. If this thought is to be found in these religions, it would be to their founders that we must chiefly look for it; but neither Moses nor Mohammed—between whom, as is obvious, we make a comparison under this point of view alone—lays claim to freedom from sin: they never even rose to this conception; nor did the adherents of their faith ever honour them as sinless beings.[2] With regard to Mohammed, the Koran makes no secret of the fact that he was guilty of failings, and he himself makes an admonition go forth from God commanding him to pray for the forgiveness of his sins: many reputed prayers of his have, moreover, been preserved in the traditions of his followers,

---

[1] Isa. liii. 9.

[2] The prerogative of sinlessness has never been laid claim to on behalf of Moses. The inadmissibility of such a notion would at once have been shown by a reference to Ex. ii. 12 and 14.

Much less can sinlessness be predicated of Mohammed. On this point the reader is referred to the Contributions to a Theology of the Koran, by Œttinger (*Tübinger Zeitschrift für Theologie*, Jahrgang 1831, No. iii. pp. 62, 63), where we find the following observations: 'Nowhere in the Koran do we find the idea of sinlessness applied to a human being. Reference might indeed here be made to the passage (12, 53) where Joseph says, "I will not acquit myself of guilt, for every soul inclineth to evil, save him on whom God has compassion." But it is evident that this expression means no more than that every man will sin unless God's mercy hold him up, which by no means implies that any one may be wholly free from sin. The Koran, in general, regards sin more as an outward than an inward occurrence, while even the prophetic vocation does not necessarily involve a perfect freedom from external and manifest transgression; though Mohammed, when his conscience accuses him,

in which he complies with this injunction.[1] But besides this, in the case both of the founder of Islam and the lawgiver of the Old dispensation, not only their lives, but even the character of their religious institutions, and their entire ministries, would have belied the predicate of sinlessness. Both of them, though in very different ways, were founders of states and leaders of armies, and, by these very circumstances, too much addicted to the use of external means to be able to maintain that purity of thought and action of which he alone is capable who, confining himself entirely to those interests which lie within the province of religion, uses none but spiritual weapons against every, even the most unjust, attack. Moreover, the doctrine and institutions of both are based only on law, and perfect holiness belongs to a higher sphere than that of law. It can exist only when the legal stage has been surmounted, and the obedience of faith and love has superseded obedience to law,—when there is no longer any need of an external law, because the law is written in the heart.[2]

This is, then, historically the state of the case: In the ages before Christ, no definite notion of sinless perfection, and where a shadow of the idea is found, an accompanying certainty of the impossibility of realizing it: since the appearance of Christ, not only the idea itself in full

or even when men reproach him for his sins, earnestly endeavours to weaken the force of such reproaches by supposed Divine revelations.' Still more decidedly is this point argued by Gerock (*Christologie des Koran*, Hamb. 1839, pp. 100, 101). It is there shown that in the Koran Jesus is indeed held up to imitation as a moral ensample, but necessarily without the predicate of sinlessness, since even Mohammed, who is greater than He, confesses to the commission of mistakes and precipitate actions. In one passage God says to Mohammed (Sur. 48, B. 1 and 2): 'We have granted thee a decisive victory, in order that Allah may forgive thee thy sins both past and future.' Again (Sur. 40, B. 57), Mohammed is reminded: 'Pray for the forgiveness of thy sins.' (So also p. 80, v. 1 seq.; p. 4, v. 104).

[1] Gerock, in the work already quoted, p. 101, note.   [2] 1 Tim. i. 9.

distinctness, but also the assured certainty of its achievement. On the one side there is a Plato, who describes the righteous man as great and glorious indeed, but still as only an ideal picture without reality; a Cicero, who calls in question the possibility of the realization of perfect wisdom; an Epictetus, who has a clearer idea of what sinlessness means, but is at the same time convinced of the impossibility of its ever being carried out in actual life. On the same side stand the founder of the Old Testament dispensation, who himself lays no claim to the possession of spotless righteousness, nor is regarded by his followers as perfectly sinless; the greatest prophet of the ante-Christian age, who had indeed an anticipation that the idea of holy purity would be realized, but not till a future time, when it should be seen in the servant of God; and, lastly, the founder of Islam, who himself confessed his moral defalcations, and who lives in the traditions of his followers as one who owned his faults and prayed for their forgiveness. On the *other* side there are the plain, simple-minded apostles, themselves reckoned neither among the poets nor the philosophers, in whom we find not only the idea of sinless holiness most clearly defined, but in whom also faith in its actual realization in the person of Jesus became a power, strong enough to conquer the world and death; and by whom was given a description of the pure and holy life of Jesus, which called forth the same faith in others also, and which must, to this very day, be regarded as an inimitable picture of religious and moral perfection.

What conclusion shall we then draw from this state of things? Shall we conclude that the apostles—like the God of Plato, who, contemplating ideas, proceeded to fashion the world—by only viewing the idea of perfection and holiness, sketched from their own internal resources the portrait of Jesus, and filled up the details of His life from their own poetic fancy? But then we must first show that that which they are supposed to have thus contemplated, had for them a real existence; and we have just seen that the opposite was the case. We must first make it appear credible that sober-minded men would have had such faith in a production of their own imagination (which they took for something real), as to sacrifice for its sake all that men usually hold dear: and in this there is a manifest contradiction. No! it would be far simpler, and far more consistent with history, to conclude that if an idea arose in all its clearness in the minds of the apostles, which the great thinkers and poets of antiquity were either utterly ignorant of, or saw but dimly, this can be accounted for only by the manifestation of a *real* life; and if an all-conquering belief in the reality of a sinless life was produced in their minds, while hitherto such a life had been esteemed impossible, the cause could only lie in the overpowering impression produced by that life *itself*, as seen unfolding before their eyes.

We shall, however, draw this conclusion with greater confidence, in proportion as this view is found to be in other respects consistent with the nature of the case. For if the idea of sinless perfection does indeed belong, of its very nature, to the human mind, and form the foundation of its whole moral development; yet, according to the laws of moral life, there can be no clear, full, and living consciousness of it, and consequently no belief in its realization, so long as sin is the ruling power in humanity. Hence, when the idea has become lucid and lifegiving, and when along with it there is the firm conviction of its realization, we are entitled to draw the conclusion that this has taken place as the result of an actual conquest of sin, and a real manifestation of a holy and perfect life. We say then: it is not possible to think otherwise than that He who called forth in His contemporaries, and through them in the Christian world, a belief strong, stedfast, and capable of transforming their whole life, in an altogether pure and holy virtue, was Himself in very deed a perfectly pure and holy Being.

We have, then—as a retrospect of what has been advanced will show—a series of facts which mutually confirm each other. The moral greatness of Christ is confirmed, in a general point of view, by that judicial and dividing effect which His appearance everywhere produced, as well as by the relation in which men of the most opposite dispositions stood towards Him:—His enemies, with their deadly hatred; the seemingly impartial, who could not, however, withdraw themselves from the influence of His spiritual power; the traitor, who, in his despair, passed sentence upon himself; and the friends, whose love and reverence endured even unto death. But more definite confirmation of the sinless perfection of the Lord Jesus is offered by the testimony of the apostolic circle,—a testimony contained partly in direct assertions, and partly in that life-portrait of Christ which forms their commentary and confirmation. Beyond and above all this, however, is the sublime self-testimony from the lips of Jesus Himself, which leaves us in no doubt of what was His own consciousness with respect to His moral character, and the relation to God and to the human race resulting therefrom. This, too, does not stand alone, but is supported and corroborated by the world-wide effects produced by Him in the sphere of religion and morality,—effects so entirely unique that no adequate explanation of them can be found, unless we allow that the self-testimony of Christ, and its echo in the evidence furnished by the apostles, is indeed corroborated by facts.

Surely all these circumstances, taken together, furnish ample security for the sinless perfection of Christ. Nevertheless, when the question is to convert the assent of the understanding into the lively conviction of the individual, there is yet another kind of testimony to adduce. And this is the individual experience which each man may and ought to make by a direct application to the original sources,—to those Gospels, whose simple, powerful, and lively portraiture can be replaced by nothing else. If this is done in a candid and unprejudiced spirit, the image of the Lord Jesus will be vividly presented to his mind; and this image will not only fill his whole soul with admiration, as some production of poetry or rhetoric might do, but will act as a moral power upon his heart, and thus take possession of his whole inner man. He will feel that he has here found that which elevates him above all that is low, earthly, and common, which directly purifies him, and penetrates him with the feeling of the Divine nearness. He will be constrained to say that, if he desires to be really in harmony with such a manifestation, he must become a radically new man; and, on further consideration, he will be persuaded that there is no other moral phenomenon on earth which produces like effects, and therefore none which thus points to a higher order of things, and to an origin beyond ordinary human experience, even an origin which is Divine.[1]

In this sense we must say that it is the moral portraiture of the Lord Jesus which, in virtue of the vital power inherent in it itself, offers the best and strongest evidence of its truth and uniqueness. As the poet,[2] in reply to the question, Whence the sun's celestial fires are derived? answers, That which enlightens the world enlightens itself: its light bears witness that its origin is light,—so may the same be said of the portraiture of Him who is the light of the moral world—

---

[1] Comp. Dorner, *Jes. sündl. Vollk.* p. 43, and Schaff *On the Moral Character of Christ*, p. 53.
[2] Schiller, in the *Bride of Messina*.

the 'Sun of righteousness.' He who beholds the light of the sun and feels the warmth of its rays, will have no doubts of its existence, nor of the power of its agency. So, too, he who has once felt in his own heart the peculiar power exercised by the Gospel delineation of the Lord Jesus, will entertain no kind of doubt as to its reality and origin.

PART THIRD.

OBJECTIONS.

AS we have before remarked, a mathematical or logically incontrovertible certainty is, with respect to our subject, impossible. Hence no proofs can be adduced which will absolutely exclude all doubts. Nor are doubts by any means lacking; for while many modern theologians have merely taken up a sceptical position with regard to sinlessness, there are others who have stated reasons which are sufficiently plausible to make a discussion of them needful. Such a discussion we are the more inclined to enter upon in the following pages, because the questions hence arising have not as yet been treated in the full and connected manner which the subject demands.[1]

The objections which have been raised may, in a general way, be classed as follows:—One class rests on a denial of the *actual* sinlessness of Jesus; the other on a denial of the *possibility* of sinlessness at all in the sphere of human life. In the former case the sinlessness of Jesus is impugned, partly on the ground of its being inconsistent with that law of development which is applied to Him in reference both to His character and His work; partly as at variance with the

[1] For a more cursory view of these questions, see Lutz. *Biblische Dogmatik*, pp. 294–299; and Schumann, *Christus*, vol. i. pp. 289–296.

idea of temptation; and partly on the ground of distinct utterances and facts recorded of Him. In the second case, the objections to the sinlessness of Jesus are drawn, on the one hand, from experience; on the other, from the very nature of the idea of sinlessness and the mode of its realization. These last objections are therefore partly empirical, and partly speculative, in their nature.

Adopting this classification, we shall proceed from that which is special to that which is general,—from that which is less important to that which is more so. That doubt is of less moment, and does not directly assail the character of Jesus, which hints that if He passed through a development at all, He must have begun in imperfection, and have risen gradually to perfection. We shall find it harder to reconcile with our idea of sinlessness, the notion that Jesus could have felt inwardly drawn towards evil when exposed to temptation; while the strongest objection of all would be a really immoral utterance or deed. But, even supposing all that might be urged under these heads were answered, this would be of no avail, if it could be proved that sinless perfection is altogether impossible in the region of human existence, if experience or the nature of the moral idea witnessed unanswerably *against* its realization in a human being.

These are the difficulties which meet us here. In endeavouring to surmount them in the order above given, we shall of course labour to keep duly separate that which is essentially distinct; but since objections of both kinds glide to a certain degree into each other, many difficulties must needs be touched upon in the first part, the more complete solution of which must be reserved to the second.

CHAPTER I.

ARGUMENTS AGAINST THE ACTUAL SINLESSNESS OF JESUS.

IF we pass by altogether, in the first instance, the question as to whether or not sinlessness be possible in humanity, and, assuming for the time its possibility, ask only, Was Jesus actually sinless? then our business is with facts; and these, if they are questionable, would be in the first instance most efficiently contested, if other indubitable and contrary facts could be opposed to them. It has been supposed that such facts are to be found in certain parts of the Gospel narratives. And in this respect attention has first of all been called to the development which took place in the life of Jesus, and therefore to a progress from a state of imperfection to one of perfection, by which, it is urged, the idea of absolute perfection is excluded. This has been made use of in two ways, —in relation, first, to the *Person* of Jesus, and secondly, to the Messianic *plan*. We must examine both aspects of this argument more closely.

Sec. 1.—*The Development of the Person of Jesus.*

The Scriptures speak undeniably of a *growth in wisdom* in Jesus,—consequently of an increase, a progress in His intellectual life; and not less distinctly do they intimate that His moral nature *became gradually perfect*. And were this not clearly taught in single passages,[1] it would naturally follow, from the view everywhere taken in the New Testament, that the entire life of Jesus was an actual human life, shorn of no quality or power proper to man. But if Jesus did advance

---

[1] For the intellectual growth of Jesus we have the classic words, προέκοπτε σοφίᾳ, Luke ii. 52: for His growth in moral perfection there are several

intellectually and grow in moral perfection, this, it is said, involves a defective beginning, and thus excludes original and symmetrical perfection.

To this we reply: Certainly the gradualness, the successive character, of the development of Jesus, must be maintained. But growth and increase do not necessarily assume transition from a state of deficiency to one of sufficiency,—do not presuppose an inner antagonism of sin, or an overcoming of the religious and moral error connected therewith. All that they really imply is, development taking place in time. There is nothing to hinder this development itself from being a perfectly pure one. The notion of growth does but furnish another proof that Jesus shared in everything that really belongs to finite, *human* nature. This is, however, as little denied by any, as it can, on the other side, be proved that mere human development, as such, necessarily involves some amount of sin. In itself it may be conceived of as a perfectly normal development, in which indeed different degrees succeed each other, each free from actual disturbance, each exhibiting in greater maturity some quality which was but prepared for in former stages, but which yet existed potentially from the very beginning.[1]

---

passages in the Epistle to the Hebrews, especially chap. ii. 10-18, v. 7-9. Compare Scholten, *Oratio de vitando in Jesu Christi historia Docetismo*, pp. 15-19; De Wette, *Das Wesen des christlichen Glaubens*, § 53, p. 269; and Riehm, *Lehrbegr. des Hebräerbriefs*, i. pp. 327, etc. Keim especially has endeavoured to bring forward the several stages of 'the human development of Jesus' in his lecture under this title. His remarks are frequently striking, but there are also many points with which we are unable to agree. Also Gess, in another, and decidedly positive sense, in his *Lehre von der Person Christi*: see many passages, but especially p. 210, and pp. 304 seq.

[1] The idea of development does not of itself involve the passing through antagonisms and conflicts, or, 'that at every step in advance the hindrances universally presented by evil have to be surmounted, and some one of its disturbing elements to be reduced to inactivity.' This is only true of the development of individuals, and of mankind, when evil has already gained

That this was so in the case of the Lord Jesus, cannot indeed be positively demonstrated, throughout the whole course of His life; but still less can the contrary be proved. Nay more, not only are we justified in inferring from the subsequent perfection of Jesus, that the manner in which it was attained was in general normal, but we have also a particular fact corroborating this conclusion, and making it evident to the mind. The fact referred to is, of course, that most significant resting-place afforded us by the narrative of His visit to Jerusalem during His twelfth year.[1] We find, even at this early age, that which ever formed the centre of His being, even the consciousness of an entirely unique relation to God; and yet this is at the same time expressed in a manner perfectly appropriate to His youthful years. This narrative is a type of His whole development; it represents His ideality in a childlike form, and therefore the ideality of childhood in general.[2]

This thought of a perfectly normal development does not by any means bring us within the regions of the magical and docetical, but rather expresses the restoration of human nature to its integrity,—nature in its primal purity and holiness; for an orderly, faultless development is proper to

---

power over them, *i.e.* when they are, morally considered, in an unnatural condition. 'But only a slavish dependence on a narrow empiricism, whose inductions will not even bear application to the sphere of nature, can lead us to represent the present form of human development as its natural and necessary one. That would be a true development in which nothing should ever be lost at a higher which had been once really possessed at a lower stage; and simply on the ground that there was nothing which it were needful and good to lose, simply because at no point was there anything which tended to interfere with or thwart the vocation of the being whose development was going forward.' See Jul. Müller's *Christian Doctrine of Sin*, vol. i. pp. 80–86 of third ed. Besides, that which specially characterizes the notion of moral development is not its negative side, viz. the conquest of evil, but positive growth in good; and it is just in this latter sense that it is applied to Jesus.

[1] Luke ii. 41–51.   [2] Lange, *Leben Jesu*, vol. ii. p. 127.

nature when interfered with by no inward or outward restraint. Nature, in its Divine origin, is purity itself. We should be on our guard, therefore, against introducing anything unnatural into the intellectual condition of Jesus, by representing Him as a precocious child, and ascribing to Him as a boy the knowledge of truth, the moral earnestness and the depth of a man. Such a condition would not be a miracle worthy of God, but an unnatural monstrosity.[1] At every period of His existence He realized just that measure of intellectual culture and moral life of which human nature is at that point capable, without ceasing to be human nature. In a word, He was exactly and fully what a man can be at each successive step of his life. As He was a perfect man, so was He also a perfect boy and youth, and of a certainty no stranger to the modes of thought and observation which are peculiar to childhood and youth; yet all was characterized by a holy simplicity and beauty. His progress was like that of a beautiful flower, to whose free growth there is no hindrance, and of which we should never require that whilst in the germ it should bud, and whilst budding, possess the glory of perfect bloom; but only that at each step in its development it should be in every respect what it then ought to be.[2]

As little ought we absolutely to deny the existence of what was individual and national in the education of Jesus,

---

[1] There is not a trace of such monstrosities as these in the sober narrative of the canonical Gospels, while, as is well known, they are to be found in the apocryphal histories of Jesus. See my work, *Historisch oder Mythisch?* § 4.

[2] The fundamental thought of all this was expressed even by Irenæus in the well-known passage, *adv. hæres.* ii. 22, where, among other things, it is said: *Ideo (Christus) per omnem venit ætatem et infantibus infans factus, sanctificans infantes; in parvulis parvulus, sanctificans hanc ipsam habentes ætatem; in juvenibus juvenis,* etc. Among modern writers it will be found in Schleiermacher, *Glaubenslehre,* ii. 178, and Olshausen, *Bibl. Comment.* i. 134.

and the influence thereon of external circumstances. Everything human is subject to influences of this nature. And as those whom we rightly call men of genius are not essentially moulded and determined by that which comes to them from without, but possess the power to employ it for the most part as a means to their own development, and to the manifestation of that which is in them by nature, we may surely conceive of a mind of which this holds true in so eminent and unqualified a manner, that everything tendered by outward conditions is simply and only the means and material of self-development,—a mind which, in the perfectly independent course of its development, appropriates nothing narrow and unworthy, but only the good and the salutary of all that its external circumstances present.[1] We do not deny that there was in the religious faith of the nation to which He belonged, and in the character of the family and surroundings amidst which He grew up, much which might naturally exercise either a salutary or restraining influence upon Him. The sacred types and teachings of the Old Testament were certainly as little lost upon Him, as the impression made by all that met His eyes, whether in nature, or among His fellow-men. But who would attempt to bring these forward as offering a sufficient explanation of the peculiarity of His whole mental life? In the case of other distinguished personages, the elements from which their characters were developed may be, as a rule, to a great degree at least, pointed out. But who is there who still conceives the notion of deriving Christianity from Essenism, or from Egyptian priest-lore, or of making Jesus Christ the happy medium between Pharisaism and Saduceeism? Or who could imagine that He had made an Abraham, a Moses, an Elijah, or any other Old Testament character His model? No; if ever there was, in the intellectual and moral realm, an

---

[1] See Martensen's *Dogmatik*, § 141, p. 315.

original, a creative, a primitive phenomenon, it was the character of Jesus Christ.[1] His development did indeed take place in a course of most lively reciprocity of action with the world,[2] but not in any dependence upon it; while aught of imitation cannot even be thought of. Together, however, with this extreme originality, is found that *universal* character which makes Him a model for the whole human race; and these united characteristics offer, at the same time, most valid security that His development was of a healthy and normal nature, because, while, apart from all disturbing influences, it resulted, in all that was essential, wholly from within, it was yet such as to place Him on a height on which He appears as the unsurpassed model of all future ages.

What has hitherto been advanced, tends of course merely to make plain the possibility of conceiving in Jesus a perfectly pure development. But at present this is all we need, inasmuch as our only aim at this point is to show that development does not of itself involve sin. The positive certainty that the development of Jesus was sinless, must be sought in another direction,—namely, by proving that it is an indispensable presupposition, if the actual condition and character of Jesus at a subsequent period is to be satisfactorily explained, and not to seem utterly out of connection with His earlier life.

Sec. 2.—*The Development of the Messianic Plan.*

With still more positiveness, and with greater force, has the objection which is based on progress from a state of imperfection to one of perfection, been urged in relation to

---

[1] Compare Schaff, p. 12, and Young's *Christ of History*, p. 197.
[2] For detailed proof, see Keim's already quoted works, pp. 12 seq.

the Messianic plan of Jesus.[1] Jesus, it has been represented, did not, at His first appearance, recognise clearly the aim of His life; His first true recognition of it was the result of a catastrophe affecting both His inner and outer life. It is allowed that, from the very beginning, the fundamental feature of His plan was the formation of mankind into a community by means of religious love; but it is contended that at first this was mingled with political views and tendencies, since He hoped, by the exaltation of Israel, to found a theocracy into which all nations should gradually be drawn. It was not till afterwards, when this notion came into conflict with the sense of the nation and its rulers, and was thereby frustrated, and its impracticability exposed, that there arose in the mind of Jesus, and that not without a struggle, the idea of a spiritual kingdom of God; and thus, we are told, it was that Jesus was transformed from a Jewish Messiah into the Redeemer of the world.

This view, which even at a former period was broached by

---

[1] The phrase, 'Plan of Jesus,' has in recent times been so much in vogue, that it may seem paradoxical to consider it inappropriate; and yet it is utterly so. The *devising of a plan* implies an activity of mind which is far too strongly individual and subjective to be ascribed to Jesus. So also the acting constantly *according to a plan*, springs from a one-sided predominance of reflection, such as He never manifested. That which He was commissioned to do and to establish was marked out for Him by God and history,—was recognised, not devised by Him. Hence, although we are not warranted in saying that there was no connection between His various acts, seeing that in all He did and said He was possessed and inspired by the loftiest idea; still, to assume that all He did was deliberately planned and intended beforehand, in the common sense of the words, reduces Him to a lower position than that which He actually occupied, as One filled with the Spirit and with God. The older terms, *office* and *work* of Christ, have much greater congruity than the modern expression *plan*. If, however, this term *plan*, having usage on its side, is to be retained, let us understand by it only, as Hase very correctly defines it in his *Leben Jesu*, § 40, 'His subjective conception of the office to which God had appointed Him, without reference to the collateral use of the word in the sense of: what is arbitrary, the mere result of reflection.' Compare Neander's *Life of Jesus*, pp. 128, etc., fifth ed.

certain of the learned, has been fully and acutely carried out in more recent times.¹ It has been, indeed, substantially retracted by its most distinguished advocate; and yet it was again brought forward, though in a modified form, a short time since.² It is a view which, if established, would evidently be followed by important results; it would essentially affect that image of Jesus which Christendom has hitherto found in its Gospels and preserved in its faith; it would banish the idea of a perfectly wise and holy Redeemer,

[1] Following in the steps of Von Ammon, De Wette, and some others, Hase, in the first ed. of his *Leben Jesu*, published at Leipsic in 1829, propounded at length the thought of a twofold plan of Jesus,—of a plan which was at first theocratical, and only became purely religious subsequently. In opposition to his view and development of the subject, appeared Heubner, in an appendix to the fifth ed. of Reinhard's *Plan Jesu*, Wittenb. 1830, pp. 394-407; Lücke, in two programmes of the year 1831, under the title, *Examinatur, quæ speciosius nuper commendata est, sententia de mutato per eventa, adeoque sensim emendato Christi consilio;* and J. E. Osiander, in his article, *Ueber die neueren Bearbeitungen des Lebens Jesu von Paulus und Hase*, in the *Tübinger Zeitschrift für Theologie*, 1831, No. i. pp. 145-148. My controversy also, in the second ed. of this work, was with Hase. To this opposition, especially as conducted by Lücke, Hase, with a noble love of truth, did justice, partly in his *Theologische Streitschriften*, Leipsic 1834, pp. 61-102, and partly in the subsequent editions of his *Leben Jesu*. He adopted from his antagonists as much as his own convictions would allow him, and sought to unite the opposed views in the following general result, § 50:—'Apart from single political institutions, which are by nature transitory, the plan of Jesus undoubtedly related to a moral reformation and a spiritual kingdom; but still the Divine law which He put in force was clearly meant in the course of time to subdue the world, or rather to pervade it as its highest general law; and He, the King of Truth, intended to become also a King of the world.' 'Jesus must, at one time or other, have examined and rejected those Messianic hopes which bore a theocratic character, for the Messianic faith could only reach Him in that form. But there is no proof whatever that He was led to this examination and rejection by hard experience in the midst of His career, and not by the clear judgment of His own mind ere He entered on His work.'

[2] Viz. by Keim in his work, *Die menschliche Entwickelung Jesu*, pp. 28, etc. He advocates the view that it was not till a certain definite period of His public ministry that the perception that the Messiah was to be a *sufferer* arose upon the mind of Jesus, and that it was at the same time that His idea of a Messianic kingdom, which was to be in the first place a Jewish one, expanded into that of a universal spiritual kingdom.

Arguments against His actual Sinlessness.

who by His spiritual greatness is able to free men from error and sin. Looked at in this light, we should not be able to feel that Jesus possessed even a high degree of insight, much less that He was perfect in intellectual strength. According to this hypothesis, He must not only in general have struggled through error to more correct knowledge, but even through such error as He might have avoided, had He carefully studied the condition of His people before commencing His work. Evidently, too, He had not well considered the whole compass of His plan; for what He would have done in opposition to the existing Roman authority and rule, when once possessed of the highest theocratic power, remains an unsolved, and by no means unimportant difficulty. He had not, in fine, that high, independent power of spirit which the moral Deliverer of humanity should and must have; for instead of fighting His way with a sure step through difficulties and hindrances, as one truly self-reliant would have done, it was the unfavourable turn which His affairs took that first brought Him to a right mind; and then, in place of joyfully and enthusiastically grasping the higher thought that dawned upon Him, He fell into sadness and dismay, as He looked back on His shattered hopes, and forward to a future in which there awaited Him a cross instead of a crown.[1] Such a Christ does not control, but is Himself controlled by circumstances; He does not distinctly and consciously propose to Himself His own aim, but has it gradually formed for, and forced upon Him, by events and accidents; He is not the Lord, but the creature of the times. If the veritable historical Christ were such a one as this, the Christian Church would scarcely be able to reverence in Him the light and Saviour of the world; nor could He satisfy the requirements which we are compelled to make of the Re-

---

[1] Hase, in the first edition of the *Leben Jesu*, § 84. Differently in the second and later editions, § 49.

deemer of mankind. Such insight into the plan of Jesus as would be attained in this way, would be dearly bought: happily, however, the view presented above has no solid foundation in fact.

The main support of the opinion that Jesus had at first a theocratic plan of the nature just indicated, is His appropriation to Himself of the character of Messiah; and the Messiah, according to the prophets, and still more in the view of His contemporaries, was to be not only a religious and moral, but also a political deliverer. It is urged: If Jesus did not mean to awaken political hopes, He would not have given Himself out for the Messiah; but inasmuch as He did call Himself the Messiah, the political element must evidently have entered into His plan. This conclusion can, however, only be drawn when certain of His utterances are isolated, and viewed apart from their connection with the whole of His teaching and works. Jesus did appropriate to Himself the idea of the Messiah as a true and eternal one; but in the consciousness of being Himself the promised One, He also glorified the idea by manifesting its high religious realization. In doing this He would have acted very injudiciously, if He had begun by theoretical discussions. His true course was rather first to realize in His own life the idea of the Messiah, and then to bring Himself forward as the promised One, under that aspect which He had thus rendered actual and evident. At the same time, however, from the very beginning Jesus declared in divers ways, that what He sought to found was a Divine kingdom of piety and love,—a union of mankind on the basis of a moral deliverance.

When Jesus spoke of His *kingdom*, it was equivalent to speaking of His plan; and at no period of His life did He leave men in uncertainty as to the true nature of His kingdom. He ever proclaimed it to be heavenly and eternal,— to be one whose commencements are within, in the heart, and which is thence to be established visibly. This is clear even from the beatitudes of the Sermon on the Mount: and these were undeniably amongst His earliest public utterances. All His parables, too, in which He gave expression to His view of the nature of the kingdom of God, are of the same purport. In them He taught, with special emphasis, that in its development the kingdom of God would be like the mustard seed, in its mode of operation like leaven. In perfect consistency with this, is the position He assigned to John the Baptist as the greatest among the prophets, but as, notwithstanding, less than the least in the economy of the new kingdom of God.[1] Not less in harmony with this representation was the whole character and tenor of His *life*,—and it was sublimely consistent throughout,—especially as depicted by John the beloved disciple. One whose object was to found a new social order on the ruins of the old, must have gone to work in an entirely different manner. For such a scheme there were undoubtedly abundant materials at hand in His own commanding spirit, and in the condition of the nation. But then something more than merely passing disturbances —disturbances which He Himself disdained—would have arisen,[2] and far more decided events would certainly have occurred. But so far removed was He from anything of this kind, that His inactivity would be inexplicable, were the supposition in question correct: His conduct, then, would have been not only without a plan, but contradictory, for no single measure can be pointed out in His course which can be regarded as having been distinctly adopted to further political ends. The nature of His operations is only intelligible on the assumption that, from the very commencement, He had in view the inward renewal of humanity. The same observation may be made with respect to His discourses. Where can we find in them a single utterance which decidedly

---

[1] Neander, *Life of Jesus*, fifth ed. p. 133. [2] John vi. 15.

announces an external theocracy? The words[1] in which He promised His disciples a hundredfold recompense in the kingdom of the Son of Man, and which might possibly be made to bear such a meaning, lose even the appearance of a reference to an external theocracy, and receive their sole appropriate explanation as a symbolical representation of future glory, when compared with other passages in which Jesus sternly repels every ambitious view of His followers, teaches them rather to look forward to the most painful conflicts, and sets forth the love which is willing and content to serve, as the true sign and seal of dignity in the kingdom of God.

Some have laboured to show that there is a contrast between the earlier and later utterances of Jesus, indicative of a change of feelings and views. This supposition is based on the fact, that whilst at His first public appearances[2] blessings fell from His lips, at a later period He poured forth denunciations against the cities which had rejected Him.[3] They have likewise inferred, from the manner in which He threatened the downfall of Jerusalem,[4] that originally it was His purpose to effect its political emancipation, and that He only renounced this design at a subsequent period. But there is no solid ground for such opinions. Not one of the blessings first pronounced by Jesus has remained in its true sense unfulfilled: as for the curses denounced against particular cities, they were the natural fruit of their unbelief. Jesus did desire, indeed, to lead Jerusalem and the Jewish commonwealth to an increased degree of civil prosperity, but only by means of a moral renewal; and for this His yearning was no less intense at the close than at the commencement of His

---

[1] Matt. xix. 27-30. These words belong in all probability to the latest period of the life of Jesus, when indeed the supposed theocratical plan is said to have been already renounced.

[2] Luke iv. 18-24.   [3] Matt. xi. 20-24.   [4] Luke xix. 41-44.

career.¹ The only perceivable difference is, that as He drew towards the termination of His mission, the ardent love He bore to His people expressed itself more frequently and more strongly in the form of grief at their perversity, until, last of all, there burst forth the prophetic warning, that their contempt of inward moral redemption must inevitably result in outward ruin.² Here was the chief ground of the sadness of Jesus, which, although more obvious and perceptible at the close of His career, had pervaded His whole life.³ His was, then, no faint-hearted depression and bitterness because of crushed hopes, but a much deeper pain. He was sad, partly on account of the degradation of His own countrymen, and partly because of the power of evil over mankind generally, —the evil which rose to its most fearful height when it caused His own death. His sadness had undoubtedly special regard to Jerusalem,—not, however, because of any discovery He had made that it was past help of a political nature, but because His fellow-countrymen had now finally rejected that which would have given them true peace and deliverance. But it is even more specially asserted, as forming a part of the 'human *development*' of Jesus, that the notion of a *suffering Messiah* found no place in His mind at the beginning of His career, and did not arise till a certain definite period, when, as an entirely new stage of consciousness, it abolished that stage which had preceded it.⁴ Let us see whether this was really the case.

We do not dispute that the notion of suffering and of death

---

[1] Compare De Wette, *Wesen des christlichen Glaubens*, § 52, p. 268.
[2] Matt. xxiii. 37-39.
[3] Osiander, in the above quoted essay, p. 147, justly finds in the constant harmony of Christ's inner life a pledge for the unity of His plans, and designates the contrast between the joyousness of the earlier period of His public ministry and the gloomy seriousness of the later, a *supposed* one. This he then satisfactorily proves by bringing forward particular instances.
[4] Keim, in the above quoted work, pp. 28-32, and elsewhere.

did but gradually attain increased power and prominence in the mind of Jesus. In conformity with this, we find that it was not till an expressly stated occasion that He solemnly disclosed it to His followers;[1] and this is but consistent with the successive development which we have already admitted. On the other hand, we decidedly contend that it was no new notion, opposed to former ideas, first making its appearance during His public ministry. For such a one could not be the result of mere development, but must rather be designated as a mighty revolution,—a total change in the views of Christ, necessarily involving a corresponding change of external conduct. Of this, if it had really taken place, we must have found evident traces, partly in the utterances of Jesus Himself, and partly in intimations by the apostles, whose perception such a state of things could not possibly have escaped. On the contrary, the exact reverse to this is found; of which fact we have ample confirmation from other quarters, without appealing to that somewhat obscure expression of the earlier days of His ministry concerning the destruction of the temple.[2]

On the very threshold of Christ's public life, we meet with the history of the temptation; and it is impossible not to regard the rejection of an externally glorious Messiahship—a rejection antecedent to any act of His public ministry—as the very essence of this narrative.[3] And if this be so, what was left but to seek another kind of glory by the path of conflicts, suffering, and sacrifice? Jesus must indeed have had but little acquaintance either with His own nation and the Roman power,—with Pharisaism and the priesthood,—with Himself and the sinful world,—if He could not foresee, even by mere human prescience, an embittered contest, and at last a tragic issue. And how does He express Himself? The ideas

---

[1] Matt. xvi. 21.   [2] John ii. 19.
[3] Compare especially Matt. iv. 8–11.

of the self-denial, the sacrifice, the surrender of life, of losing it that it may be gained, of the dying of the corn of wheat that it may bring forth fruit, run like a red thread through all His discourses from first to last. He sends forth His apostles as sheep in the midst of wolves, announces to them calamities of every kind, and impresses upon their minds this one thing, that it is enough for the disciple to be as his Master.[1] Even in the Sermon on the Mount He predicts hatred and persecution for His name's sake, to all who should believe in Him;[2] He acknowledges as His true disciple only him who denies himself and takes up his cross;[3] and knows that His people will everywhere have, not power and authority, but service, subjection, patient endurance of wrong, to the very uttermost. Have we, indeed, in all this the image of an outwardly triumphant Messiah? Certainly not; but rather of one who would Himself take up the cross before all others, and precede them on the path of suffering, even to the very extremity of self-sacrifice. And that the Lord recognised Himself as the Messiah in this sense, is already shown by His own words, even at a very early period of His ministry, without appealing to the above-mentioned more obscure passage.[4]

In this point, as well as with regard to the plan of Jesus, we cannot but hold fast the essential oneness of His views; and though we do admit a development, it is only such a one as by no means presupposes the existence of any internal discord in His mind.

Sec. 3.—*The Temptation.*

The very difficult problem now awaits our consideration, whether Jesus ever experienced any *inclination to sin?* Our

---

[1] Matt. x. 16–25.   [2] Matt. v. 10–12.
[3] Matt. viii. 34, 35; Matt. x. 38, 39.
[4] *e.g.* Matt. ix. 15. For more on this subject, see Dorner, *Jes. sündl. Vollk.* pp. 31, 32.

business is specially with the application of the idea of *temptation* to Jesus, and the difficulty lies in the question as to whether He could be really tempted, and yet remain absolutely sinless. Temptation implies allurement to evil; allurement involves a *minimum* of evil itself, and that is inconsistent with perfect purity.

We may very easily get rid of this difficulty by refusing to recognise one or the other of the two sides which should here be held in conjunction with each other; *i.e.* by affirming either that Jesus was not really tempted, or that we must not be so precise in our view of sinlessness. And there are not a few who do either deny the reality of the temptation, or sacrifice the strict conception of sinlessness. But the problem is not solved in this way. On the contrary, since Scripture teaches both the temptation and sinlessness of Christ, it becomes the duty of theology to furnish an answer to the question whether both can be held without prejudice to either, or whether the one necessarily excludes the other. Our proper guide in answering this question is the well-known passage in the Epistle to the Hebrews.[1] Jesus was tempted in all points, yet without sin; *i.e.* He was tempted so as it is possible to be without the entrance of sin. We must conceive of His endurance of temptation with the qualification that He continued free from sin; and of His sinlessness, as having stood the test of every species of temptation. According to this, there must be temptation without sin, and temptation with sin: there is a limit within which temptation is without sin, beyond which it involves sin. Our task is consequently to determine the point at which temptation does become sin; and in order to accomplish this, we shall need to examine more closely the relation between sin and temptation. If our investigation be conducted on right principles, it will

---

[1] Heb. iv. 15. See on this subject Riehm, *Lehrbegr. des Hebr. Br.* i. pp. 317, etc., and 321, etc.

tend greatly to diminish the difficulty presented by the narrative of the actual temptation of our Lord.

Our inquiry into the nature of sin has shown us that, although its focus is in the will, we are not to regard it as confined to that faculty. The life of the man in all its essential aspects must be taken into consideration. Reciprocity is the law of our constitution; and in virtue thereof, not only does the will, when affected by sin, act prejudicially on the other spheres of our life, but these latter also, when they are sinfully incited, exercise a corrupting influence upon the will. Sin does not take place simply by an abstract act of the will,—it is consummated only where there is a simultaneous darkening of the intelligence and imagination, by means of a stirring up of false and sensual emotions. The actual influence exerted by these different sides of our being varies according to the peculiarities of individual constitutions, and to the measure of our sinfulness. At the same time, however, with respect to the various spheres of our life, we must carefully distinguish between that which arises from their natural orderly action, and that which is already a beginning of sin.

We cannot consider it sinful that that which is evil should present itself to the understanding and imagination, partly as objectively existent, and partly as a possibility; for this is just one of the things which man, as a moral being, cannot avoid. Nor can it with any greater reason be looked upon as in itself sinful, that a sense of the opposition between pleasure and pain should be called forth within us by distinct thoughts or images, and that the one should exert an attractive, and the other a repulsive, influence. Such experiences owe their existence to the fact that man is endowed with sensibilities and a physical body, which being inalienable parts of his nature, must be recognised as of Divine ordination.[1]

---

[1] In the fact that Jesus had a body, and consequently sensibility, no ground or direct occasion of sin was involved. Σάρξ is ascribed to Him in

The presentation of evil through the understanding or imagination only implies sin, when the thought or image rises from within ourselves. Then we consider its presence sinful, because it presupposes the groundwork of our soul to be corrupt. But in case the thought or image is suggested by the surrounding world, we are only chargeable with actual sin if we dwell thereon with approval; for then our moral

a perfectly good sense, with reference, of course, to human limitations and lowliness, but with no reference at all to sin. In opposition to this, it is maintained by some, chiefly persons tinged with fanaticism,—as for example, formerly, by Dippel, Eschrich, Fend, and Poiret, and recently by the well-known Irving, through whom this point became the subject of a religious controversy in England,—that to Christ must be ascribed not simply flesh, but *sinful flesh;* and that, though in respect of His spirit and will He is to be held perfectly free from actual and habitual sin, it must yet be granted that in the matter of the senses and their sinful impulses, He was not different from other men. It is plain that these persons are somewhat lax in their views of sinlessness; for it is involved in the true idea of sinlessness that the sensuous impulses do not act independently of, and in opposition to, the spirit, but are altogether ruled by it. Moreover, the words of the apostle, to which they appeal, do not furnish a sufficient warrant for the doctrine. In the passage, Rom. viii. 3—ὁ Θεὸς τὸν ἑαυτοῦ υἱὸν πέμψας ἐν ὁμοιώματι σαρκὸς ἁμαρτίας—the word ὁμοίωμα refers only to σαρκός, and not at the same time to ἁμαρτίας, and the meaning is, 'God sent His Son in such a form of flesh and corporeity, as was of like kind with ours, which have, through sin, departed from their original condition,—not like with respect to sinful inclination, which would make the apostle contradict himself (2 Cor. v. 21), but of like kind with respect to finiteness, limitation, the wants of physical life: Christ, though not sinful Himself, was yet a man just like us who are sinners, and subject to the same conditions of sensuous existence. Compare Flatt, Tholuck, and other commentators on this passage. For more extended discussions of this point, see Müller's *Doctrine of Sin,* i. 407 ff., and especially pp. 434–459, third ed.; and Nitzsch's *System of Christian Doctrine,* § 129. J. E. W. Gericke, in an article on the effects of the death of Christ with respect to His own Person (*Stud. u. Krit.* 1843, ii. pp. 261, etc.), has lately brought forward the view that, in virtue of His participation in the flesh of the human race, its hereditary corruption—though only in the smallest degree—was transmitted to the human *nature* of Jesus; yet that this sinful incentive in Him, ever conquered and kept far from His person by the Divine principle within Him, was fully abolished by His death and resurrection. This view also, apart from other objections, is without a firm scriptural foundation, and inconsistent with the fundamental views of the New Testament.

judgment begins to be darkened, and an inclination towards evil to be felt. In like manner, the sensations, whether mental or bodily, of pleasure and pain, of the desirable and repulsive, can only be called sinful when they owe their rise to an opposition between spirit and flesh, already active in our personal life; or, at all events, they first acquire a sinful character when they prepare the way for the action of this antagonism, and produce desires whose satisfaction would be a transgression of the Divine order of our life.

It cannot be denied that evil does enter man through the channels of thought and imagination, of feeling and sensibility. At the same time, however, it must not only be acknowledged that the real decision of the matter rests with the will,—because it is only by a determination of the will that man really appropriates evil, and makes it an internal or external act for which he is responsible,—but we must also keep in view the fact, that in the spheres of thought and imagination, of emotion and sensibility, there are boundary lines very clearly separating between that which is natural and that which is sinful.

Our inquiry concerns, then, the relation which temptation bears to evil. In order to answer this question, we must bring before our minds the idea and nature of temptation.[1] By temptation, we mean every influence by which a personality intended for moral action may receive an impulse from good towards evil, every enticement to sin produced by any kind of impression, and especially such a one as, proceeding from some other person, is purposely designed to lead to sin. That which tempts may lie either in the man him-

---

[1] For the usage of the expressions πειράζεσθαι and πειρασμός in the New Testament, see Tholuck's *Commentary on the Sermon on the Mount*, pp. 432 ff., and Kern's *Brief Jacobi*, p. 125 ff. This subject is also further discussed in Köster's *Bibl. Lehre von der Versuchung*, Gotha 1859, and Palmer's article, *Versuchung*, in Herzog's *Theol. Real-Encycl.*

self, in the form of disorderly desire or inclination;[1] or be presented from without, in the shape of a motive to sinful action. Still, a temptation coming from without, must enter the mind through the medium of thought or fancy or sensuous impression, or else it is as good as not present. It must also exhibit the appearance of good; for mere evil, as such, does not tempt any but natures already Satanic. If evil is to tempt at all, it must appear as good; it must take the illusory form of a desirable possession, enjoyment, or other coveted result.

Every being is liable to temptation whose nature is on the one hand susceptible of good, and does not on the other necessarily shut out the possibility of evil. God cannot be tempted, because the holiness of His nature exalts Him *above* all temptation. Irrational creatures cannot be tempted, because, being incapable of true good, they are also *below* temptation to evil. Man alone, free to choose, can be tempted, because he is a moral, though not yet in his inward nature a holy, personality. Temptation begins for him when evil is presented, at some point of his inner or outer life, in such a way that he can directly take it up into his own being. But man is exposed in two ways to the possibility, and seductive power, of evil. On the one hand, he may be drawn to actual sin by enticements; and, on the other hand, he may be turned aside from good by threatened, as well as by inflicted, suffering. The former may be termed positive, the latter negative, temptation. The one is notably illustrated in the story of Hercules at the two ways, the other in the sufferings of Job.[2] As evil, when it lays hold upon us, affects our

---

[1] This is the ἐπιθυμία of which St. James speaks as the usual commencement of sin in man (Jas. i. 14). This kind of temptation presupposes a germ of evil already within the man himself, and is irreconcilable with moral perfection in the strict sense.

[2] Luther places temptations through suffering on the left hand, and those through pleasure on the right, and thus declares the latter to be the stronger and more dangerous (*Works*, B. vii. p. 1165).

life in its entirety, so does temptation assail us at different points, in order to gain possession of our will. Hence we may be tempted as truly through the thoughts and imaginations as through the emotions and senses; and in each case the temptation may be either a seduction to evil or a preventive from good, by means of either pleasure or pain.

Where, then, is the point in temptation at which sin begins, or at which it becomes itself sin? It is there where the evil which is presented to us begins to make a *determining* impression upon the heart. We do not say an impression in a general sense,—for without making this, it would be no temptation at all,—but a determining impression, that is one which, first creating commotion in the mind in general, then seizes upon the will in particular, and inclines it towards an opposition to the Divine order.[1] Then we find that a conflict is awakened in man which is inconceivable without the presence of sin, be it only in the least degree. Disorderly desire and inward bias towards evil are themselves the beginning of sin; and if such desire has its root and source in our own inner being, it not only leads to sin, but presupposes the ground of our life to be already corrupt. At this stage it is sin itself that entices to sin,—sin as a condition leading to sin in act. But temptation does not imply sin, when the evil, as a thing coming from the world without, merely offers its allurements, and is repelled by the indwelling energy of the spirit; or when we are shaken by sufferings, whether of body or soul, and instead of giving way to ungodly states of feeling and tendencies of the will (as in certain circumstances we might do), endure patiently, and are sustained by our inner moral power.

Contemplating the life of Jesus from this point of view,

[1] Luther well distinguishes between *sentire tentationem* and *consentire tentationi*. Unless the tempting impression be felt, there is no real temptation; but unless it be *acquiesced in* or *yielded to*, there is no sin.

we can understand how He might be tempted, and yet remain free from sin. He was tempted in all points,—that is, He was tempted in the only two possible ways, specified above. On the one hand, allurements were presented which might have moved Him to actual sin; and, on the other hand, He was beset by sufferings which might have turned Him aside from the Divine path of duty. These temptations, moreover, occurred both on great occasions and in minute particulars, under the most varied circumstances, from the beginning to the end of His earthly course. But in the midst of them all, His spiritual energy and His love to God remained pure and unimpaired. Temptations of the first order culminated in the attack made on Jesus by Satan; temptations of the second order assailed Him most severely during the struggles of Gethsemane, and when He felt Himself forsaken by God on the cross. It will therefore be necessary to consider these two events more closely.

At present we shall consider the *narrative of the temptation*[1] only in *one* aspect, namely, in its relation to the sinlessness of Jesus, with respect to the difficulty it may present in the way of a full recognition of that sinlessness.[2] At the same time some reference to the different modes of understanding that narrative will be unavoidable. In some explanations the sinlessness of Jesus is regarded as beyond all question; in others, on the contrary, it is imperilled. On this ground it

---

[1] Matt. iv. 1–11; Mark i. 12, 13; Luke iv. 1–13.
[2] The following essays, which advert to my own earlier view, may be compared in this connection: Usteri, *Ueber die Versuchung Christi, Stud. u. Krit.* 1829, 3, and 1832, 4; Hasert in the same, 1830, 1; Hocheisen, *Bemerkungen über die Vers. Gesch.*, in the Tübingen *Zeitschrift f. Theologie*, 1833, 2; Kohlschütter *zur Verständigung über die Vers. Gesch.*, in Käuffer's *Bibl. Studien*, Jahrg. 2. The most recent discussions of the subject are by E. Pfeiffer in the *Deutsche Zeitschrift*, May 1851; and by Rink in the same periodical, September 1851; also by Laufs in the *Studien und Kritiken*, 1853, 2.

will be necessary to pass the different interpretations briefly in review, and to decide to which our adherence shall be given.[1]

Among such views of this narrative as are by no means at variance with the doctrine of Christ's sinlessness, may be regarded those which see in the accounts of the evangelists no actual occurrence, but simply a product of early Christian thought. The opinions of those who take this view are divided as to whether the account originated with Jesus Himself under the form of a parable, or with His immediate followers under the form of a myth. Whatever our judgment may be of explanations of this nature, it is quite clear that they do not endanger the sinlessness of Jesus. Neither as a parable, in which Jesus set forth the fundamental maxims according to which all efforts on behalf of His kingdom should be regulated, nor as a myth, in which His Church glorified Him as the conqueror of Satan, would it involve anything really at variance with His sinlessness. But though circumstances have helped to decide the preference of some recent theologians, amongst whom are Schleiermacher and Usteri, for the parabolical mode of interpretation, we cannot see our way clear to the adoption of such a method of escaping the difficulties; and simply for the reason, that we hold the view which underlies it to be an utterly inadmissible one. The entire character of the narrative, and especially the position it occupies between the baptism and public appearance of Jesus, argue too strongly that we have to do with facts, and not with parable or myth. And even if it be true, which at present we do not stop to consider, that some portions of the account cannot be in every respect regarded as actual history, and must be looked upon as drapery, still we should have to hold fast a kernel of fact. When we reflect that it was involved in the human nature of Christ that He should be tempted; further, that the Gospels

[1] At present briefly; more fully in a special appendix.

throughout know nothing at all of a Saviour who was not actually tempted; and finally, that it lay in the nature of the case, that that which could be a temptation to Him should present itself with special force at the commencement of His career,—we shall see the necessity of maintaining a substratum of fact in this history.

But even when maintaining that we have before us the report of actual temptations undergone by Jesus, there are still, as is well known, a variety of possible explanations from this point of view also. Before entering on an examination of these, it will be advisable to come to some decision as to the essential meaning of the history, and thus to ascertain clearly that which must hold true under all circumstances, whatever may be the mode in which single points are treated.

The narrative is undoubtedly set forth as an essential item of the gospel of Jesus as the Christ, as a constituent part of the life of Jesus as the Messiah. In this quality it is placed between that baptismal act which should, and did, inaugurate the Messiah, and the actual appearance of Jesus as the Messiah. By this we are indirectly, but notwithstanding plainly enough, taught that the temptation bore reference to Jesus in His Messianic character; that it was not merely a trial of the general human kind, but specially a trial of the Messiah. This is clear from the third temptation,—the offer of worldly dominion. But it is also distinctly hinted at in the two others, in the words, *if Thou be the Son of God* (Matt. iv. 3, 6); for these words do not relate to the human nature which Jesus had in common with us all, but to His higher dignity. Moreover, both these latter temptations manifestly presuppose a person, like the Messiah, endowed with extraordinary powers from God, and under special Divine protection. We may accordingly determine the essential feature of the temptation in one aspect to be, that Jesus, at a point of His career in which His whole future was involved, repelled, with all firmness and decision, the seductions of an external conception of Messianic glory, as ungodly and sinful, and decided, once for all, upon aims and modes of operation which were pure and well-pleasing to God.

Linked together in this way, the individual temptations may be conceived as follows. The first, which was the temptation to change stones into bread, contains a call to the Messiah to employ His miraculous endowments for the satisfaction of His own immediate and pressing wants. In the second temptation, which was to cast Himself down from the pinnacle of the temple, He is urged to put that protection which is promised to God's chosen One to the test, by wilfully running into manifest danger.[1] The third temptation, in which the kingdoms of the world and their glory were exhibited before Him, appeals to Him to employ worldly means for the realization of His idea of a world-wide theocracy. The rejoinders show that such is the significance of the temptations. To the first, Jesus answers that *man does not live by bread alone*,—by that which only relieves his physical necessities,—*but by every word that cometh from the mouth of God;*[2] to the second He replies that *we may not tempt the Lord our God*,—we may not tempt arbitrarily, and unnecessarily call for His protection; to the third He rejoins,—making reference to the fact that an external empire like those which had been spread out before Him could only be established by the service of the Prince of this world,— *Thou shalt worship the Lord thy God, and Him only shalt thou serve.* All three temptations converge in *one* central and fundamental thought—the thought of a kingdom which, al-

---

[1] The supposition that the second temptation calls for a miracle of display, now seems to me to come far behind the explanation given above. Compare Kohlschütter in Käuffer's *Bibl. Studien*, Jahrg. 2, pp. 75, 76.

[2] According to another view, we must not anticipate the command of God, who has a thousand means of preserving life.

though apparently Divine, is in reality only worldly, and opposed to the true kingdom of God, which is first founded in the hearts of men, and thence attains external visible realization.[1] The only way to the establishment of such a kingdom was through the prostitution of His higher Messianic endowments to the satisfaction of the desires of His physical nature and self-love; through a presumptuous confidence in Divine protection in paths of danger chosen by Himself; and finally, through a league with, and an entrance into, the service of the Prince of the world. On the contrary, it was only in a spirit of voluntary self-denial in the way prescribed by God, and by a distinct rupture with all the power and glory of this world, that the true kingdom of God could be founded. It was, consequently, the essential opposition between a kingdom which, corresponding to the views of the carnal mind, might be speedily and compulsorily set up, and one of self-sacrificing love, which could only be gradually established from within, and in the divinely ordered way, that now presented itself to the mind of Jesus. He who was sent to found a true theocracy was thus called upon, as He entered on His mission, for a distinct, full, and final decision on one side or the other.

This is unmistakeably one aspect of the temptation of Jesus; but we cannot confine ourselves to it. Were we to do so, our conception of the whole matter would be far too abstract. The Tempter does undoubtedly appeal to Jesus as the Son of God, and very obviously endeavours to influence Him as such; but there must be no separation made between the Son of God and the Son of man. In fact, the temptations endured by Jesus were real and genuine, for the simple reason, that whilst they tried Him in His character of Messiah, they also assailed Him as a man. A merely theoretical choice between a false and a true conception of Messiah would have

[1] Compare Neander's *Life of Jesus*, fifth ed. p. 118.

been no temptation at all. It was indispensable that the false conception should have in it something of a blinding and bribing nature,[1] something that might prove seductive to the self-love of His sensuous nature. That such an element was present, is as unquestionable as it is evident that Jesus could only be open thereto so far as He shared the general human sensibility to pleasure and pain, to joy and sorrow. Only on this supposition could it be said of Him that He was tempted in all points like as we are.[2] In this sense His temptations have *a general human* as well as a special Messianic character. They exhibit the spiritual Head of our race as tried like our natural, physical head, but with contrary results.

The seductive element in the several suggestions seems, so far as its human aspect is concerned, to have consisted partly in that which would prove tempting to human nature in general, and partly in that which would be specially alluring to men of a higher order, who are called to a higher vocation. There was, first of all, the inclination to use the gifts of God in the service of self; then there was the liability to entertain the fancy, that One entrusted with a Divine mission, and under the special guardianship of God, might unhesitatingly incur any danger, and even arbitrarily expose Himself thereto; and lastly, there was the desire for this world's power and glory. To temptation of the first kind men are exposed, as men; to seductions of the second kind, those are peculiarly liable who have the consciousness of a higher mission; by allurements of the third kind, those are mainly affected who feel themselves destined to rule. Jesus was exposed to all alike, for He was a man like ourselves; He had the certain consciousness of the

---

[1] Special emphasis is rightly laid on this point by Kohlschütter, pp. 68–71.
[2] Heb. iv. 15, where the words καθ' ὁμοιότητα are not employed without purpose.

highest mission, and He could say of Himself, *I am a King*. Here, however, again, the three temptations converged and united in one all-inclusive and fundamental temptation; and this lay in the choice between enjoyment and sacrifice, between self-will and the Divine order, between the service of the Prince of this world and the exclusive service of the holy God,—between the one as the essential principle of a kingdom of this world, and the other as the essential principle of the kingdom of God.

We may hold, however, that this is the true significance of the temptation, and at the same time that the history is substantially a record of facts, and yet form very different conceptions of the facts themselves. For instance, the matter has been represented as follows: that Jesus brought before His own mind the chief features of the Messianic notions of His contemporaries, and consequently that the choice between a false and true Messiahship was made as a purely mental transaction. Such a view is, however, evidently too spiritualistic, and out of harmony with the character of the Gospel narrative. The words of the evangelists undoubtedly demand that we should form a more realistic conception of the whole event. They point out that the seductive thoughts were brought to Jesus from without, by means of an objective and personal power exterior to Himself. Thus to have contended with him who is in the highest and most general sense the Tempter, gives, too, to the conflict and victory of the Lord Jesus an unmistakeably sublime and universal significance, with respect both to the person concerned and the principles involved. Nevertheless, whatever stress we may lay upon the objective feature of the transaction, we must always at the same time admit that if it was anything more than the mere semblance of temptation, and is to be regarded as real, the seductive thoughts must have entered into the mind of Jesus, in such a manner that He did not merely hear, but also thought and felt them,—that, in short, they made an impression upon Him. Then there arises the question, which for us is the most important of all: Could such seductive thoughts, in whatever way they came, *enter the soul of Jesus* without sullying His moral purity,—without putting an end to His sinlessness?

We answer that this is quite conceivable. Two suppositions must, however, be most carefully avoided in connection with this matter. The one is, that the producing cause of these seductive thoughts was in any sense in the soul of Jesus Himself; and the other, that they gained any determining influence over the heart, the will, the life of Jesus. That neither was the case may be clearly shown.

Undoubtedly, if the thoughts in question were *produced* in the soul of Jesus, the conviction would be forced upon us, that its ground was morally impure, corrupt, and that sin was present in Him in the shape of evil desire. But there is nothing whatever to warrant such a supposition. And further, we strike at once at the root of a hypothesis of this nature, when we hold by the recognition of a tempter who appeared objectively to Jesus. If we were even to admit that it was by the agency of His own mind that the Lord Jesus brought forward the false idea of the Messiah as an object of contemplation, any misgiving which might thereby arise is immediately obviated by distinguishing between the presentation and the origination of a thought. The expectation of a worldly Messiah was not a notion which had yet to be conceived; on the contrary, it was one everywhere rife, and which Jesus must have inevitably encountered on all sides in the world around. Nay, He could not carry out the true idea of the Messiah in its full extent, without also taking up into His thoughts its spurious counterpart. The full and decided appropriation of the one necessarily involved the rejection of the other; consequently, also its presence before His soul. In any case, then, we have only to do with the thought of something already actually existing; and such a thought, though its object might include every element of sin, could not, of itself, be by any possibility defiling.

There is of course another thing yet to be taken into consideration. If we are not to deem the moral purity of Jesus to have been stained by the presence of the seductive thoughts, we must not suppose them to have exerted any *determining influence* on His inner life: and this seems difficult to maintain, when we take the idea of temptation in right earnest. One concession must be made in this connection—viz. that the mere thinking of evil does not in itself constitute a temptation, and that, in order to its being a temptation, the evil must appear adapted to, and must be enticing to, the self-love of our sensuous nature. The false conception of Messiah, whether suggested by the devil or by the world, was of this nature. Moreover, there can be no doubt that Jesus, as being a real man, was susceptible of its influence. For to the nature of man enjoyment is always dearer than privation, honour than disgrace, and a throne than a cross. Not that we are to conceive the enjoyments of life, honour, and rule to be essentially sinful. They are that only under certain conditions. Nor do we necessarily contract defilement through our sense of the pleasantness of these things. Only when it has a corrupting effect on the moral feelings, disturbs the judgment, and gives an ungodly bias to the will and activity, can this be affirmed. But the narrative of the temptation exhibits the direct opposite of all this. Not like the first parents[1] of mankind, did Jesus dwell with pleasure on the temptation which was laid before Him. That was precisely the cause of their fall. Neither did He suffer a 'yea, hath God said,' to arise in His mind. With a quick resolution that is obvious from the whole narrative,

[1] Gen. iii. 6.

without any lingering or longing hesitancy, He trampled the allurements under foot; and so directly did He in the thrice repeated 'It is written' oppose to each seductive suggestion the sword of the Spirit, that no ground whatever is left for the assumption that evil entered within so as to disturb and stain His feelings or imagination, His heart or will.[1] It is, however, the character of His whole subsequent life, and the moral consciousness expressed in every part of it, which is our strongest guarantee that His purity was maintained on this occasion also. So spotless was the purity that shone through all His acts and words, that it is inconceivable that the temptation, though real, should have involved for Him aught like the beginning of a fall, or aught of sin.

The positive temptations of Jesus were not, however, confined to that particular point of time when they assailed Him with concentrated force.[2] They returned as often as impressions were made on Him from without, whose tendency was to draw Him away from complete faithfulness to His love of God, and from pure and holy activity on behalf of the kingdom of God. But still more frequently in after times was He called to endure temptation of the other kind,—the temptation of suffering; and this culminated on two occasions —viz. in the conflict of Gethsemane, and in that moment of

---

[1] Therefore, as Hocheisen justly observes in the Tübingen *Theolog. Zeitschrift*, 1833, 2, p. 115, no parallel can be drawn between the temptation of Christ and Prodikus's story of Hercules and the two ways; for a hesitation of choice between two ways cannot be spoken of in connection with Jesus. In order to anticipate and cut off possible difficulties, Menken, in his *Betrachtungen über den Matthæus*, i. 104, would have the whole transaction termed *trial* instead of *temptation*. But the Scriptures do not sufficiently justify this change. Inasmuch as Satan comes before us πειράζων, we may fairly apply the distinction made even by Tertullian: Deus *probat*, Diabolus *tentat*.

[2] In Luke iv. 13 it is said *Satan departed from Jesus* ἄχρι καιροῦ: and Jesus Himself speaks of His temptations in the plural number (Luke xxii. 28).

agony on the cross when He cried, *My God, my God, why hast Thou forsaken me?*

The whole life of Jesus, as depicted by the evangelists, was pervaded by suffering. They were griefs of the intensest kind which pierced His soul during the contest of His loving will with the sin of the world; and to these were added bodily pains. Both conjoined reached their climax in the tortures of the cross,—than which no agonies can be conceived higher or more intense. Jesus never expressly sought, or capriciously exposed Himself to, suffering. Nor did He need to do so, for it came unsought. Still less did He purposely avoid it, seeing in it as He did an essential constituent of His Divine calling. He resigned Himself cheerfully to all that befell Him, and thus displayed a power of endurance, which, whilst never inconsistent with the human, always ensured victory to the Divine.

The two events in question might be alleged as revealing a state of mind at variance with our assumption,—namely, the conflict of Gethsemane, in which suffering of soul is peculiarly manifest, and the moment on the cross in which the physical pain, added to the agony of soul, reached its highest point. In both instances Jesus seemed not to maintain the strength of mind consistent with sinless perfection, but to succumb to the weakness of human nature.

There have not been wanting those who have found in the *conflict of Gethsemane*,[1] especially in the supposed struggle against death, something inconsistent with the greatness of Jesus in other respects; and in order to remove from the image of Jesus a feature which, in their view, disfigures it, they have resorted to the desperate means of declaring the whole incident unworthy of credit.[2] But the portion of the

---

[1] Matt. xxvi. 36–47; Mark xiv. 32–43; Luke xxii. 39–47.
[2] See Usteri, *Studien und Kritiken*, 1829, 3, p. 465. Usteri thinks that if the tradition were true, he must rank Jesus under Socrates. On the other

Gospel narrative in question is too well attested, both externally and internally, to justify any such violence. We must therefore endeavour to understand this paradox also of the life of Jesus. And in fact, when we look at it with an unprejudiced mind, it not only loses much of its strangeness, but gives besides a peculiar significance to the Person of Jesus, and to the relation in which He stands to ourselves. The incident exhibits Jesus to us in the full truth of His humanity, in His perfect nearness to men. Jesus, as a man, could not have had a heart filled with holy love, without feeling sorrowful, even unto death, at the hatred He encountered in return for His self-sacrifice,—a hatred manifesting, as it did, the dreadful degree to which the power of sin prevailed in the world. He could not have possessed that fulness of fresh and sensitive life which He everywhere revealed, without shuddering at the approach of a death of torture. But there is nothing sinful in the grief felt by love at unmerited hatred; nor in the wrestlings of a lofty soul with the sin of the world; nor in the natural recoil from death experienced by one whose life is healthy and energetic,—for this must not be confounded with a reflective shrinking from and resistance to death.[1] These are purely human conditions, and as such they were involved in the fact that the body and soul of Christ were of like nature with our own. They would have passed into sin, only if they had produced some alteration in feeling or will. And that such was not the case,—that, on the contrary, the spiritual nature of Jesus and His love to God rose victorious over the agitations of

side, compare the beautiful parallel between the death of Jesus and that of Socrates, in de Wette's *Wesen des christlichen Glaubens*, § 53, p. 270. Rousseau says, in his pithy manner, 'If Socrates suffered and died like a philosopher, Jesus suffered and died like a God.'

[1] Hasert justly remarks, *Studien und Kritiken*, 1830, 1, p. 72, that the impulse of our physical nature to secure itself against destruction is a natural expression of our life, belonging essentially to its character, and therefore not necessarily involving sin.

His feelings and the pains of His body,—is testified by the words, *Father, not as I will, but as Thou wilt.* These words cast a light and a glory on all that preceded them,—they tell of the complete inward victory gained by the Lord Jesus,—and prove that, even in the midst of such mental agony as this, He maintained a spotless purity.

But the sufferings of Gethsemane were only a foretaste of those which in full reality and force preceded and accompanied His death on the cross. And on the cross His agony rose to such a point that He had a sense of being *deserted by God*,—to which feeling He gave utterance in the well-known words of the 22d Psalm, *My God, my God, why hast Thou forsaken me?* Desertion by God must not, in this case, be conceived of strictly, as objective, actual withdrawal of God from the Person of Jesus, but only as a subjective feeling of desertion. Efforts have, however, been made to do away even with this, on the supposition of its being unworthy of the Lord. Jesus, it is said, though He certainly cried out only in the first words of this Psalm, yet had in His mind its whole contents, and especially its close, which, far from being of a desponding nature, expresses the utmost confidence in the future victory of God's kingdom. To give matters this turn is, however, perfectly arbitrary, and, in opposition to the situation, transposes the whole from the sphere of direct spontaneous feeling to that of reflection.[1] We ought rather to take that which is historically recorded in all its significance and force, and at the same time to adhere to the rule of not treating a single saying as isolated and cut off from the connection in which it is found.

The frame of mind and exclamation in question are manifestly an intensified counterpart of the agony of Gethsemane. Jesus had in fact, for the moment, the feeling that He was deserted by God, when physical tortures burst in upon Him

[1] Matt. xxvii. 46, and Meyer's Commentary on this passage.

Arguments against His actual Sinlessness. 143

in all their fearfulness, in addition to the deepest sorrow of heart. But this feeling was only a *momentary* one with Him whose whole being was rooted in God, although, in the circumstances and at the time, it made its presence known with the involuntariness of a force of nature. In no sense did it continue, or exert any influence over His inner life. It immediately gave way before, and yielded its due place to, a sense of His true relation to God. As in the conflict of Gethsemane the full submission to the will of the Father soon triumphed over His natural reluctance to drink the cup, so here, that sense of Divine desertion which rose involuntarily in His mind was at once swallowed up in the higher feeling, expressed first of all in the words, *Father, into Thy hands I commend my spirit*,[1] and then in the crowning exclamation, *It is finished*.[2] Nay, it is manifest that the higher feeling had already begun to work, from the words in which Jesus expressed the sense of desertion; for He did not exclaim simply, *O God! O God!* but, *My God! my God!* He thus appropriated the God by whom He felt Himself forsaken as *His* God, and clung firmly to His fellowship with Him, notwithstanding the sense of desertion. Moreover, this feeling was something in itself so thoroughly strange to Him, that He expressed it, not in the form of a positive assertion, but of a question: thus hinting at its incomprehensibleness, —one might almost say, at its impossibility.[3]

The perfect purity of Jesus shone forth, therefore, even in such circumstances as these. At the same time, we see and

---

[1] Luke xxiii. 16.   [2] John xix. 30.

[3] Both, in fact, were implied in the passage from the Psalms, of which Jesus availed Himself; yet if it had not fully expressed His actual feelings, He would either not have used it, or have altered it to suit His need. But even the passage in the Psalms itself does not express the feeling of desertion alone, nor speak of this as a permanent state of mind, as the whole context plainly shows. Even in the Psalmist's mouth, the saying cannot be taken in an absolute sense, much less in that of the Lord Jesus.

feel throughout that He was a man, and, as such, mightily moved and keenly sensitive. Nor could it be otherwise. The whole delineation of the Gospels forbids our making of the character of Jesus an ideal of stoical apathy and imperturbability.[1] In respect of wants and woes, of the susceptibility of His mind to emotion, and the sensibility of His body to suffering, He was a perfect type of humanity. We cannot, however, for this reason consider Him as ranking below, but above, the wise man of the Stoics. It is precisely in this particular that the morality of the Stoics is untrue. Man's highest moral task is not to realize the anti-human, but the purely human,—it does not consist in repressing his natural capacities, which, because natural, are ordained of God, but in employing them in, and glorifying them by, the service of the Divine Spirit and holy love. This is what we find in Jesus; and the most rigid moral judgment, so far from seeing therein anything sinful, must rather confess that it is this that brings Him so near to us, that shows Him to us as our Brother, and makes Him capable of being a real example to man. Nay, only on this condition could He also be a truly human Redeemer,—*a High Priest who was Himself tempted and tried, who Himself in the days of His flesh offered up prayers and supplications with strong crying and tears, and is therefore touched with the feeling of our infirmities.*[2]

Sec. 4.—*Other Acts and Expressions of Jesus, as Arguments against His Sinlessness.*

If, then, there is nothing in the facts that Jesus underwent a temporal development, and that He was tempted, which

---

[1] As among the Fathers, Clement of Alexandria was inclined to do, and therefore applied to Christ the expression, ἀνεπιθύμητος. For examples, see Hagenbach's *History of Doctrines*, i. §§ 66 and 67.

[2] Heb. iv. 15, v. 7.

compromises His sinlessness, another question arises, namely, as to whether we do not find in His *works* and *discourses* themselves, much that is inconsistent with moral perfection. An affirmative answer to this question would constitute the most striking and satisfactory refutation of what has been hitherto advanced. Several things of this nature were urged even by the contemporaries of Jesus. Others have been brought forward more recently. Some of these seem almost frivolous, and scarcely worthy of notice. Yet the removal of even subordinate misunderstandings may be useful, when they threaten to deface so elevated a form as that of Jesus.

Amongst the scanty traditions of the *earlier* period of the life of Jesus, has been preserved that account of His peculiar ripeness at twelve years of age (Luke ii. 41–52), which we have already several times brought forward as very significant in relation to His mental development. But there is the appearance of a blemish even in connection with that remarkable circumstance. The boy might be reproached with disobedience, with wilfulness, for remaining behind in the temple. In examining the matter, however, more closely, this apparent blemish vanishes. Not a word hints that His parents looked upon Him as in fault for remaining behind. The exclamation of His mother was simply the spontaneous expression of tender concern. Further, we can easily conceive of many circumstances arising, where the family relationships were less constrained, which might give occasion to the separation, without neglect on the part of the parents, or self-will on the part of the Son. On the other hand, we may discern even in the boy the same Jesus, who, as a man, rising above the narrow limits of family connections, and subordinating everything that was private and peculiar to His vocation, could say, *Who is my mother? who are my brethren?* and on another occasion could address His mother, *Woman, what have I to do with thee?* His energies were to be devoted to the whole of mankind, and the spirit requisite thereto must needs have been manifested at an early period.

In the properly *Messianic period* of the life of Jesus there were many things at which even His own contemporaries cavilled. Scrutinized, however, more closely, they only furnish one proof more of the elevated nature of His moral life. Of this kind are the reproaches, that He did not live ascetically like the Pharisees, nor even like John the Baptist, but ate and drank like ordinary men; that He associated with publicans and sinners; that He broke the Sabbath by healing the sick; and the like. But it was precisely in opposition to such narrow-heartedness that Jesus manifested by word and deed the grand principles of a freer morality, —of that morality which flows from the fountain of Divine love, and which raises the gospel so far above the level of all legal service: precisely then did He take occasion to defend the simple and genuinely human cheerfulness of a truly pious life, which is marred by no spurious asceticism, but receives and uses all God's gifts thankfully and temperately: precisely then, too, did He propound those simple doctrines, that the disposition is the test of genuine morality; that love is more than sacrifice; that ordinances are for man, and not man for ordinances, and lay them down as eternal truths in forms appropriate to the time.

The evangelists have artlessly recorded many doings of Jesus with that unreflective objectivity which is peculiar to them, without ever thinking that they might give moral offence. It is only the sensitiveness of the modern world that has found them strange and offensive. Some things of this kind scarcely deserve examination; as, for example, *the cursing of the fig-tree.*[1] The reproach, that He was interfering with the property of others, is in no sense well founded, and is almost too frivolous to be mentioned. And even the

[1] Matt. xxi. 17-22; Mark xi. 11-26.

notion, that Jesus here manifested personal irritation against a lifeless object, disappears as soon as we remark that He was performing—and that too, undoubtedly, with perfect self-possession—a work of prophetically instructive import, designed symbolically to announce the destruction of the spiritually unfruitful Jewish people. There are other things which do in part present real difficulty, and therefore demand a more careful consideration. With greater apparent justice might Jesus be accused of interference with the rights of property in that noteworthy *act* in the *country of the Gadarenes*,[1] where it cannot be denied that the cure performed by Him was directly coupled with damage to the inhabitants of the district. Almost all commentators on this passage have believed it necessary to offer an apology for Jesus; and naturally this has been done in various ways, according to the different points of view of the writers. We should hesitate to excuse Jesus, as many recent commentators have attempted to do, on the ground of His not foreseeing the result;[2] for this is at variance with the idea which the evangelists give of Him. And, on the other hand, we might justly urge that Jesus acted here, as He did generally in His miracles, as the Plenipotentiary of God. When God, in the pursuance of higher aims, destroys single things, when He permits the destruction of human possessions by natural forces, who dare charge Him with injustice? The complicated system of the universe requires it, and particular occurrences are ordered on the plan of a wisdom which is beyond our comprehension. Jesus also stood on this position of higher wisdom and authority; and whoever objects to His acting out of the fulness of Divine right, can hardly justify Him in a manner that will harmonize with the general representation of the Gospels. But it has been urged, and not

[1] Matt. viii. 28-34; Mark v. 1-20; Luke viii. 26-39.
[2] Hase, *Leben Jesu*, third ed. § 75, p. 134.

altogether without reason, against this mode of treating the question, that it lies out of the proper sphere of an apology, whose business it is to justify Jesus according to the general laws of human action. We take our stand, therefore, entirely on the ground, that Jesus, on this as on every occasion, was fulfilling His mission; not indeed without foresight of the consequence of His acts, but without suffering Himself to be influenced thereby. The aim of that mission was to save the lives and souls of men; and the possible destruction of irrational creatures, or the contingency of a loss which might be replaced, could not possibly restrain Him therefrom. Nay, His conduct on this occasion rather serves to place in a clearer light the high value which Jesus attached to man as the image of God.

But if we are not justified in regarding Jesus as under the influence of passion when He cursed the fig-tree, there is another occurrence recorded by the evangelists, in connection with which we can scarcely avoid such a supposition,—namely, *the driving out those who were buying and selling in the temple*.[1] It is even possible to describe it in such a way as to give it the appearance of a low and violent action.[2] There is, however, nothing to authorize such a delineation; for it was certainly not the employment of external chastisement or threats, but His holy earnestness and personal dignity, which gave to the action of the Lord Jesus its impressiveness and efficacy. Their feeling that He was in the right, and they in the wrong, drove the traffickers out of the temple. Notwithstanding, there do remain traces of angry ebullition in the act, which contrast with the usual mildness of Jesus. The disciples themselves were sensible of the presence of a devouring zeal in His conduct on this occasion.[3] But here

---

[1] Matt. xxi. 12-17; Mark xi. 15-19; Luke xix. 45, 48, compared with John ii. 14–18.
[2] As Pécaut does in very strong terms, p. 252.   [3] John ii. 17.

the distinction must be observed between personal passion and the noble anger felt by one entrusted with a high calling. It is not as a Jewish Rabbi that Jesus stands opposed to these Jewish traffickers, but it is as the divinely appointed Purifier of the theocracy that He stands opposed to the desecration of the sanctuary of God; and this position gave Him the right to act in a way which need not be justified according to traditional rules. Even if the doubtful *jus zelotarum* were recognised, it would not be necessary to appeal to it in order to clear the conduct of Jesus from blame. 'He was wielding that power of chastisement which is truly connected with the office of Prophet,—that power which has been and should be exercised in all ages and among all peoples by higher natures called with such a vocation, whenever earthly relations and the course of justice, according to existing laws, are unable to stem the growing corruption.'[1] Such an action, however, could never have been performed but under the influence of an overpowering earnestness and an intensely indignant zeal. Such zeal for the Divine honour is, however, not unworthy of the purest; and in periods of corruption, nothing that is truly great can be accomplished without it.

The relation between Jesus and Judas also offers peculiar difficulty.[2] If Jesus knew Judas, why did He enroll His future betrayer among the apostles? And if He did not see through him, what have we to say on behalf of the moral penetration of Jesus? In either case, did not Jesus here make a mistake? In giving a satisfactory answer to this question, all depends on our conception of the moral condi-

---

[1] See Lücke's *Commentary* on this passage, Pt. i. pp. 536, 537; and Dorner's *Jes. sündl. Vollk.* p. 17, note 1.

[2] Compare on this relation, and the different modes of conceiving it, Dr. Gust. Schollmeyer's *Jesus and Judas*, Lüneberg 1836. See also Neander's *Life of Jesus*, fifth ed. pp. 192, 679-689; and Hase, *Leben Jesu*, § 110, p. 182 ff. third ed.

tion of Judas when called to association with Jesus. Substantially, there are three different views of this matter possible, each of which leads to a different solution of the difficulty. According to the first, Judas, at the time of his acceptance by Jesus, had already within him the germs of his after sins — ambition and covetousness, but the good was still predominant in his soul; and further, Jesus hoped to accomplish his complete renovation, and then to avail Himself of the strong nature of Judas as an able instrument for the advancement of His cause, but was foiled in His gracious intentions.[1] According to the second view, Judas, when he came into contact with Jesus, had already fallen irrecoverably a prey to evil;[2] and Jesus chose him, not only with the distinct knowledge that he would be, but—since it was *necessary* that treachery should bring to pass the death of the Redeemer— also with the intention that he should be, His betrayer. He chose him, moreover, that in him a most striking example might be given how even one so utterly corrupt could but subserve the execution of the Divine purposes. According to the third view, when Judas was called to be an apostle, evil was, indeed, already predominant in him, but not absolutely supreme. His proximity to Jesus might influence him for good or for evil, and it was worth while to make the attempt to recover him. If Judas were gained to the side of the good, he would prove one of the most powerful of the

---

[1] This hypothesis is carried out in a manner correspondent to the state of theological science at the time of its publication, in the Essay entitled *Wie könnte der grosse Menschenkenner Jesus einen Judas zum Lehrer der Menschheit wählen?* See Augusti's *Theologische Blätter*, B. i. pp. 497–515.

[2] This is Daub's conception of Judas in his *Judas Ischarioth, oder, über das Böse im Verhältniss zum Guten*, Heidelberg 1816. See especially No. I. pp. 16–20. Judas is there described as the evil which has utterly cast off all humanity, as a devil in the flesh, who becomes the betrayer of the incarnate God, and in whose (predestined) despair there was no stirring of good. Not quite the same, yet similar is the view of Olshausen. See his *Biblical Commentary*, vol. ii. p. 438 ff. (German ed.).

Arguments against His actual Sinlessness. 151

apostles; if he were lost, he must still of necessity serve the plan of Jesus. Jesus was prepared for any issue: He saw, even at an early period of their connection,[1] how Judas would decide; but He did not then cast him out, partly because He would act towards him with the utmost forbearance, partly because the proximity of Judas, even in the case of his yet deeper fall, would answer His further purposes.

The first of these views not only supposes that Jesus was deceived, which is irreconcilable with the depth and acuteness of His penetration, but rests also on a misconception of the true nature of moral development. In order to reach the degree of evil at which we find Judas, its influence over him must have been for a longer period growing stronger and stronger, and working its way into all the parts, into the very tissue of his being. Had he entered into the fellowship of Jesus with a predominant susceptibility to good impressions, the result would have been different. Moreover (and this is decisive), this view clearly contradicts the declaration of John,[2] that Jesus knew the traitorous designs of Judas even at the earliest stage of their intercourse. The second view rather cuts than unties the knot. It considers the matter only in its relation to the end aimed at, whilst primarily it ought to be examined from the point of view of the determining cause; it makes a leap from the region of the historical to that of the metaphysical, and explains the obscure by that which is still more obscure: it further supposes a degree of wickedness in Judas that strips him of everything human, and this notwithstanding that his repentance, although perverse in its operation and results, testified to some

---

[1] The expression ἐξ ἀρχῆς, John vi. 64, need not necessarily be referred to the period *before*, or to the exact time of, the call of Judas. It means, as in John xvi. 4, *in the first period*, soon after he was chosen, and long before he manifested his real disposition in the act of betrayal.

[2] John vi. 64, 70.

remains of goodness,—notwithstanding, too, that even his violent and desperate death exhibited traces of his former greatness. Finally, it assumes that it was necessary that a member of His most intimate circle should betray Jesus, which does not by any means seem to have been the case when we bear in mind the publicity of His life.

The first two views being untenable, only the third remains for our adoption. This has also its difficulties, but will be justified by the remarks which follow. It was the destiny of Jesus, in His entire manifestation, to divide the Divine from the ungodly, the good from the evil,—to awaken and quicken the one, and to punish and spiritually overcome the other. Even whilst on earth, He thus manifested and judged the hearts of men. In and through Him were the thoughts of the heart to be revealed: He was to be for the rising again and the fall of many. Either of the two results, considered in itself, might have followed in the case of Judas. He was still a man, and, as such, capable of salvation: he might fall, but he might too, like Peter, rise again—a ray of holy love might yet penetrate his soul. That this would not take place, was not clearly to be foreseen; for evil, being in its nature arbitrary, its development cannot be calculated with certainty. Looking to the possibility of a change for the better, Jesus chose him. But by an act of wickedness, which is at the bottom as incapable of rational explanation as evil generally is, Judas hardened himself, even whilst in communion with the purest goodness. Thus that Divine love which might have saved him, only worked his destruction. And just as all evil must finally serve the good, so Judas, when the process of hardening had once set in, was compelled to further the ends of Jesus. In contrast to the purity of Jesus, he exhibited sin in all its abominableness; and by bringing about the catastrophe of the death of Jesus, he helped on the accomplishment of the work of redemption. Through him it became possible for Jesus to enter into the suffering of death, without seeking it. Himself. Finally, too, by his own desperate death, he testified to the purity of Him whom he had betrayed. In all this, however, we must not seek the end, the reason, but only the result of the choice of Judas by Jesus. The choice was dictated by the motives indicated above, and these cannot but be acknowledged to have been pure, since they were based on the hope of the salvation even of a Judas.

But it is finally and almost triumphantly asked, Did not Jesus *Himself* decline the predicate 'good,' and thereby deny His sinless perfection? Did He not answer the young man who saluted Him as 'Good Master,' with the plain words which it is impossible to misunderstand, 'Why callest thou me good? there is none good but one, that is, God?'[1] What more can be needed than the testimony of Jesus Himself against the notion of His sinless perfection?[2] To this we reply: It is indeed true that Jesus did decline the predicate 'good,' but not in such a sense as to exclude the idea of His perfection. His words have a totally different tendency; and here, as in other instances, everything will be found to depend upon the occasion which gave rise to them, and the connection in which they are found.

The young man who accosted Him, believed, as the sequel shows, that he had already fulfilled the whole law, and was under the delusion that in this respect he lacked nothing. He wanted to learn from Jesus, as from a master undoubtedly capable of instructing him, what exceptionally 'good thing' he must do to obtain, besides the blessings promised by the

---

[1] Matt. xix. 17; Mark x. 18; Luke xviii. 19.
[2] See Strauss, *Glaubensl.* ii. 192; Fritzsche, *Comment. de ἀναμαρτ. Jesu*, ii. 1, p. 7; and Pécaut in his above-named work, p. 268. Among modern expositors the contrary view will be found advocated by J. Müller, *Lehre von der Sündl.* i. 143, and Dorner, *Sündl. Vollk.* p. 12; also Wimmer in the *Theol. Studien und Kritiken*, 1845, i. pp. 115-153.

law, eternal life. Can it then be supposed that Jesus would have responded to a young man of this kind,—one who used a word so full of meaning as 'good' twice in one breath, in so light and thoughtless a manner,—by imparting to him information concerning the moral constitution, and indeed the moral imperfection, or even the sinfulness of his own person? It is evident that instruction very different from this was needed by the young man. With all his good intentions, his whole moral nature was infected with self-complacency and shallowness. What he lacked was self-knowledge, acquaintance with the Divine holiness and his own sinfulness. This Jesus perceived from his words, and it was towards this end that all which He said to him was directed. And first of all He takes up his just uttered salutation, 'Good Master,' and at one mighty stroke, as it were, shows him, in the most forcible manner — even though for the moment He might not be fully understood by His hearer — the fathomless depth, the immeasurable fulness, contained in that little word 'good.' God alone, says the Lord, is 'good;' but what He more specially meant by this, must be determined by the meaning of the expression 'good' in this place; and when we reflect how it was used by way of contrast to its inconsiderate application by the young man, and take into account the entire character of this address, this meaning can be none other than the most pregnant of which the term is susceptible.

Undoubtedly there is a sense in which goodness can be attributed to God alone, and another in which it may also be applied to man. The first is its absolute sense; and that this is the sense which it bears in the passage in question, is obvious so soon as the whole purport of the saying is considered. In this sense God is good, as the eternally perfect and unimpeachably holy One who can be nothing else but good Himself, and is at the same time the original source of all good in others. But if Jesus, by this intimation, would

Arguments against His actual Sinlessness. 155

exclude all that is not God from goodness, there are two things which He certainly would *not* do. He would neither, as older theologians suppose, indirectly allude to His own Divinity,[1] nor, as more recent ones assert, represent Himself in general terms as not good, and consequently sinful. The first notion would be an allusion of too vague and artificial a nature; the second a self-contradiction of so glaring a kind, as no one would venture to put into the mouth of Jesus.[2] On the other hand, He undoubtedly did intend to reject the attribution to Himself of goodness in that absolute, that purely Divine sense, of which we have spoken. And not without reason. For His moral perfection did not appertain, as that which was purely Divine, to the sphere of eternal being,[3] but to that of temporal existence; His goodness was not, like the Divine goodness, absolutely unexposed to temptation and raised above all change, but a goodness capable of development, and to be perfected by temptations, conflicts, and sufferings. He was as yet in the very midst of His great mission, and the heaviest trials and sufferings still awaited Him. Thus viewed, the expression by no means excludes the perfection which is possible within the sphere of human existence. It only declines an attribute which is absolute and Divine; it does not deny that the moral nature of Jesus is sinless, but it does affirm that it is liable to temptation. We have here the testimony of Jesus Himself to His genuine and proper humanity in a moral point of view, and a noble expression of the humility which knows that the victory has not yet been won, as contrasted with the self-complacency

---

[1] As also Stier, among recent theologians, though he rather hints at than expressly advances such a view, *Reden Jesu*, Pt. ii. p. 282.

[2] It is opposed not only to John viii. 46, but even to John x. 14, and other passages.

[3] Such a τελείωσις as is spoken of in Heb. ii. 10-18, v. 7-9, and elsewhere, with reference to Christ, cannot be attributed to God, who is in and by Himself absolutely τέλειος.

which could inquire, 'What lack I yet?'—but by no means a confession of sinfulness.

We have thus, we trust, solved all the graver difficulties offered by particular occurrences.[1] Yet a few more general remarks seem desirable with reference to the French author,[2] who has of late most strongly insisted upon them. This author occupies a very peculiar standpoint. He desires to appear, not as decidedly opposing, but rather as seriously doubting, the sinlessness of Christ. Yet his questioning points far more to a negative than an affirmative reply. On one side, he not only willingly acknowledges, on the ground of the Gospel delineation, the peculiar moral greatness of Jesus, but often speaks of it even with enthusiasm, and adheres, after his own fashion, to the belief that He was a teacher of the very highest excellence.[3] On the other side, he sees between this relative greatness—even granting it to have attained the very highest degree—and absolute perfection, an abyss[4] which his faith cannot pass. He is hindered partly by the consideration that the moral nature of Jesus is not laid open to us as to the inmost motives of His heart, nor during every stage of life,—partly by a regard to certain actions and expressions which seem to place insuperable difficulties in the way of admitting His sinless perfection.[5] We cannot regard such a standpoint as

---

[1] The instances derived from John vii. 8, 10, and from Luke xxiv. 28, are too trifling for detailed discussion. In the first passage the difficulty disappears if οὐκ is taken, as in John vi. 17, in the sense of οὔπω; in the second, if προσεποιεῖτο is referred not to the intention of Christ, but to the impression which the disciples, who were His fellow-travellers, received from His conduct.

[2] Pécaut, in his already frequently quoted work. For a review of the whole treatise, see Waizsäcker in the *Jahrb. für deutsche Theol.* vi. 1, pp. 178, etc.

[3] Pécaut's above-named work, Letter xvii. pp. 244, 247, etc.

[4] The same, pp. 241, 242.   [5] The same, Letter xvii. p. 237.

tenable. If we once go so far as to admit that the moral greatness of Jesus is of so superlative a kind that nothing surpassing it is to be found within the sphere of human nature, and if we do this on the ground of the Gospel delineation, we shall be constrained to take the further step which leads to a belief in His sinless perfection. For the same Jesus whom, from the Gospel statements, we acknowledge to be so great, is He who, in the same documents, constantly attributes to Himself a moral and religious nature and position which we — in the sense which He Himself furnishes—designate no otherwise than as absolutely perfect. If, however, we either cannot, or will not, take this step, we have no choice but to retreat from our former position, and, by relinquishing the historical ground of the Gospels, to declare the general greatness of Christ to be altogether doubtful. In short, if Jesus, as we know Him from history, is as great as Pécaut admits, He is also perfect; but if, according to the given conditions, He is not perfect, then He is not truly great in any sense: the greatness ascribed to Him dwindles to such a degree, that it becomes altogether inappreciable.

With regard to the difficulties offered by certain particulars, we are certainly not of opinion that they are at once to be disposed of; on the contrary, we have done our best to solve them. But even granting that neither the explanations which we or others have offered should be found sufficient to obviate all objections, does it follow that the sinlessness of Christ must be given up, or even regarded as utterly problematic? By no means. For the sinless perfection of our Lord is no individual view or sectarian tenet, no hobby of this or that theologian, but the firm persuasion of all Christendom in every age,—a persuasion arising from the overpowering impression produced by His whole life and character. A persuasion of so universal a kind, and one confirmed by its effects, will not be given up, like some doubtful hypothesis, because difficulties are encountered in certain obscure passages, which it is not easy to solve, or whose solution by others is not deemed satisfactory. In a phenomenon of such unfathomable depth, of such immeasurable greatness, as the personality of Jesus Christ, there must necessarily be, from the very nature of the case, points which will ever be enigmatical. Divine truth could not be such if it were in all respects on a level with our understandings, and presented no paradoxes to our minds. In the case of such phenomena in general, we must, first of all, abide by the unquestionable impression produced by the whole, and thence endeavour to appreciate and understand particulars. In the case of Scripture especially, we must not make what is obscure the standard of what is more clear, but, on the contrary, must determine the meaning of the less comprehensible by that which is plainer. If these rules are granted, their result in the present case is obvious. The testimony of Scripture to the sinlessness of Christ is as clear as noon-day, while the purport and references of those passages which might excite a doubt of it, are by no means so transparent as to justify us in taking them as our criterion in deciding on the moral character of Jesus.

Our opponent repeatedly insists upon the axiom,[1] that the conduct of Jesus is to be estimated only according to ordinary moral standards, and not according to some superhuman code. This he applies to certain expressions and requirements of Christ, especially to His address to His mother, on the occasion of His first miracle,—His saying to the Canaanitish woman,—and His command to the disciple, who desired first to bury his father,[2]—which he finds unnecessarily harsh

---

[1] *E.g.* p. 255, and often, besides, in individual instances.
[2] John ii. 4; Matt. xv. 22–28; Luke ix. 59, 60. See in Pécaut, pp. 257, 259, and elsewhere.

and severe. Our reply is as follows:—If this axiom is to be so understood as to include those moral principles which were first introduced into the world by Christianity, it is not in itself incorrect. It becomes so, however, if these principles are excluded, and only an abstract general morality left. And this is the manner in which Pécaut holds it. He everywhere ignores that *mission* of Jesus which can never for a moment be separated from His Person. In all these cases, indeed, the Lord Jesus spoke and acted, not as some chance individual usurping undue authority, but as one undoubtedly certain of being the Founder and Head of the kingdom of God. What He said or did in this sense, always bore the distinct impress of a regard both to the stage of development which this kingdom had at the time reached, and to the special spiritual necessities of the individuals in question, whose faith might need to be encouraged, to be tested, or to be guarded against relapse, by means more or less vigorous, nay, even sharp;—not that such a regard could indeed alter the general principles of morality in His case, though it might give to their application that form which the nature of the kingdom of God demanded. Now the fundamental law of this kingdom is self-denial and self-renunciation,—its chief requirement, that it should be regarded as the supreme good, with which none other can stand in competition. To such a standard, and to such a standard only, did the Lord Jesus conform His demands, and by it was a sharper line of action prescribed to Him, with all His gentleness, in certain cases, than would have been becoming to an individual in a more ordinary position.

CHAPTER II.

ARGUMENTS AGAINST THE POSSIBILITY OF SINLESSNESS IN GENERAL.

WHEN the arguments against the actual sinlessness of Jesus, taken from matters of fact, are found to be inadequate, the *possibility* of sinlessness in the domain of human life may still be called in question. For if, indeed, such perfection were intrinsically impossible to human nature, it could not have been realized in the Lord Jesus, in so far as He shared that nature. Such an impossibility has been asserted, and reasons have been urged in support of it, which are partly drawn from *experience*, and partly from the *nature of the moral idea*, and the mode of its realization. The examination of the reasons of both kinds thus brought forward, is now, therefore, incumbent on us.

Sec. 1.—Arguments drawn from Experience.

In many cases, undoubtedly, the fruit of experience in connection with the moral relations of life, is distrust of the purity of human virtue, and unbelief in the existence of true goodness and greatness amongst men. The more earnestly we examine the phenomena of human life around us, and the workings of our own hearts, the harder is it to attain the conviction, that there ever did live one who was wholly pure and perfect. Whithersoever our eyes are turned, we find concealed, under a thousand captivating forms, vanity and ambition, the pursuit of possessions, power, and enjoyment; malevolence and envy; and, above all, that evil of evils, selfishness, which in the subtlest way creeps into volitions and acts of a nobler character. Seldom does it fall to our lot to rejoice at the sight of a really pure deed; never have we the happiness to discover a man whose life is an unblemished picture of moral perfection. The eye of our spirit becomes, in consequence, so accustomed to the constant spectacle of imperfection, to this *chiaroscuro* of human life, that we are in danger of ultimately losing the power of recognising a character of perfect moral purity, when presented before us. And it is an undeniable fact, that the knowledge of human nature on which many plume themselves, ends in the miserable and comfortless result of absolute moral scepticism.

But that acquaintance with man which leads to such a conclusion really begins with the principle of mistrust; and there must have been beforehand an inclination to discover defects, and either not to pay attention to the good, or to attribute it to bad motives. Besides, such a knowledge is proved to be spurious, by the fact of its giving a result that tends to destroy our best powers, faith and love, and that blights at the root all self-sacrificing effort for the welfare of mankind. *Moral scepticism*, consistently carried out, possesses no firm ground on which to base a moral judgment, and does in fact ultimately undermine all those higher relations which rest upon such a judgment.[1] In opposition to such a system, the mind of man, when unaffected by sophistries, will ever cleave to the belief that it is possible—at least from the tendency of a whole life—to recognise moral differences between man and man, not indeed infallibly, but still with sufficient certainty to satisfy an earnest and modest mind. Such a mind, pursuing its inquiries in a spirit of love, will never renounce its faith in human virtue. And there will be less danger of this, because such a faith does not entirely rest upon mere experience: it is based also upon something far higher,—upon the perception of the purposes of God in and for mankind. Hence faith in humanity, as well

[1] Comp. Reinhard's *Moral Theol.* iii. cap. 1, § 329.

as faith in God, with which it is connected, is independent of experience, nay, often maintains its power in opposition to experience. Man is destined to good by God, and the law of his being is not selfishness and sin, but holiness and love. What, then, could justify us in believing that, universally and necessarily, *only* exceptions to this law are possible, and that never and nowhere can there be a fulfilment of it? If we have a strong and living faith in the destiny of humanity, we shall always be ready and willing to acknowledge that some one can become, and to recognise that One actually has become, what man should properly be,—an image of his holy Creator. If we have sufficient evidence to warrant our believing that there has been such a realization, no experiences of a contrary kind, however numerous, should prevent our reception of this *one* fact. Nor must we allow it to stand in our way, that this has not lain within the range of our own direct experience. A resolution in moral matters to admit only that which falls under our own observation, would make our circle of vision an exceedingly contracted one. Not only would our faith in the absolutely pure virtue of the Redeemer be overthrown, but even our faith in the moral excellence of all beyond the limits of our own sphere of life. The moral nature of man devolves upon him the duty of believing in general in higher virtue, even when it does not occur within the sphere of his own individual experience; and we cannot, therefore, rightly refuse faith in a perfect and pure virtue, when there is satisfactory evidence of the fact of its historical realization.

It may, however, be further asked: Is it not a *universal*, indubitable *truth*, that the very nature of man renders it *impossible* for him ever to be perfectly good? Does not experience show us that, to be human at all, involves both *sinfulness and actual sin?* The question thus started is of a very comprehensive nature; and we shall do well to examine, one by one, the different elements of which it is composed.[1]

And, first, it has been urged that, 'if we ascribe to Jesus the possibility of sinning, we must also conceive of Him as subject to sinfulness; for sinfulness consists precisely in the possibility of sin, and not in the sum of actually committed sins. Sinfulness implies necessarily a *minimum* of sin, and therefore excludes absolute sinlessness.'[2] On the assumption that Jesus was a true, a real man, it cannot of course be denied that it was possible for Him to sin. This possibility is directly involved in human nature, in so far as this is to be morally developed. And if we assume that the possibility of sin means exactly the same as sinfulness, then it must be at once conceded that a germ of sin is implanted along with a moral nature. But the term sinfulness manifestly expresses far more than the mere possibility of sinning. Along with the latter, it is possible to form a conception of the free-will being in a state of perfect indifference to evil or good, and of a development from a condition of simple innocence to one of conscious virtue, without the intervention of sin. The former, on the contrary, presupposes a positive inclination to evil, from which there then arises actual sin. Hence, in acknowledging the possibility of sin in Jesus, we do not at all concede the existence of sinfulness, or even of the least trace of actual evil.

It is a further question, whether, besides that possibility of sin which we necessarily attribute to a personal being as such, there was not in Jesus that bias towards evil which we term original sin? The answers given to this question vary,

---

[1] The difficulties which may be raised in this connection are most fully expressed by De Wette in his *Christliche Sittenlehre*, Pt. i. pp. 182-193, where the entire section on *Christus der Heilige* should be compared. De Wette speaks more positively in regard to the sinlessness of Jesus in his work entitled *Das Wesen des christlichen Glaubens*, § 53, p. 272 ff.

[2] De Wette, *Sittenlehre*, Pt. i. p. 188.

of course, according to the varieties of theological opinion. We merely evade, not solve, the difficulty, when we reply by affirming that there is no such thing as original sin,—when we assert that man enters life innocent, in the full possession of his moral powers, and that there is nothing in himself to prevent his development being perfectly pure, especially when circumstances are favourable. We cannot indorse this answer, because, as we have plainly declared in the first section, we recognise in human nature a prevailing inclination to sin. Neither are we able to agree to the view, that the result of this inclination is only that we labour under 'a difficulty of good,'[1] but possess also a freedom capable in each separate instance of deciding in favour of that which is right, and hence rendering a perfectly sinless development conceivable. For as soon as the moral power is regarded as one which has to contend with inward difficulties, a perfectly pure beginning is no longer possible, and an internal discord is assumed irreconcilable with that sinless development which we attribute to the Lord Jesus.

On the assumption of universal sinfulness among men, there remains, therefore, no other way of accounting for the perfect purity of the life of Jesus, than by supposing that a creative Divine influence was at work in the origin of His personality.[2] Because God so willed and effected it, a new link was introduced by a direct creation into the chain of sinful life; and the individual thus created was endowed with pure, fresh, and unblemished moral powers, in order that a perfectly holy, godly life might be first realized in Him, and then through Him in humanity. The objection, that the case is in this way transferred to the region of the

[1] Augustine calls it *difficultas boni* in his earlier writings.

[2] 'All individual life rests on an original and specifically determined form of being, which points back to the Creator' (Hase, *Leben Jesu*, § 32, p. 58). For a further carrying out of this proposition in relation to the sinlessness of Jesus, see the *Streitschriften*, No. iii. pp. 105-109.

miraculous, need not mislead us. The new commencement of moral and religious life in Christ is undoubtedly a miracle, and inexplicable save on the assumption of direct Divine causality. The new thing, however, which is thus called into existence is not contrary to nature, but the re-establishment of nature in its original purity.[1] Besides, the origin of Christianity, and of all true religion in general, can only be explained on the condition that God should enter into real fellowship with humanity, and exert a creative influence on its development. This, again, is inconceivable, except on the supposition that the influence should manifest itself in a special manner in individual persons, and in every portion of the being of these persons. They who think they can explain the commencement, progress, and perfection of the religious life, and especially the origin of Christianity, apart from Divine agency, utterly misconceive its real nature.

It has been objected, and with greater apparent force, that in this way we destroy the significance of the life of Jesus as an example to men. If Jesus was in His origin free from sinful taint through special Divine influence, and if He was endowed with new moral power by special Divine gift, He cannot be, it is said, in respect of His moral perfection, a true, binding example to those who are not similarly favoured. To this we reply: The doctrine that Christ is an example for our imitation, must first of all be rightly understood. It evidently does not refer to *all* that Jesus was and did. He had a work to perform of an utterly unique kind, which, in its turn, required and assumed a unique personality. In this work, none of course can imitate Him in such wise as to do a like work—as to be a like person. He can only be

---

[1] Christ as the second Adam. Gess, *Lehre von der Person Chr.* pp. 338, etc., defines the religious and moral disposition of Jesus as a natural *nobility of soul*, ever powerfully attracting Him towards God and towards good, yet by no means exempting Him either from temptation and conflict, or from the necessity of ever fresh resolutions and self-denial.

regarded as our example with reference to religion and morality in general, to His perfectly holy disposition and conduct;—and even in these respects, not in the sense that we are to *be* as He was, but in the sense that we ought to *become* like Him, to attain to a conformity to Him, to be transformed into His glorious image.[1] This is a goal not to be reached at once, but one set before us throughout the whole course of our earthly existence, and even beyond its limits. Now Jesus could not be a perfect and universal example of this kind unless He were absolutely pure and holy; and this, again, would be impossible if any impediment to a perfectly normal development were found in the basis of His personality. On the other hand, it is asserted that none but one absolutely like ourselves in all things, the original inclination to sin not excepted, could really be an example to us. But if this be the case, we shall find ourselves obliged either to give up the idea of a really perfect example, or to demand that it should be given by one naturally incapable of so doing. Hence the choice left us is—either we have no perfect example, or we must admit that this was furnished by a personality who was even in his moral constitution extraordinary. We need the less scruple to accept the latter alternative, since in other spheres, also, parallel instances occur.[2] In those of poetry and art, that which is truly typical and classical is ever the production of minds of extraordinary endowment; yet it never strikes any one that these, if they are to be examples to others, must necessarily have worked their ways through all the hindrances and difficulties to which the rest of the world is subject.

Again, it is argued, that 'so far as the virtue of Jesus was really human, there must have been a *sensuous* element

---

[1] 2 Cor. iii. 18.
[2] *Parallel*, not *identical*. The differences are well stated by Gess, *Lehre von der Person Christi*, pp. 339, etc.

in it, for no human virtue is quite free from such an admixture; but imperfection is involved in such a subjection to the law of our sensuous nature, and thus an end is put to any absolute moral perfection.'[1] There is undoubtedly an element of truth in this observation also. We cannot deny the presence, in the virtue of Jesus, of that sensuous admixture which gives the freshness of life to our own willing and acting. Body and spirit in Him were connected in the same manner as in other men. But there is nothing to justify the assertion that there is something intrinsically sinful in this sensuous element of our volitions and acts. Provided that the highest principle of our constitution, the spirit (*pneuma*), is the ultimate and decisive source of our volitions and acts, they are good, although either at their origin, or during their progress, the freshness and vigour of our purposes may be owing to an inevitable admixture of the sensuous element. The sensuous part of man's being is only evil when it sets itself in opposition to the higher, the pneumatic part. By branding it as essentially sinful, we necessarily bring an accusation against the Author of our nature.[2] But it is impossible to show that the sensuous impulses in Jesus were in any single case, to an unwarrantable degree, the moving spring of a determination of His will; or that, when called into natural play, they ever came into conflict with His higher nature. The general character of His words and acts is not passionate excitement, but the most deliberate calmness and self-possession.[3]

Last of all, the objection has been raised from this side, that 'the feeling of humility in Jesus must have arisen from a consciousness of the imperfection and limitation of some

[1] De Wette, *Sittenlehre*, Th. i. p. 188.
[2] Compare Müller's *Lehre von der Sünde*, i. 405 ff.; and with special reference to the perfect holiness of Jesus, pp. 439–442.
[3] This is beautifully unfolded in Sack's *Apologetik*, second ed. p. 207 ff.

minimum of sinfulness. Such a feeling is the means by which man frees himself from the guilt which cleaves to him: consequently Jesus was in this respect also our pattern, that He humbled Himself as a finite being before His heavenly Father.'[1] If we are to uphold the unity of the inward life and being of Jesus, we cannot admit this assertion; for the same Jesus who declared Himself free from all sin, who was certain throughout His whole life that He was glorifying the Father, could not have humbled Himself from any consciousness of imperfection, but only from that feeling of piety, which evidenced itself in perfect submission to God, and in loving condescension to man. And, in fact, humility does not arise from a consciousness of sin. To regard it in this light, would make it synonymous with the feeling of guilt. Humility really arises from that inward relation of an individual towards himself and others, which removes all over-estimation, all vainglory, even in the midst of the most evident superiority,—which does away with all efforts to exalt self and to dazzle others. It prompts, in its judgment and treatment of others, to a spirit of gentleness, appreciation, and kindly sympathy, so far as the interests of truth permit. In this sense only was Jesus humble; but in this He was a perfect model of humility. He laid claim to nothing for Himself, but received all that was given Him of the Father. He pleased not Himself, and would have none but God called good in the very highest sense. He never placed His own dignity in a conspicuous light, but sought, on the contrary, to conceal it. He made Himself as he that serveth, even to His disciples. He condescended to all, and was ever ready to cast the beams of His light and His love, not only on the meanest and weakest, but even upon the most sinful. Such humility by no means presupposes the presence of indwelling sin, and the necessity of freeing Himself from it,

[1] De Wette, *Sittenlehre*, Th. i. p. 192.

on the part even of Jesus, but is, on the contrary, quite consistent with perfect moral purity.

Sec. 2.—Arguments drawn from the Nature of the Moral Idea.

In the last place, a word must be said on the position taken with regard to the subject under consideration by modern *speculative criticism*.[1] This decidedly opposes the sinlessness of Jesus, and does so chiefly on philosophic grounds, *i.e.* upon such arguments as are derived from the *nature of the moral idea and its development in humanity:* we are therefore under the necessity of meeting these objections also.

Modern speculation does indeed leave to Jesus a certain residuum of greatness, in virtue of which He was capable of being the 'occasion' of the rise of a new faith. Yet this greatness is of an indefinite kind, and in no case constitutes a specific distinction between Him and all other men. As a proof of this equality, two maxims are brought forward which are evidently regarded as fundamental axioms. One of these axioms is, 'that the first in a series of developments cannot at the same time be the *greatest;*' the other, 'that it is not the manner of the idea to realize itself in a single individual, but only in the sum-total of individuals,—in the *genus.*' If the first axiom held universally and necessarily true, we should be driven to conclude that the moral greatness of Jesus did not surpass the succeeding links of the chain of development realized in the Christian world; and

---

[1] The literature of this subject is well known. I therefore merely mention, on the one side, Strauss's *Schlussabhandlung zum Leben Jesu*, and the christological portion of his *Glaubenslehre*, especially pp. 153-240, vol. ii.: on the other side, the essays of Alb. Schweizer on the *Dignität des Religionstifters*, in the *Studien und Kritiken*, 1834; and on Strauss's *Leben Jesu*, also in the *Studien und Kritiken*, No. III. 1837; my own treatises in the work *Historisch oder Mythisch*, Hamb. 1838; Fischer's *Prüfung der Straussischen Glaubenslehre*, Tüb. 1842, Heft ii. p. 10 ff.; and De Wette's *Das Wesen des christlichen Glaubens*, §§ 6 and 46.

the relative eminence of Jesus, His character as our pattern, would thus be destroyed. But if the former axiom were shown to be inadmissible, and there remained only the second, this latter would, if applied to Jesus, at the least exclude the possibility of believing in His *absolute* moral greatness, and consequently do away with His typical relation to men.

In both these propositions, individually considered, there is a certain amount of truth; but in the application made of them to the founder of Christianity, we find but another exemplification of the erroneous tendency of modern speculation to merge the particular in the general, the concrete in the abstract; and this tendency we cannot but decidedly oppose. It is perfectly correct to say that in certain spheres of life the first in a series of developments is not at the same time *the most perfect*,—the commencement is not also the fulfilment. But it is no less true that in other spheres the first of a series *must* be also the highest, as certainly as that there would be no development at all were it otherwise. For our present purpose, we shall distinguish between the spheres of science, of art, and of the moral and religious life. In the first department, all is dependent on the range of knowledge; in the second, on the inventive intuition of genius, and the distinctive capacity to give shape and form to that which is imagined; in the third, on the entire inner life, in so far as it takes up a special position to things human and Divine. *Knowledge* is by nature progressive, because, on the one hand, it is dependent on experience, whose circle is widened only gradually, and by the co-operation of many; and, on the other hand, because it is based on processes of thought, which become ever deeper in their course. Consequently, if this progress goes on unimpeded, the later inquirer ordinarily surpasses the earlier. Here the axiom mentioned previously, holds good as a general rule. It is not possible that one man should comprehend in himself all that can be known. Least of all can this be expected of him who is the pioneer in any special branch of science or knowledge. Every inquirer and knower is complemented by other inquirers and knowers. It is true that at certain epochs giant minds arise, which either unite the elements they find at hand in higher combinations, or sagaciously anticipate the future; but even they cannot pass beyond certain definite limits, and it cannot fail that some of those who follow after may gain a higher eminence. It is quite different even in the sphere of *art*. There only those individuals accomplish anything great who are endowed with special creative powers, and with remarkable talents of execution; there, the most important works owe their origin not to a co-operation of many, but to the intuitions and technical skill of individual genius. In this department, supposing that the masters who arise, possessed of higher genius, do form schools, they ordinarily surpass their scholars and successors, and thus, whilst first in the order of time, are also relatively the most eminent. It is even conceivable, that a master endowed with the very highest powers should produce works in his department, which remain pre-eminent and unequalled in all subsequent times. The case is different, again, in the matter of *religion*. Religion has indeed an element of knowledge in common with science, and one of intuition and representation in common with art; but in its inmost nature, it is a peculiar state of being affecting the whole life of man,—it is that reference of the life of the individual to God which governs every thought and action. Here the personality, as such, is all in all. Everything depends on the manner in which it stands inwardly related to God. To speak of the gradual introduction of an essentially new form, of a principle of religion, by the combined exertions of many, is almost preposterous; for the life, the consciousness, is not the joint product, the joint result of the efforts of a community, but must originally reside in One, from whom it then passes on to others. He through whom a new religious life and consciousness are produced in others, is the founder of a religion; and he will naturally be the most perfect, as well as the first, in the series of development of which he is the originating cause. Only once can a peculiar religious consciousness be said to dawn for the first time; only once can there be a really original religious life; and of necessity the life and consciousness will be present with the greatest freshness, purity, and energy in the spirit of him in whom they take their rise. He who should surpass the founder of the system to which he belongs, in the intensity and energy of his religious life and consciousness, would himself become the founder of a new religion, and be the first in a new series of developments.

A speculative system which treats religion as a mode and branch of knowledge, and considers it, in contrast with philosophy, but an imperfect, elementary, childish knowledge, may find it very natural to conceive of piety as gradually progressing from a lower to a higher state (like all things else), and may consequently be unable to consider the founder of a religion as even relatively the greatest, for he is in its view only the occasion of its existence. But it is quite incredible that such should be the actual state of the case, because religion is not mere knowledge, and therefore its development is governed by totally different laws from those which hold good in the case of science. In one aspect, undoubtedly, religion may be classed as knowledge; that is, so far as it is a doctrinal system. On this side, religion may undergo a development through the co-operation of many. This is the domain of theological science, and in it the later may far surpass the earlier. But surely the more recent theological science is generally acknowledged to have gained at least one step,—to have established the principle, that religion is not properly knowledge, that Christianity is not originally a system of doctrine, and that the nature and functions of theology are quite distinct from those of religion. In religion there is ever an element which is primitive, underived, direct, which does not gradually arise, but is present perfectly, undividedly, and originally; and this is the case simply on account of its being life, consciousness, a peculiar state of the whole soul. No thought of individuals supplementing each other, especially when the institution of a religion is concerned, can possibly be entertained. If a new religion is to arise, that which constitutes its vitality must at first exist in a single individual. And if this has once been the case, there is neither room nor need for others to contribute aught else to this its essential foundation. Sound sense, on the contrary, will not fail to recognise in the originator of the new religious life the greatest in his own peculiar sphere; and in fact there is no historical religion which does not in this sense place its founder at the head of its community. Moreover, a glance at actual history necessarily raises *the* question: If Christ is *not* to be considered the most perfect in that whole series of development, of which He was the first, *who* in the whole Christian world, during its successive ages, is to be regarded as having actually surpassed Him? A most expressive and intelligible silence is its only answer.

Still Jesus might, as the founder of Christianity, have been the greatest within the Christian community, without being therefore absolutely perfect. We may admit that He is an example, without absolutely regarding Him as our prototype. Against the latter criticism urges, that 'it is not the manner of the idea to realize itself in *one* individual, and grudgingly to deny itself to the rest; it realizes itself in the *totality* of individuals, in the *race*. Consequently, where an individual is represented to be the absolute embodiment of the idea, there is a transference to it of that which properly holds good only of the genus, for the individual is but a symbol of the totality.' In this objection also there is an element of truth. The idea does undoubtedly realize itself in humanity as a whole. Otherwise what significance could we attach to the existence and development of mankind? But in order to get at the whole truth, the other side must be taken into consideration, namely, that the idea realizes itself in humanity only in and through individuals. So far from the former excluding the latter, it is not even conceivable without it. All development in humanity has its ground in personalities: the higher the sphere thereof, the more certainly is this true. All great men derive their chief significance and importance from the fact that their life is not something isolated, but that whilst itself having its foundation in the foregoing development of humanity, it passes over into and becomes part of the succeeding development. The more fully this can be affirmed of any person, the greater he is; and if there existed a spirit possessing the capacity to diffuse and expand its inner life till it should become the life of entire humanity, we should be under the necessity of esteeming it absolutely great.

In connection, however, with the question as to the realization of the moral idea, everything will depend on the way in which we define the idea of humanity. The idea of humanity does not relate to any special sphere, such as that of science, or art, or political wisdom; nor can be said to have attained its realization in the perfection of any endowment which belongs exclusively to one of these spheres. The idea of humanity comprises in itself that which all men, as men, are bound to accomplish,—that for the performance of which, each, apart from his special talents, is endowed with the requisite capacities,—that which may be described as the universal task,—the task which all men, as such, are bound to accomplish, whatever other powers or gifts may have fallen to their share. Now this absolutely universal thing is religion and morality. These belong to all men alike,—make man in the full sense man, in relation first to himself, then to human society, and specially in the highest relation of all,—that, namely, to his holy Creator, Lawgiver, and Judge. If we recognise the highest aim of all humanity, and of every individual, to be the attainment of perfection in piety and morality, or, in other words, the state of perfect union with God, and the holiness which has its ground therein, we shall be driven to concede at once, either that this ideal perfect condition is never realized at all, or, that such realization takes place, first in the individual personality, and then, through it, in a greater or less number of individuals, but not in the race as such.

The fundamental thought ever firmly embraced by modern criticism is, that the idea is by no means a something lying beyond actuality,—a mere 'ought,'—but that it necessarily enters into real existence. This is, moreover, equally the result of our conviction, that the idea of man, which we recognise as Divine, but which we can only regard in God as creative, would, if it remained unrealized, be but empty and unreal. For if the idea of man originated with God, and if man must therefore have been conceived of as perfect, as fulfilling, and not in conflict with, his destiny,—if, moreover, we are necessitated to ascribe reality to the thoughts of God,—we must assume that the Divine idea of man will in some way, and at some time, arrive at realization. But where is the realization to be met with? Modern speculation points us to the race, to the totality of human individuals forming a complement to each other. But from this standpoint, though original sin is denied, it is confessed that, taken together, we are sinful and imperfect beings.[1] Whence, then, is the realization of the idea to come? A series of imperfect beings,

---

[1] Strauss, *Glaubenslehre*, B. ii. p. 184.

even if it is continued indefinitely, can never produce one that is perfect; the totality of all sinful men will not originate one who is sinless. Religious and moral perfection is a thing complete in itself, and can never be attained by the supply on the part of one imperfect being of that which was lacking in others. It must either be perfectly and completely present, or not at all. If the individuals are not moral and religious, the race cannot be said to be so.[1] In this method we should be driven to look upon the idea as a thing which ought to be,—as a goal ever revolved about, but never attained; and a notion of this kind cannot be called, even by modern criticism, an idea at all, but a mere fiction.

In maintaining that the idea bestows itself in its fulness on one individual,—a thing which we find, at all events, to be approximatively the fact in all departments, and specially in art,—we are far from implying that it is for this reason *niggardly* towards all other individuals: we mean, in truth, just the reverse. That special bestowment on one, is the commencement of the historical process by means of which alone it is possible for all the rest to become participators. It is eminently requisite that the idea should be realized in an individual, when a perfect manifestation of God is to be made, when a perfect atonement and deliverance are to be effected, and, by means of both, a perfect religion is to be

---

[1] Julius Müller remarks very justly, in his *Christian Doctrine of Sin*, i. 265, that 'the moral idea demands complete realization—a realization that embraces all its fundamental aspects—in the life of the individual: it endures no division of the task; it does not allow one person to limit himself to the exercise of one virtue, and to leave to others to supplement him by the cultivation of the other virtues. It is one of the most flagitious attacks on the majesty of the moral idea, to refer its claims to a reciprocal compensation of men, which shall make up for the shortcomings of one by the virtues of the rest.' Schaff (*On the Moral Character of Christ*, p. 52) observes, that 'the realization of the idea in an individual is no more contradictory than its realization in the race,—that, on the other hand, what is true in the idea must necessarily be realized in individual life, and that all history points to such realization.'

established. If the establishment of any definite historical religion presupposes one who is the greatest as regards that stage of the religious life, one who is therefore a pattern, how much more must the establishment of the perfect religion presuppose one who is not only relatively the highest, but altogether perfect in the sphere of religion, and who is consequently our prototype! It is a sheer contradiction to call Christianity the absolute religion, and yet to declare its founder morally or religiously imperfect. The fundamental requirement of all religion is the union of God and man. This is allowed by modern speculation: but it makes the effecting thereof an infinitely light and easy matter by its pantheism, by its regarding God and man as directly one. But, apart from the objection, that union can only be spoken of as taking place between two objects essentially distinct from one another, the most important point of all is entirely lost sight of, viz. sin, which, wherever it exists, necessarily causes a separation between God and man. If the reality and significance of sin are admitted, union with God can only be conceived of as *reunion*, brought about by the breaking down and taking away of sin,—in other words, by atonement and redemption. But it is evident, again, that atonement and redemption, if they are to be accomplished by an individual, require the appearance at the head of the human race of one perfectly free from sin, well-pleasing to God, and in full communion with Him. Hence in this respect, also, we are reduced to a choice between two alternatives, —either religion is reduced to an unaccomplished 'ought,' or the religious idea was perfectly realized in its founder. But so far is the idea from being niggardly to others through its realization in one person, that, on the contrary, it is therein alone that efficient means exist for rendering the attainment of perfection possible to others, and for giving it the greatest possible extension.

PART FOURTH.

INFERENCES FROM THE FOREGOING FACTS AND ARGUMENTS.

IF it is clearly established, in opposition to all the objections which have been raised, that Jesus Christ led on earth a life of sinless perfection, such a fact, being a realization of that which is best and highest in the sphere of human life, must be admitted to be in itself of incomparable importance. At the same time, however, this fact — as has been already hinted in the Introduction — is so constituted, that we cannot, as in the case of other extraordinary phenomena, stop at its simple admission. On the contrary, we shall find ourselves compelled to look both backwards and forwards from this point, and thus to reflect on its hidden reasons and connection. It will then quickly appear that we have here to do with a phenomenon of the most far reaching and widely influencing significance.[1] For sinlessness is manifestly a con-

---

[1] Dorner treats on the importance of the sinlessness of Christ in Christian apologetics, in his already so frequently quoted work, § 4, pp. 49–58. He well shows that, in proving the Divine authority of Christianity in these days, more stress is to be laid upon the *miracle of love*, manifested in the moral character of Christ, than in those *miracles of power* which have hitherto been more appealed to for this purpose, because the special and most essential nature of God is to be found rather in His holy love than in His omnipotence. But, true as all is which he advances from this point of view, it is to be regretted that the author should in this section have stopped at general allusions, instead of going into details.

dition which cannot possibly occur as something isolated and disconnected: it presupposes the whole nature and character of the person of whom it is predicated, to be peculiar. Furthermore, it will not suffice, nor indeed shall we be able, to look upon the person whom we regard as thus peculiarly constituted as existing merely for himself: we shall be compelled to attach to him a significance for the whole human race. One so exalted above all who are sinners as to be absolutely perfect, must necessarily exist for all, and must, in all that he is and does, stand in a peculiar and important relation to the inner life of all. Thus the sinlessness of Christ is a central point from which light is shed on all sides, first upon the Person of Jesus Himself, to enable us more fully to know and understand Him; and then upon His position with regard to the human race, that we may be more capable of appreciating it.

We started from the point, that perfect religion and the work of salvation could only be conceived of as personally effected, and that by a person who should be himself in perfect union with God, and therefore absolutely perfect. Hence we inferred that if a person proved to be thus absolutely perfect should really appear in the midst of the sinful human race, there would be every reason to believe that, in and through him, the perfect religion would have been manifested in a personal form, and the foundation laid for the salvation of mankind in all ages. We have now to apply this to Christ and His work. And in doing so, we shall naturally direct attention, first, to the Person of Christ, independently considered, and then to the position He occupies towards mankind. With regard to the first point, we shall have to show what are those inevitable inferences from the sinless holiness of Christ, which exhibit Him in all respects as One in whom the relation of man to God and of God to man, and therefore the religious life in all its purity, fulness, and power, was realized. With regard to the second, it will be our task to make it evident that conclusions which prove that it was Jesus Christ exclusively who obtained salvation for the whole race of man, cannot possibly be avoided. It is self-evident that, in the treatment of our subject, we shall not go into minute details concerning the Person and work of Christ. Our purpose will be answered by bringing forward those more general and fundamental features which are, on the one hand, more closely connected with our own starting-point, and which, on the other, may best subserve the end we have mainly in view, viz. to prove that Christianity is the divinely appointed and perfect way of salvation.

CHAPTER I.

SIGNIFICANCE OF SINLESSNESS WITH RESPECT TO THE PERSON OF JESUS.

JESUS CHRIST, viewed simply as a sinless and holy being, is undoubtedly a phenomenon of extreme significance, and must be admitted, on this account alone, to be invested with incomparable dignity and unimpeachable majesty.[1] But when this fact of sinless perfection is admitted, it is directly felt that this cannot, like many other qualities, be present only in one or in another condition of the mental life, but that

---

[1] The immeasurable pre-eminence of Jesus, as the absolutely perfect One, is shown especially in the fact that no delineation of His life and character can possibly exhaust its subject, and that His moral greatness does but appear the more exalted in proportion to the elevation attained in a moral sense by him who contemplates it. It might be said that, in this case, as in that of lofty mountains, the whole altitude is not apparent until the observer stands upon an opposite height. The comparison, however, fails, because it deals with an elevation which, after all, it is possible to attain and to measure; while the moral eminence of Jesus, on the contrary, is a height over unattainable by us. The absolute and

it necessarily presupposes a totality of this life, from which it then springs forth as its best and loveliest blossom. Sinless perfection, being itself extraordinary, either requires, in the person in whom it is manifested, something else which is extraordinary, or will produce this as its natural consequence. If we would, however, know what this something else is, we must first of all learn it from the lips of Him who is *Himself* sinlessly perfect. For, apart from the consideration that, even in this respect, He alone could know with certainty who or what He was, His own statement on the matter must have, *à priori*, decided authority for us. Even in the case of a person distinguished for mental and moral eminence in a general sense, we should lay special stress upon such disclosures as he was pleased to make concerning himself; how much more, then, upon His, who is so supremely pre-eminent! But while, in the former instance, a claim to be somewhat extraordinary might seem to justify us in questioning and investigating the fact, the case is altered when this claim is made by one who, whether in living, dying, or suffering, proved Himself to be sinlessly perfect. When He who is holiness calls Himself also the Truth, and when He who has proved Himself to be the true Son of Man, represents Himself to be at the same time the Son of God, and ascribes to Himself a relation entirely peculiar with respect both to God and man, such a statement commands a reve-

majestic pre-eminence of the moral phenomenon presented by the life of Christ, as bearing on it the direct impress of the Divine, has been well brought forward by Ph. A. Stapfer in his *Versuch eines Beweises der göttlichen Sendung und Würde Jesu aus seinem Charakter*, Bern 1797, rendered into French in Vinet's *Mélanges Philosophiques par Stapfer*, Paris 1814, vol. ii. pp. 464–514: see especially pp. 467 and 493–95. To the two sublimities asserted by Kant, viz. the starry heavens *above*, and the moral law *within* us, Stapfer beautifully adds a third, viz. the fulfilment of the moral law *without* us, in the Person of Jesus Christ (p. 494, note 1). I would also refer the reader to Dandiran *sur la Divinité du Caractère Moral de Jesus Christ*, Geneva 1850.

rential and believing acceptance, by virtue of the holiness of Him who makes it. It is in this sense that we may well lay down the axiom, that a perfectly holy being is that which He plainly and decidedly declares Himself to be. It is not, however, our purpose to appeal, in this case, to the sayings of Christ alone as valid authority, apart from any other consideration. On the contrary, we shall endeavour, at the same time, to prove that those inferences on which faith in Jesus Christ, in the sense intended, is grounded, are the natural consequences of His sinlessness.

It must be always in a measure detrimental, in the case of a personality of essential unity, to represent it according to the several elements of which it is composed. The impression of dismemberment thus given is at variance with that organic connection with a common centre which really exists. And yet it is only by viewing an object, first in one, then in another, of its individual aspects, that we arrive at a comprehension of the whole. This method, then, must be pursued even in our contemplation of the Person of Jesus Christ, yet in such wise as to maintain our consciousness of the ever vital connection existing between its separate components. In this sense, but in this sense only, do we propose to contemplate, each by itself, the different sides of His Person, for the purpose of considering what light is thrown upon it by His sinless perfection. Our remarks, then, as is self-evident, will relate to those two chief sides of His nature, according to which our whole subject is divided,—to the human and the Divine, the Son of Man and the Son of God.

Sec. 1.—*The Human Nature of Jesus.*

As we have seen at an earlier stage of our inquiry, although sin has its true home, its central abode in the will, yet it is not limited to this sphere of our being. On the contrary, the whole spiritual and physical life of man, though in varying proportions, is ever found in sympathy therewith. The same thing may be affirmed of sinlessness, only in an opposite direction. Wherever sinlessness is realized, it cannot at all be conceived merely as a quality of our volitions and actions alone, but must ever be regarded as inseparably co-existent with the perfect purity and full development of all the powers of our nature.

This applies first to *intellectual knowledge* in matters which concern religion and morality. Such knowledge is not indeed the sole, nay, not even the highest and most prolific, element in the religious life; and yet it forms so essential a component thereof, that the existence of perfect religion in general is inconceivable apart from it. On the other hand, if the sinless perfection of any one person is proved, this will be the most valid and direct guarantee that he is possessed also of perfect and complete knowledge in the spheres of religion and morality.

In this sense, above all, does Jesus express Himself. Even when speaking in general terms, He ever combines the knowledge of Divine truth with the moral condition. It is in the Sermon on the Mount [1] that we hear from His lips that great saying—'Blessed are the pure in heart, for they shall see God,'—which lays down purity of heart as the fundamental condition of the highest, *i.e.* the intuitive knowledge of God, and, at the same time, regards the latter as the blessed effect of the former. Elsewhere He makes veracity of doctrine, and consequently that knowledge which must be its foundation, dependent upon the seeking not our own glory, but the glory of God; [2] and, consequently, upon a full surrender of ourselves to God. Again, He points out as the surest way of being convinced that His own doctrine was indeed from God, an earnest desire to do the will of God.[3] In other words, He says plainly enough, that in religion it is not he

[1] Matt. v. 8. [2] John vii. 18. [3] John vii. 17.

who desires only to know who will attain this end, but he alone who actually does the will of God as far as he yet knows it, and thus proves the moral sincerity of his efforts. Moreover, Christ makes the most direct application to His own case of that which has been here advanced. This He does rather more obscurely, when He declares the reason of His teaching by the Father, and of His continual abiding with the Father, to be, that He does 'always those things that please Him.'[1] He does this, however, in the very plainest manner, in that chief passage in which He chiefly testifies to His own sinlessness,[2]—'Which of you convinceth me of sin?'—by immediately adding to these words, '*And if I say the truth*, why do ye not believe me?' He here, with a certainty which leaves nothing to be desired, makes His sinlessness the pledge of the truth of His doctrine. Nay, we cannot but say, that to prove His doctrine to be truth, is, properly speaking, the very aim of His discourse; for He bears testimony to His sinlessness, not so much for the sake of this testimony itself, as for the purpose of thus authenticating Himself as the announcer of Divine truth. There would be no need, He seems to say, for your believing a sinner in things Divine; but you must of necessity acknowledge that one who can confidently appeal before God and man to the sinless purity of his life and character, cannot but be also a trustworthy and infallible witness.[3]

The infallibility which the Lord Jesus thus simply claims in this concise but forcible manner, follows also from the very nature of the mental faculties. The human mind, however psychology may divide its powers and activities, is not really separated into different departments. It is absolutely *one* mind, though manifesting itself in various manners, and ex-

---

[1] John viii. 28, 29.   [2] John viii. 46.
[3] Compare the discussions of this subject in Stier's *Reden Jesu*, Pt. iv. pp. 427, 310; and Goss's *Lehre von der Person Chr.* pp. 364–372.

erting itself in different directions. The threads of our whole intellectual life are so subtly and inextricably interwoven, that 'every stroke (on one) strikes a thousand connected therewith;' that every influence from without affects the whole mind; and that in every action from within, each power of the mind in its measure participates. The man as thinking cannot be separated from the man as willing, nor the man as willing from the man as knowing. It is this indivisible unity of the mind which makes it inconceivable, that the same person should, with regard to religion and morality, be perfect as to volitions and acts, and defective as to knowledge. It is indeed very possible that the special talents belonging to some one department of life may, by a vigorous but one-sided cultivation, attain to a degree of development which is lacking to all the other mental powers. But it cannot hence be inferred that in the general department of the highest relations of human life, the practice may reach the degree of perfection, while knowledge remains in a state of imperfection. As sin here exercises a darkening influence on the reason, so, on the other hand, does purity of life secure purity of knowledge, while the latter is also the condition of the former. In fact, in this region there cannot be said to be a truth which belongs merely to *one* side. Whatever deserves the name, whatever is so called in holy Scripture, is in reality *life*-truth,—truth in which the knowledge of God, and the desire to do His will, are by mutual interpenetration combined into a perfect unity. This being the case, the very existence of sinless perfection presupposes an infallibility of knowledge in things religious and moral, and therefore a *freedom from all error*.[1] Hence we are

[1] Hase defines 'infallibility' as the other side of religious perfection, with respect to the possession and communication of knowledge (*Leben Jesu*, § 32). Comp. Schleiermacher's *Dogmatik*, ii. 223, and his fourth *Festpredigt*.

justified both in inferring the former from the latter, and in regarding sinlessness in purpose and action as a pledge of the absence of all error in knowledge and doctrine;—to which must indeed be added, that this can, in fact, be fully applied to none but *Him* who, alone of the whole human race, has made good the claim to absolute perfection.

That Jesus was fully conscious of possessing such infallible knowledge of things religious and moral, is obvious from the very manner of His teaching. We read in the Gospels that 'He taught them as one having *authority*, and not as the scribes;'[1] that the people were astonished at His teaching;[2] that the officers sent by the priests and Pharisees to apprehend Him testified, 'Never man spake like this man;'[3] and that the Apostle Peter exclaimed in the name of his fellow apostles, 'Lord, to whom shall we go? Thou hast the words of eternal life.'[4] Is it asked in what did the power of His words consist? We reply, not in the force, beauty, or perfection of diction, which may in other cases make human eloquence powerful and influential; for, however appropriate even the very words of Christ, in all their abundant variety, may be, artistic effect is the very last thing to be thought of in this connection. On the contrary, their power lay entirely in the fact that they were in perfect unison with His personality, and that this personality was of a nature which made His words incomparably important as to their matter, and powerfully affecting as to their form.

The teaching of Jesus was no delivery of lectures on the general truths of religion and morality, but the living testimony of facts and realities. The fact that the kingdom of God had already come, its nature, constitution, and future prospects, and, above all, His own position therein as its Head and King, as He in whom the Father was to be glorified, and

---

[1] Matt. vii. 49.
[2] Matt. xiii. 54, xxii. 33.
[3] John vii. 46.
[4] John vi. 68.

the human race to find redemption,—such was the main purport of His teaching. Its manner, however, was that of self-testimony and self-manifestation. This is the reason that it exhibits nothing of sudden and violent exultation, no unexpected bursts of enthusiasm, but always that same peace, and that same undisturbed tranquillity, by which His actions were also pervaded. There is, however, another feature, which may be regarded as its most distinctive mark; and this is, its absolute elevation above all that is uncertain and problematical,—its utter exclusion of all doubt or hesitation. On the contrary, it claims a supreme authority, and is supported by a certainty and confidence on the part of Him who imparts it, which we meet with in no other teacher. There is in it a tone of Divine demonstration which, notwithstanding the humility of the speaker, declares that that which He advances is perfectly unanswerable. When the external effect of such a manner of teaching is considered, we are constrained to acknowledge that, viewed in conjunction with the indwelling truth and saving power of His announcements, it must have given to the words of Jesus the greatest possible emphasis, and have secured for them the most abundant results. When regarded, however, with respect to the teacher Himself, such a mode of instruction could only be justified and explained in the case of one in immediate and secure possession of that which He announced, —of One who spoke that which He knew, and testified that which He had seen.[1] None but one perfectly sinless could thus have spoken. Teaching of this kind, whether we consider its matter or manner, would, in the mouth of a man that was a sinner, have been the grossest presumption. But from the lips of Him whose life was one uninterrupted communion

---

[1] John iii. 11, compared with Matt. xi. 27. Some excellent remarks on this feature of Christ's teaching will be found in Young's *Christ of History*.

with God, it was both the natural and necessary expression of His inmost nature, of His entire personality. If testimony, powerful in itself, and capable of resounding through the whole world, was to be given concerning a higher state of things, this could have been done only as Jesus did it; but, on the other hand, none could have so given it, but One who, in virtue of His sinless perfection, was an unerring witness in things pertaining to God.

That which has been advanced is not, however, important with regard only to the intellectual side, but is equally applicable to the *emotional* and *imaginative* powers, nay, even to the *physical* basis of life, to the whole man in general. In all these respects, sin, on the one hand, proceeds from a spurious excitement which both disturbs and destroys the true unity of life, and, on the other, begets such an excitement in an aggravated form. With sinlessness, on the contrary, an entirely opposite process takes place. We cannot conceive of sinlessness otherwise than in conjunction with a simple and harmonious movement of the feelings, with a pure and spotless activity of the imagination, and with a condition of physical life in which the spirit that rules the whole man finds its appropriate expression, and a well-ordered and sufficient instrument, for the execution of its higher aims and purposes. It will be, moreover, wherever it exists, the foundation for an undisturbed and healthy development of the life in all these aspects. Sinless perfection can only grow from a life whose whole condition, and all whose functions are in every respect pure. Of such a life it is the noblest fruit. And while it is thus the natural result of such a state, it becomes again, in its turn, the power which maintains the entire life in health and purity.

It was precisely this which was exemplified in the historical manifestation of Him whom we know as the only sinless man. Jesus participated in every human *feeling*, from the most powerful to the tenderest, and appreciated such feelings in others in the most open and delicate manner. At the grave of Lazarus He wept with them that wept, and at Cana He rejoiced with them that rejoiced. His indignation overflowed against the Pharisees and the desecrators of the temple, while He ever manifested the tenderest compassion towards all who were in need of His help. He exhibited in presence of His enemies a heroic readiness for conflict, and to His friends a love willing to lay down life for their sake. In all His sorrow, however, as in all His joy, there was no worldly element, but that deep and Divine seriousness which gave to every emotion its due proportion. His indignant zeal never degenerated into violence, because it was aroused for the honour of God, and His pity never sank to weakness, because it aimed at the real good of those who craved His assistance. And as even on the cross He had thoughts of peace for His bitterest foes, so, when truth demanded it, He had words of sharp rebuke for His nearest friends. His every emotion and every frame of mind, moreover, bore the impress of holy purity, while peace, which was the distinctive mark of His whole nature, was shed forth over all.

Such, too, was the case with respect to everything belonging to the sphere of *the imagination*. We perceive from His discourses how truly and clearly He had stored up in His mind the phenomena of nature, and the various conditions of human life; and how all these were at His command for the freest and most varied use.[1] It is, moreover, from the very use He makes of these in figures, parables, etc., that we perceive how pure must have been the springs of that soul in which all was thus reflected, and then formed into the aptest vehicle for the conveyance of eternal truths. If the material

[1] Comp. Keim, *menschl. Entwickelung Jesu*, p. 13.

is derived from nature, it is always those simple, every-day objects most familiar to men's senses which serve as the foundation, while their treatment manifests the utmost originality, and the finest and most genuine feeling for what is natural. If, on the other hand, it is taken from human life, it is always its great and ever-recurring events which are invoked, and all is so represented that these appear in their actual and genuine nature, and are called by their right names; so that in the very figure, apart from its application, we already find a purifying and enlightening power. Nowhere do we recognise anything far-fetched, distorted, or variable; on the contrary, we everywhere feel that nature and human life have been viewed with a divinely correct and single eye, which has derived from them whatever seemed adapted for expressing and conveying Divine truth. And when this truth is thus popularized, and in the noblest sense embellished, we are at the same time fully impressed with the fact, that the reason why it was thus expressed was not to polish or beautify it, but to bring it to bear with the most striking effect and the greatest power upon those who heard it.[1]

History offers but very little in the shape of fact, to enable us to say anything definite concerning the physical condition and appearance of Jesus. Hence arose the possibility that very different, and indeed opposite, views could be entertained on the subject at an early period of Church history. One of these views maintained the perfect beauty of His external

---

[1] Weisse, the author of the *Reden über die Zukeruft der evang. Kirche*, p. 220, strikingly remarks, that ' to the moral sinlessness of the Saviour there is a correspondent equally inborn æsthetic spotlessness in His manifestation; and the moral greatness of His nature is reflected in the exalted beauty both of the thoughts He uttered, and of the expressions He employed, to convey the fulness of His meaning,—expressions which seemed on every occasion, and with ever equal force, to be always at His command.'

appearance; the other asserted that He was deficient of all beauty, and even unsightly. These views being, however, supported only by inadmissible applications of passages from the Old Testament,[1] are of no special importance. Yet, even in this respect, we are not without grounds for more tenable conclusions, especially if we take into consideration the inseparable connection between the external and the internal. Sound natural sense will always take for granted that the intrinsic dignity of the Lord Jesus was expressed in His external appearance; and that though it might seem incongruous to attribute to Him a dazzling beauty, yet we may well picture Him to ourselves as possessing a comely and dignified exterior, calculated both to inspire reverence and to awaken confidence. In fact, it is self-evident that a mind of so unique a character must have set its mark, as such, even upon His countenance; and equally so, that the office undertaken by our Lord justifies the supposition that His body was in all respects an instrument perfectly adapted for its accomplishment. In this aspect, we have also a right to insist especially upon a perfectly pure and moral physical development as an element of decided importance with respect to our subject. If there ever existed a personality of whom it might be said that the integrity and well-being of even the bodily organization were preserved by the power of the moral element, and that the corporeal itself was transfigured by the spiritual, it was in the case of Him who was sinlessly perfect. His body was indeed, and in the fullest sense of the term, the temple of the Holy Ghost;[2] and we cannot possibly conceive that which so justly deserves to be called a temple of God as aught else than a form of majesty and dignity. Besides, certain undeniable facts testify that we do not err in drawing such a conclusion. On the one

---

[1] The former by Ps. xlv. 3; the latter by Isa. liii. 2.
[2] 1 Cor. vi. 19.

hand, there is the powerful impression ever made upon all kinds of people, and under every variety of circumstances, by the mere appearance and presence of the Lord Jesus. On the other hand, there is the manner in which He indisputably did accomplish His mission, with all its self-denial, exertions, and conflicts,—a fact utterly incomprehensible, even in its physical point of view, without a corresponding amount of bodily health and vigour.

Thus in Jesus, the sinless One, we have, in every respect, the model of a perfect man. And that designation, 'Son of Man,' which He so often applied to Himself, though used chiefly in another sense and with reference to His Messianic office, may yet most rightly be bestowed upon Jesus, as expressing also, that in Him all that was truly human was as clearly impressed as was necessary, if the Divine favour were to rest upon Him, and if a type and example of the true position of man with respect to God were to be given. The sinless and perfect Jesus was *the* Son of Man, bearing every feature of humanity, but imparting thereto a Divine glory; enduring every human sorrow, but rising superior to all; entering into the very depths of human weakness, yet elevating human nature to a height far surpassing its native powers.

Besides these general features of His human nature, there is another and special feature inseparable from His whole agency and manifestation, which we must not omit to bring forward. This characteristic is one which is not only of the greatest importance in a general point of view, but which, when contemplated from that of His sinless perfection, becomes specially significant, and has much light thrown upon it. We mean the *miraculous* element in the manifestation of Jesus, upon which we now propose to add a few words.

The miraculous feature running through the whole manifestation of Jesus Christ, stands in very close connection with His sinless perfection. To be convinced of this, we have only to take a just view of the relation existing between them. We might entertain some scruples—especially in an argument intended for the present times—in making the miracles which Jesus performed, or which were accomplished in Him, the foundation of our faith in His mission and Person. But the case is different when, from reasons found in Himself and His actions, we recognise Him of whom so much that is miraculous is related, to be absolutely holy. Then miracles appear as only a further consequence of that peculiarity already involved in His personality; as such they are but the expression of the same fact in a physical, which sinlessness is in a moral sense. And far from being either a stumbling-block or offence, their absence, in the case of such a Being, would, on the contrary, be regarded as a deficiency. But we must more closely explain our meaning.

The appearance of one sinlessly perfect in the midst of a sinful race is *itself* a miracle. For thus the continuity of that sin which is everywhere perceptible is broken through, and a new beginning, a perfectly original creation, introduced. And if the essence of a miracle be the appearance, in the ordinary course of nature or history, of something totally new, which can only be referred to a Divine causality, such a feature is found in this instance in its full completeness. Nay, we may even call this appearance the *supreme* miracle—the miracle of miracles.[1] For while other miracles are wont to recur, this moral miracle appears *but once* in

[1] The poet V. Zedlitz is said a short time before his death to have uttered these significant words: 'One might have thought that the miracle of miracles was to have created the world, such as it is; yet it is a far greater miracle to lead a perfectly pure life therein.' At all events, one perfectly sinless is as great a miracle in the moral, as one risen from the dead is in the physical world. Comp. Orelli, *Kampf des Rationalismus mit dem Supernaturalismus*, p. 26.

history. Nor is it merely a miracle of power, but a miracle of holy love; and hence, not accomplished by one single transaction, but only through the sacrifice of an entire life passed till its very last breath in a manner well-pleasing to God. With this prime and fundamental miracle, moreover, the principle of the miraculous in general is combined with the Person and life of Jesus Christ; and we cannot but expect unique and extraordinary acts and events in the case of One who was Himself thus unique and extraordinary. And first, this is true of the Person of Jesus, independently considered. The connection ordained by God between sin and sorrow, and especially between sin and death, had no application to Him, for the very reason that in Him was no sin. Death could not have had the same significance for Him as for those who are subject thereto, because they are sinners. If He then suffered death, He could not suffer it as the wages of sin; nor could it have the same power over Him as over sinners. In this sense, His resurrection stands in the very closest connection with His freedom from sin.[1] And if this miracle, on which so much depends, is certainly regarded in Scripture as pre-eminently the work of God in Jesus, we shall be constrained, at the same time, to acknowledge that this very act of Divine power has its hidden cause in the Person of Jesus Himself,—namely, in the fact that He was in truth the Holy One of God,[2] and that, as such, He already possessed perfect life in Himself.[3]

But what has been said applies also to the miracles which Jesus performed on others. Sinless holiness naturally presupposes a freedom and power of will, a purity and fulness of vital energy, in virtue of which we should infer in Him

---

[1] See a further discussion by Doedes, *Dissert. de Jesu in vitam reditu*, Utrecht 1841, p. 192. Comp. also Reich, *die Auferstehung des Herrn als Heilsthatsache*, Darmstadt 1845; especially pp. 208-270.

[2] Acts ii. 27. [3] John x. 18.

in whom it was found, a power of reacting upon His own physical nature, and of exercising an influence upon the nature of other men, and of the world around Him, such as we could not believe possible in the case of those whose minds and wills were enslaved by sin.[1] At the same time, it is a self-evident notion to every one who seriously believes in the existence of a personal God, ever carrying on His operations in the world and in mankind, that this God will communicate Himself with infinitely greater fulness and abundance where constant intercourse with Himself is found, and vital fellowship with Himself is undisturbed by any kind of sin, than where sin has separated between Him and His creature. Such communication, moreover, will not consist merely of gifts for the benefit of the inner life, but also of powers, by the employment of which it may be shown how the Omnipotent manifests Himself—not only in His moral perfections, but in His control over nature—in His perfect image on earth.

The sinless nature of Jesus was at the same time the source of His perfectly consistent use of miraculous power. In this respect, also, it was holy love which ever determined Him; and this quality is so clearly impressed upon His miracles, that even if no other tokens thereof were bestowed upon us, we might in these alone recognise its distinctive characteristics. Here, too, as everywhere, Jesus was the merciful, condescending, and self-sacrificing Saviour, untiring in His offices of love to the meanest and most wretched, even when of ten that were healed, one only showed any gratitude.[2] Yet, even when He stooped the lowest, all that He did ever kept the highest aim in view,—all was directed towards the glory of God and the salvation of man. He

---

[1] Comp. my letter to Strauss in my work, *Historisch oder Mythisch?* pp. 135, etc.
[2] Luke xvii. 12–19.

ever turned attention from Himself to the Father who had given Him such works to do; and even when He bestowed bodily healing or temporal benefits, the higher and eternal blessing was ever His special and ultimate aim. It was this which formed the background, so to speak, both of each separate miracle, and of all His miracles viewed as a whole, the purpose of which was to secure and support the introduction, and furnish the foundation of the whole work of salvation.

These are the chief points in which the sinlessness of Jesus affects His personality, viewed on its human side. In this aspect He shows Himself to be, in all respects, and especially in His position towards God, *a perfect man*, who being in His own inner nature a miracle, is also surrounded by the miraculous, whether in the deeds which He wrought, or in the lot which He submitted to. But it is this perfect man, thus gifted with miraculous powers, who, in the most decided manner, directs us to something beyond Himself—something still higher in His own Person: hence this Jesus cannot be the perfect *Son of Man*, unless He is also, what He declares Himself to be, the *Son of God*. It is in this sense that we now proceed to consider the sinlessness of Jesus with respect to His Divine nature.

Sec. 2.—Inferences in respect to the Divine Nature of Jesus.

The Christian Church, in all its genuine branches, confesses and teaches, besides the true humanity, the *proper Divinity* of Christ, and has from its earliest days laid down, in very definite formulæ, the manner in which the Divine and human natures are inseparably united, and yet distinct, in the Person of the God-man. To test these formulæ, or even to enter into any general examination of them, is beside our purpose, which aims rather at an apologetic than a doctrinal treatment of our subject. On the other hand, it is, however, quite in keeping with this, to direct attention to the fact that the article of faith which is now in question is not a matter of merely ecclesiastical or doctrinal detail, but one founded upon primitive evangelical testimony. It rests, moreover, not on the testimony of the apostles only, but on that of Jesus Himself. In this last respect, then, to treat of the internal verification of this testimony, is to deal with a matter which has a very decided bearing upon the sinlessness of Jesus. And here we would, first of all, call attention to the following facts: how the Lord Jesus, with a confidence raised above the very slightest degree of hesitation, makes Himself the central point of His work of redemption, the object of saving faith, and the beginning and end of His mission. He attributes to His death the most wide-reaching results for all mankind, and combines with His own exaltation the sending of the Holy Ghost. He institutes baptism as the sacred act by which all nations are to become His disciples, and the Lord's Supper as a celebration of His death until His coming again. He says of His words, that though heaven and earth shall pass away, they shall not pass away. If, then, no other particulars of His life were known to us than these, we should even then be constrained to infer that He was assuredly conscious of being more than man. In all this, the limits of the human are far surpassed; for it is absolutely unbecoming in any created being to make himself an object of faith, an *object of religion and religious worship*, and to place his own person in such a position with regard to the salvation of the whole human race, as Jesus undoubtedly does.

Besides, it is no less certain to all unprejudiced minds, that He ascribes to Himself in plain terms, besides human *existence*, a nature *superhuman, heavenly*, and *Divine*. And this not only in sayings recorded in St. John's Gospel, but also in sayings essentially agreeing with these in the other three Gospels. The very manner in which He calls God 'the Father' *His* Father, points to a relation of a peculiar kind; still more so, that in which He represents Himself as 'Son of God,'—not as a son, but as *the* Son, in a sense unparalleled; for it is only He, as being this Son, who fully knows the Father, and is, on His part, fully known by Him.[1] All true knowledge of the Father is brought about by Him alone, and no man cometh to the Father but by Him.[2] The Father is glorified in Him, and He in the Father.[3] He that seeth Him seeth the Father; nay, He and the Father are one.[4] Moreover He, in the most decided manner, attributes to Himself Divine attributes and operations: an existence before the world was, in and with God,[5]—the office of judging the world,—the power of quickening whom He will.[6] In the institution of baptism, He connects His own name with that of the Father, and that of the Holy Ghost; and at His departure from the world, He announces to His disciples that all power is given Him both in heaven and in earth, and that He will be with them alway, even to the end of the world.[7] In short, He represents Himself as One who, from the beginning to the close of His earthly existence, participates in and experiences all that is human, but who, at the same time, bears within Himself the fulness of the Divine nature and life.

What, then, is the relation between this self-testimony of Jesus and the doctrine of His sinlessness? Evidently this: that if there are good grounds for accepting the latter, there must be equally good grounds for believing the former. The two must stand or fall together. He who was perfectly pure

---

[1] Matt. xi. 27; Luke x. 22; John vi. 46.   [2] John xiv. 6.
[3] John xvii. 1, 4-6, xiii. 31, 32.   [4] John xii. 45, xiv. 9, x. 30.
[5] John viii. 58, xvi. 21, xvii. 5.
[6] John v. 21, 22, 26, 27, xvii. 2, xi. 25; Matt. xxv. 31, etc.
[7] Matt. xxviii. 18-20, with which connect xi. 27 and xviii. 10.

and sinless, and who must therefore have been most moderate and conscientious, could never have affirmed aught concerning Himself of so supremely exalted a character, unless He had felt a certainty, surpassing every other certainty, that such pre-eminence was indeed His own. Besides, the bare fact that a being actually appeared who, on the one hand, assumed such a position with respect to God and a higher world, and, on the other hand, displayed such mental and moral sublimity, is inexplicable, on moral or psychologic grounds, unless this position to God and a higher world be a true and genuine fact. The reverse would indeed be far more incomprehensible. It would be a mental aberration, to estimate whose greatness no standard could be found, and utterly incompatible with every established fact of a mental and moral kind, which has been handed down to us concerning the Lord Jesus. If, in this highest of all respects, either self-delusion or wilful deception of others were found, such an error would be one which must necessarily pervade the whole nature of Jesus; and, in this case, far from being the sinlessly perfect One of the Gospels, He could not be the mentally and morally exalted character which even rationalism esteems Him, but something for which the correct expression has yet to be invented.

Nevertheless, in this respect also, it is not our purpose to appeal to the expressions of Christ Himself as our sole authority. Here, too, the doctrine of His sinlessness furnishes an internal proof of the doctrine in question, which, in an apologetic point of view, must be by no means overlooked.

In our contemplation of the moral phenomenon presented by the life of Jesus, we saw that there was everywhere originality and absolute independence, that it exhibited a harmony in which all the antagonisms of human existence were reconciled. A life of such perfection gives a direct impression of being the result of a *Divine* operation. Where the human is the only element, we ever meet with some measure of dependence and imperfection, some conflict between flesh and spirit, some antagonism between the intellectual and the moral, or some other disproportion or irregularity. Where, however, we find the reverse of all this, we already discover in this very fact a trace of the Divine. To this same inference are we also led by that quality which we recognised to be the principle of the life of Jesus. This principle is holy love. Now holy love constitutes the nature of God Himself; hence, in the same proportion in which this principle is found to be present and effective in a personality, are we constrained to conceive God Himself to be present. Consequently, where a perfect manifestation of holy love takes place, there must we believe also in a perfect indwelling of God.

But to say this, might seem to be affirming a principle of gradation, which might in its application to the Lord Jesus exhibit Him as merely possessing in the highest degree that which others shared in their measure. We perceive, however, in Him something besides, and that a thing entirely *peculiar*,—even the grand peculiarity of His *sinless holiness*. Others may be found truly pious, glowing with holy love, and in whom, therefore, God's more abundant presence must be assumed; but we do not meet with one who is sinless,—one who, absolutely conscious of His sinlessness, succeeds in making Himself acknowledged as such,—however carefully we may scan the boundless field opened before us by the history of the known races of men. An explanation, then, of this absolutely unparalleled phenomenon[1] is required, and this

---

[1] Pelagianism denies that Jesus was an utter exception in a moral point of view. It is therefore driven to maintain that it is possible for other men to be sinless. If it was possible for Jesus in His human nature to remain sinless, it must also be possible for others, inasmuch as, according

leads us to recognise in Jesus Christ a relation to God which, as well as the effects resulting therefrom, must be regarded as of an entirely exceptional kind.

to the Pelagian doctrine, all men enter life with their moral powers in perfect integrity. Even if Christ were the only example of sinless perfection hitherto seen, there is no reason why there may not arise another like Him in the course of time. This particular view is connected with the entire Pelagian conception of Christianity, in which the idea of the Redeemer is left quite in the background, and example and doctrine alone are considered to be essential. Along with Pelagianism, Nestorianism has been reproached with holding the same view: this was so, at all events, in the West, where it was supposed to be connected with Pelagianism. It was argued, that if the Divine and human natures are distinct, and holiness and sinlessness are regarded as the privilege only of the human nature, it follows that other men may attain the same moral elevation, without special communion with God. Compare Gieseler's *Ecclesiastical History*, Pt. i. § 86, especially the Observ. p. 447. This was, however, an inference from his doctrine, which Nestorius would never have conceded; for he did not in reality maintain such a separation of the Divine and human, and the presence of such a complete moral power in human nature in its present condition, as that deduction presupposes. It is a remarkable fact, that a renowned teacher of the ancient Church, the father of orthodoxy, Athanasius, seems, although from an utterly different point of view, to assume the sinlessness of other human individuals besides Jesus. He says not only generally, ἐξ ἀρχῆς μὲν οὐκ ἦν κακία· οὐδὲ γὰρ οὐδὲ νῦν ἐν τοῖς ἁγίοις ἐστίν, οὐδ' ὅλως κατ' αὐτὸν ὑπάρχει αὕτη (*Contra Gentes, ab init.* t. i. p. 2, edit. Colon), but also, developing the thought with greater specialty, he observes further, that the character of the Divine image, of the Divine Sonship in Christ, cannot consist merely in moral unity with God, because in that case other spiritual beings also, and especially men, might be designated sons of God: hence the peculiarity of Christ must rest rather on His oneness of nature with God. In the sense of moral unity with God, he adds, patriarchs and prophets, apostles and martyrs, and even Christians now living, might be called the sons of God; for they resemble God, and are compassionate, like their Father in heaven, —they are imitators of the Apostle Paul, as he imitated Christ (*Contra Arianos*, Orat. iv. t. i. p. 455, and especially pp. 462, 463, edit. Colon). Still we cannot with perfect certainty conclude from these expressions that Athanasius distinctly held the view that other individuals were sinless besides Jesus. In the first passage, it is to be remarked that the word κακία is too general and indefinite. In the other passages Athanasius avails himself of the thought of a repeatedly occurring moral perfection, only to strengthen another doctrinal line of argument; and it is doubtful with what degree of definiteness, and to what extent, this notion was applied by its author.

By viewing sinlessness as an attribute of the human nature of Jesus, we have maintained the notion that a human development characterized by perfect purity is possible, because neither human nature, considered simply as such, nor the idea of development, necessarily involves any element of sin. But then the question arises: If this be the case, how comes it that experience furnishes only one example of freedom from sin? Why have not others of the human race risen up from time to time, making the same claim, and compelling their fellow-men to acknowledge their pretensions? Why is there not at least one besides Jesus, who had the same faith in himself, and was able to beget it in others? This cannot be the result of accident. The reason must be, that sinlessness, though not unattainable by human nature, as such, is not, neither has been, nor can be, attained by man in his *present state*, because sin has gained a mastery over the whole human race, by virtue of which it is not possible for man, by his own unaided powers, to maintain a perfect freedom therefrom. But if man's own strength is not sufficient for this, it can only be effected by a power which is exalted above the sphere where sin prevails, and which, notwithstanding, enters into that sphere without contracting defilement; and this is precisely the *Divine* power. Consequently, when we meet with a man who has actually proved himself sinless in his conduct, we have grounds for inferring that a Divine power has in the fullest sense been operating within him,—that here is one who was indeed man, but who was also more than man.

But this point must now be more fully elucidated. If all men are sinners,—and, with the exception of the Holy One of the Gospel, not even one is sinless,—it is a plain proof that a principle of sin is implanted in human nature, not indeed by original constitution, but, certainly in its present state, that sin, although not the true, is still the second nature of man, that it pervades and rules the whole race. The principle of sin being in such a manner ingrafted in human nature in the condition in which experience presents it to us, only one supposition can render intelligible the existence of a sinless man,—namely, that the chain of sin has been broken, and that, in consequence, a personality has arisen in the midst of the sinful race, endowed with perfect soundness, with powers thoroughly pure, and amply sufficient for leading a life entirely in accordance with the will of God. But this is only possible as the result of a Divine creation. Such a person could not be the product of a race infected with sin. In this aspect, He in whom there really was the possibility of being sinless, is a *totally new man*, the *second Adam*. He is that Person in whom a new beginning of the higher life was to be made, and from whom a new race, a race new in this sense, might proceed.

But the moral development and office of this second Adam evidently differ from those of the physical ancestor of the human race. He was not, like the latter, introduced in a state of full consciousness into a world as yet untouched by sin, but was born as an unconscious infant into a world in which sin had already become a power. In this world He was not, for His own sake alone, to preserve in its purity the yet unspotted Divine image, but to restore to mankind, by His conquest of sin, that image which had been lost or obscured. In the same proportion as the task set before Him was incomparably higher, was the difficulty of accomplishing it infinitely greater. This difficulty lay chiefly herein : that a human life was to be developed in perfect purity *from its very earliest stages*, and that, nevertheless, this development could only take place in the midst of a sinful world. If the soul had entered at once into conscious possession of its freedom, it might have been capable of directly waging war against all that was carnal and sinful, and of carrying on such war to a successful issue. But the moral, as indeed the whole mental life in man, as now born into the world, comes forth in the midst of a state at first unconscious, then semi-conscious and half dark, and but gradually attaining to the full light of complete consciousness. Under these conditions, if sin comes upon him from his surroundings, it gains possession of him before he knows it; and when he has attained to fuller moral consciousness, it has already obtained a footing in some form or other.[1] Thus perfect sinlessness is excluded, and a development perfectly free from sin is inconceivable, *under the given circumstances*, by merely *human* means. But if, as we have found in Jesus, such a development has, notwithstanding, been brought to pass, we ought not to feel any hesitation in assuming the presence of something over and above, and in union with, the integrity of constitution originally given. In Him whose development was thus sinless, there must have been an *infallible sureness*, enabling Him during its whole course, and even at those stages of it when He was not as yet awakened to full consciousness, to reject everything impure, untrue, and sinful, and to appropriate for His inner life only the pure, true, and good, from that which the surrounding world presented to Him. If we regard this merely as the result of a Divine care, operating from without, of a continuous Divine agency, we could not then understand why God should have suffered His grace to be thus efficient in this one Person only, and not in others also. Besides, we should thus be assuming that, in the case of Jesus, sin was ever on the point of breaking forth, and was only repressed by a Divine influence exerted from without. Our only reasonable course, then, is to conceive it as the result of a principle which acted from within. And indeed only such a principle could have worked with the required infallible certainty, and have separated and

[1] Comp. Gess, *Lehre von der Person Chr.* pp. 229, 239.

rejected the sinful as something alien and hostile to its own nature. It must therefore be conceded, that a *Divine* principle conditioned the original integrity of Jesus, and was a constituent element of His personality, which, developing in perfect harmony with the human element, did not hinder, but on the contrary favoured, the natural progress of the latter, and maintained its perfect purity. Clearly, however, we cannot understand by this Divine principle merely something akin or bearing a resemblance to God, such as is in every man; for sin can, and actually does, co-exist therewith in every man. We must therefore conceive it as the Divine in its uncorrupted and true *essence*. In this way we are led from the sinless Son of Man to the Son of God, and the recognition of the pure humanity of Jesus ends in the conviction of His true Divinity.[1]

Summing up all together, we may say then, Jesus was sinless as a man, for the idea of sinlessness is only applicable to human nature; not, however, in the general sense of the term, man, not, in short, as a 'mere man,' but as *the man*, in whom the humanity was on the one hand endowed with extraordinary powers, and on the other hand was pervaded, animated, and energized by a Divine principle. In a word, He was sinless, because He was the second Adam, and the

[1] What has been advanced, must not, as is self-evident, be so understood as to make the Divinity of Christ a mere auxiliary proposition to the conceivability of His sinlessness. For this would be to place that which should fill the highest place in a subordinate position. Our purpose is only to show how the sinlessness of Jesus points from itself to His Divinity. We may with equal correctness say, because God was in Christ, Christ was free from sin; or, because He was sinless, we have grounds for believing that God was in Him. The first proposition pertains more to the doctrinal, the second to the apologetic point of view; and since it is with this that we are here concerned, the latter naturally occupies the more prominent position. For the manner in which the results deduced from the development of the doctrinal side of the question coincide with those to which we are led, see Liebner's *Dogmatik aus dem Christolog. Princip dargestellt*, B. i. pp. 291-352.

God-man. Only in virtue of the former condition was a development in any sense, and therefore a sinless development, possible to Him: only in virtue of the second could He accomplish it in face of a world full of evil, and which on all hands enticed Him to sin. Thus, although His sinless holiness was a quality of the human nature of Jesus, it had its proper roots in His character and essence as God-man. From His sinlessness, therefore, we may equally infer His pure and perfect humanity and His true Divinity; and inasmuch as we can only conceive of both as in complete unison and interpenetration, we infer further that He is *God-man*.

Such are the inferences with respect to the Person of Jesus resulting from His sinlessness. The peculiarity of His moral character and conduct in the midst of a sinful world, testify, as well as His own assertions, that in Him we have to recognise a Person in whom God and man are entirely one;—a Person, therefore, who on one side as much commands our reverent adoration, as on the other He stands before us as the pattern of a perfect life in and before God. That *the last and highest stage*—so far as the *personal realization of the perfect religion* is concerned—is thus attained, is self-evident; for in this respect nothing can surpass the indwelling of God in human nature undisturbed by sin, and a human life passed in the spotless purity resulting from union with God, and terminated by an act of supreme self-sacrifice.

The question, however, which now arises, is, how far—if Christianity is proved to be the perfect religion—did this Person furnish and accomplish all the conditions essential to the true and eternal salvation of the sinful human race? In this respect also, as we shall proceed to show, most important conclusions may be deduced from the sinlessness of Jesus.

CHAPTER II.

SIGNIFICANCE OF THE SINLESSNESS OF JESUS WITH RESPECT TO HIS RELATION TO MANKIND.

IT is obvious that a personality constituted as we have seen the Lord Jesus to be, must have a significance for the entire human race. It is as evident that this significance must be sought in that point in which the being and nature of such a personality is most essentially comprised and concentrated. Now the earthly life of Jesus, from its commencement to its close, the purpose to which it was entirely devoted, was to make the true relation to God and to His fellow-men a living reality. Hence, too, His life-task, and the aim of all His outward acts, was to bring men in this highest of all respects into their right position, and thus to found their true, their imperishable happiness on God, the source of all life and blessedness.

This, however, was to be accomplished, not in a race in whom the Divine image was still pure and unobscured,—the moral power, vigorous and unscathed. It was to be effected in one in which sin had attained a supremacy, which had eclipsed the image and the knowledge of God, in which the true fellowship with God had been destroyed, the moral powers enslaved, and a principle of discord and ruin introduced even into the relations between man and man. Hence what was needed could not be merely to give greater firmness and stability to a bond of Divine fellowship already in existence, and to cherish and render still more energetic a life already based on such communion. The question, on the contrary, was to form afresh the bond which sin had destroyed, —to plant anew, in the midst of a sinful condition, an entirely new life. The question was to bring about a *re*-union with

God, to produce a *new* creation of human life — new to its very roots and sources; and this could only.be effected by actually breaking the power of sin, and doing away with its guilt, — by taking away all that was either destructive or obstructive. For such a purpose, the influence of instruction and example, though of the most perfect kind, was by no means adequate. On the contrary, an atonement, a redemption, a *mediation*, were of absolute necessity. This being the case, it is evident that the being who is to intervene between the holy God and the sinful race of man, for the restoration of true and vital fellowship between them, can be none other than one standing in a relation towards God which is uninterrupted by sin, and at the same time impelled by holy love to enter into the very depths of human nature, and to take its entire condition upon himself. Jesus is such a being, by reason of His sinless perfection; and it is this very quality that makes Him capable of being the one mediator between God and man.

If it be then asked what was needed for the purpose of bringing the human race, which through sin had become estranged from God, and at variance among themselves, into saving fellowship with God, and of laying in that race the foundation of a truly satisfactory state of life, the reply, if it is to be at once complete and particular, must embrace the whole work and scheme of salvation. We may, however, reduce that which falls within our present aim to a few general essential features. These seem to us to be the following: first, the revelation of the will of God to all men, so far as this is necessary for their salvation (knowledge of the method of salvation); secondly, the removal of all that separates the sinner from God, and the establishment, in its place, of a new life of fellowship with God (atonement and redemption); thirdly, the institution, upon this foundation, of a community whose aim and purpose should be wholly of a religious and moral character, — a community of fosterers and guardians of the new and Divine powers (foundation of the kingdom of God and of the Church); and fourthly, the assurance to the living members of this community of a final victory over all opposing powers, and of eternal glory (pledge of eternal life). All these we find in the Person of Jesus Christ. But we find them only in so far as He is sinless, and should not be able to find them in Him unless this were really the case. Had He been a man with the slightest taint of sin, He would not have been able to fulfil these necessary conditions. As the sinlessly perfect One, however, who stands in that oneness with God which He Himself asserts, He is, in the most direct manner, the personal revelation to us of the nature and will of God,—the true mediator between sinful man and the holy God; the royal founder of the kingdom of God and the Church, the highest of human communities; and the perfect pledge of everlasting life, and glorious victory to this community, and to its members united to Himself by a living faith.

We shall now proceed to consider Him in each of these several aspects.

Sec. 1.—*The Sinless Jesus as the personal Revelation of God.*

Sinlessness, in the case of Him to whom it cannot but be conceded, is of itself a powerful guarantee of perfection, both in the knowledge of things Divine and moral, and in the doctrine arising therefrom. Sinless perfection and religious infallibility mutually condition each other; and Jesus Himself appeals, as we have seen, in proof that He spoke the truth, and that His doctrine was not His own, but His that sent Him, to the impossibility of convicting Him of sin, and to the fact that He did at all times such things as were pleasing to the Father.[1]

[1] John viii. 28, 29, and 46. See above, pp. 182-188.

But doctrine, simply as such, is not *revelation*. It is, indeed, a component, but only a deduced and secondary part of revelation, and everywhere presupposes—but most especially in Christianity—a more primitive and more comprehensive whole,—a series of *actual* Divine announcements. Doctrine, at best, can but tell us what we ought to think of God: from revelation, on the contrary, if we regard the term in its full meaning, we expect that it should *show* us what He is,—that it should manifest His nature. Without needing to adduce evidence, revelation will of its very nature be itself the strongest actual proof of the Divine existence and government, by bringing the God of whom it is the witness and lively image as near to our soul as is possible, and above all by disclosing to us His very nature, and making it an object of contemplation. In this sense, that alone can be a perfect revelation which is accomplished by means of the totality of a personal life. For God Himself, as the infinitely perfect, self-conscious Spirit, is essentially a person; and the true relation of created spirits to Him cannot be otherwise conceived of than as that of person to person. Hence that manifestation of God to man which completes all revelation, in which both the relation of God to man and of man to God is perfectly realized, must have that same form which we recognise as the highest form of life, viz. the personal. Only in this form can the fulness of the Divine Spirit and the Divine love suitably manifest the whole sum of those qualities which, in a moral sense, constitute the nature of God. Only thus can God draw so near to man, that he, according to the measure of his capacity, may become a partaker of Him. Only thus can the true relation of man to God be expressed by an actual and genuine life, and a restorative, creative, vital power be implanted in the history of mankind in such wise that, from henceforth, the higher life of man may be renewed and developed by organic connection with this its true centre. Hence we may say that, the more personal the Divine revelation,—the more it is expressed, not merely as religious instruction, or as the delivery of law, but as personal life,—the higher is it in degree ; and that the final and perfect revelation must necessarily be one which is essentially manifested in a holy personality, in one whose life and conduct bring before the very senses of man the nature and will of God.

It is in this sense that Jesus is the revelation of God. It is He Himself that is this revelation, both in His own Person and in the totality of all that proceeded therefrom, whether in word or deed, of all the suffering and the glory, the humiliation and the exaltation, that was accomplished therein. It is thus that He represents Himself. He says,[1] 'I am the way, the truth, and the life,'—thus most expressly declaring that for the attainment of everlasting life everything depends upon His Person, and that in this respect He would be regarded not merely as one who teaches truth, but as truth impersonate, as truth manifested in life. In like manner, He designates Himself as one who has manifested unto men the name of the Father, *i.e.* the whole extent of His nature, so far as it could be revealed in the world, and to mankind.[2] He also asserts that no man can attain to the true knowledge of the Father but he to whom the Son will reveal Him;[3] and in that passage in which He speaks of a knowledge which is at the same time eternal life, He directly combines with the knowledge of the only true God that of Jesus Christ, whom He has sent.[4] Besides, wherever He speaks of a perfect and saving knowledge of God, He always represents this as brought about by means of His own Person; while it is undoubtedly Jesus who is intended, when subsequently the Son is designated in the apostolic circle as He through whom,

[1] John xiv. 6.   [2] John xvii. 6.
[3] Matt. xi. 27.   [4] John xvii. 3.

as being the brightness of His glory and the express image of His Person, God has, after divers previous revelations, in these last days fully revealed Himself.[1]

We have, moreover, this revelation of God in a personal life in Jesus, inasmuch as He was sinlessly perfect. His whole life breathes of God, is rooted in God, is inexplicable apart from God. There is not, nor can there possibly be, a stronger evidence of the existence and government of God than such a life. If God is not to be seen and felt here, where, we may ask, is He to be found? But that He is to be found by, and that He is the rewarder of, them that seek Him, is told us by every word and act of the Lord Jesus, and is powerfully declared by His whole manifestation, in which the reality of a higher and a heavenly order of things is so overwhelmingly evident. And not only does the existence of God become a certainty through Him, but He is also the means of disclosing the nature of God, and that—as is indeed demanded by the very notion of revelation—under an entirely new aspect, an aspect which had not as yet become an all-pervading consciousness. Hitherto the power, the glory, the unapproachable dignity of God had been clearly perceived, while but a faint and distant idea of His grace had been entertained. But now, in the sinless Jesus, who died for a sinful world, in the 'only begotten of the Father, full of grace and truth,' that which constitutes the essential nature of God,—that which, as has been aptly said, is most God-like in God, even His holy love, His preventing, sin-forgiving, death-conquering, and life-giving grace,[2]—is brought out in the clearest light. In the sinless One, who lived only for sinners, God was for the first time revealed in the manner needed for the salvation of a sinful world. Nor was this done in the way

---

[1] Heb. i. 1–3.

[2] Compare Dorner, *Jesu Sündl. Volk.* p. 57, and the fourth section generally.

merely of doctrine and declaration, but very chiefly in that manner in which alone such a revelation could exercise creative energy, even by acts of direct intervention, by a totality of saving deeds and saving operations, centering in the divine-human Person of Jesus Christ Himself, the living exemplification of the holy love of God. In that miracle of Divine love—the whole being and life of Jesus—the nature of God, as love, is manifested in a manner than which it is impossible to conceive aught higher or more perfect; and therein is fulfilled that profound saying of St. John:[1] 'The law was given by Moses, but grace and truth came by Jesus Christ.'

But a revelation of God concerns itself not merely with His nature, but also with His *will*. In this aspect it is still more apparent how Jesus the sinless One was the personal revelation of God to humanity. Looking at the moral side, we find that two conditions absolutely require to be complied with, if sinners—and all men are sinners—are to become well-pleasing in the sight of God. In the first place, they must be brought to know their *sin*, and to repent of it in their inmost soul; and further, the *good* must be set before their minds in its whole compass by means of a living and powerful example. Both these things—self-abasing knowledge of sin, and quickening knowledge of good—are effected in an incomparably excellent way by the manifestation of holy life given us in Jesus; and this manifestation is a moral revelation of God, because its true foundation is in Him.

Without doubt, even the moral law, both in its positive and in its unwritten form in the conscience, produced *knowledge of sin*, and *sorrow* on account of it. But evidently mere knowledge of and sorrow for sin in themselves are not all,—everything depends on their *purity* and *depth;* and

[1] John i. 17.

here it must at once be acknowledged that a concrete life will have quite a different effect from an abstract law.[1]

The knowledge of sin may always be measured by the knowledge of good. The more complete and certain the latter, the truer and deeper the former. Now it is unquestionable that no law is able to communicate so sure and full a knowledge of good, as the life of one truly holy in all relations and circumstances. Conscience, when tenderly cherished and cultivated, does indeed speak with great certainty, but it is never infallible. It takes its tone in part from our own inward state; it is itself entangled in that web of sin which is thrown around our whole being; and, as a thousand instances prove, it may go astray, it may even fall into a state of most fearful blindness, if it is not guided and enlightened by an external standard clearly held before it. The positive law, being more fixed and definite, is of course surer than the law in the conscience, but both lack that living completeness which is necessary for giving true knowledge of the good. They stand above and outside of our life: the commands they issue are abstract and general. Even the law as we find it in the Old Testament does not present the standard of good in its greatest perfection, not in the whole depth of its free inwardness. These defects are all overcome and supplied in the holy and sinless life of Jesus. There we have a sure standard. His life is conscience outwardly realized. We find there a perfection of good as to principle, and a carrying of it out in action, in all relations, which can never be surpassed. Consequently, in the presence of this exemplification of holy life, an entirely different knowledge of sin is awakened,—a knowledge much purer, deeper, more certain and complete, than any which arises from mere law.

That which thus holds true with respect to the knowledge of sin, is equally true as regards *sorrow* for sin. 'Is it not

[1] Martensen's *Dogmatik*, § 109, p. 233.

natural that he who gazes on absolute righteousness and truth, realized in the living example of Jesus, who beholds there the transcript of human nature and the human will in their original purity, and who therefore comes to know the beauty and perfection, the glory and excellence of the holy Divine will, should humble himself more deeply and truly than the man who can merely oppose a stern commandment to himself and his inclinations?'[1] In His realization of the good, Jesus always referred to God, not to the law. Hence it is that, as we stand in His holy presence, we become more truly conscious, than in any other circumstances, of *that* quality of sin, in virtue of which it is rebellion against God, unfaithfulness towards Him; and thus, too, of the deep guilt which sin involves. Inasmuch, however, as Jesus sacrificed His own pure life in the conflict with sin, the sinner may at the same time see in Him the love which went even to death for his sake: and how much more genuine and inward a sorrow for sin must this awaken than the mere thought of having transgressed the law! In this aspect, the life of Jesus had the effect of separating most distinctly good from evil, and did in the true sense discern and judge men. Through Him a direct judgment was executed on sin, which is shown to be Divine by its purity and holiness. In His Person man possesses a living power capable of awakening the knowledge of sin, and of calling forth sorrow for it,— a power which they who experience it will confess to be of Divine origin, and a constituent part of revelation.

More important still, however, is the *positive* side. Not only was the whole strength of sin laid bare, but man was made also to see and feel the whole purity and fulness of life possessed by the good; for how could he be brought to the determination of making goodness the substance and aim of his life, unless he saw its beauty and loveliness? It is not of

[1] Words of Nitzsch in the *Deutsche Zeitschrift*, 1852, No. X. p. 81.

course to be questioned that a susceptibility for the ideal of moral perfection is implanted in man along with his moral capabilities; but precisely at the moment when we feel that in this ideal there is nothing which contradicts and is foreign to *true* human nature,—that, on the contrary, it really belongs to our nature,—the question presses itself most strongly upon us: Why, then, do we not universally find in mankind a full belief in the existence of perfect goodness, and living examples of its attainment? And why was it that, when it did appear in full distinctness, it was but gradually, with much difficulty and after much resistance, that it penetrated the minds of those who beheld it? The simple reason is, that man cannot possibly produce what does not previously live in himself. The image of the perfect good, however, could not live in him, because sin did not permit its free development. It *slumbered* in him. It must have done so, or no power could ever have awakened it in his inner being, and it would always have remained incomprehensible to him. But it did not *live* in him, else would he have had a distinct and full consciousness of it. Proofs enough that such an ideal did not live in him, are furnished by history. The idea of justice, of a self-complacent virtue which prudently keeps the mean between two extremes, the idea of accordance with the laws and with that which is commended by all reasonable men,[1] was the highest point to which educated reason rose before the appearance of Christ; and even this idea was more a matter discussed in the schools, than a universal persuasion. On the contrary, the picture of one who is filled with holy love,—of a love of the good for the sake of God,—of a love which compassionates the souls of

---

[1] For references as to particulars, see Rothe's work on the *Berechtigung der Sinnlichkeit nach Aristoteles, Studien und Kritiken*, 1850, 2, p. 265 ff.; and Schaubach's *das Verhältniss der Moral des class. Alterthums zur Christlichen*, likewise in the *Studien und Kritiken*, 1851, 1, p. 59 ff.

others, seeks, and sacrifices itself for their salvation, was foreign even to the most cultivated reason; nay, not only foreign to it as mere natural reason, but even unnatural and overstrained. Such an ideal could only be introduced amongst men through the medium of facts, of an actual life. The life by which this is effected cannot be regarded as a mere product of humanity, a climax reached by existing human nature; but, because an entirely new element, even true holiness, is there revealed, it must be viewed as the work of the Spirit from on high, as the operation of God. It is, in fact, a communication of God to humanity, and is as truly a revelation in connection with the department of morals, as what is usually so designated in connection with religion.[1]

This ideal has been set before us in the Person of Jesus, in Him who was the sinless One, who, because He lived only in God, was not merely a perfectly righteous man, but also manifested a love which proclaimed itself Divine by its holy earnestness and unbounded devotion. He is man, as God would have Him be, and therefore is He also the full and living expression of the Divine will to humanity. In Him, the Son full of grace and truth, has the Sun of Righteousness arisen upon man; in His light it is that we first see light, even in a moral sense, in its full brightness.

The presence of such a distinct, fixed, and elevated standard must unquestionably be of infinite value for the moral development of humanity. The significance of the matter becomes still greater, when we consider the mode and circum-

---

[1] 'Christology must no longer be merely a chapter in dogmatics, but must take its place also as a chapter in ethics.' So speaks Ackermann in a beautiful review of Harless's *Christliche Ethik*, in Reuter's *Repertorium*, 1852, 4, p. 39. We may even speak still more strongly: not only must Christology become *one chapter*, but *the fundamental principle*, of ethics. Christ is as truly the principle of the *moral*, as of the religious revelation. Compare De Wette, *Lehrbuch der Christlichen Sittenlehre*, Berlin 1853, §§ 3, 41-52.

stances in which it was accomplished. Such ideals and examples of the good and noble as are to be found before the coming of Jesus, all wanted power to affect and actually to transform the depths of man's life,—to transform humanity as a whole. The reason thereof was partially that they were not in reality the highest, but more because they were only products of *thought*,—products of intellect in a higher state of cultivation than was commonly attainable. Even when, as under the old covenant, these examples came before men clothed with Divine authority, and in a shape which the common understanding might lay hold of, they only appear as *requirement*, not as fulfilment. It is otherwise in Jesus. In His case, the ideal of perfect goodness is not merely set forth *by* a personality as a product of thought, but is realized *in* its life. Hence arises the extreme value it has in relation to moral intuitions and knowledge, and its boundless influence on our moral volitions and acts.

There is a further superiority, also, of this realization in Jesus, that it has both an all-inclusive and a universally intelligible character. The image of goodness in Jesus, we say, is *all-comprehensive*. It exhibits before us that which is true and universal in human nature under the very conditions to which every man is subject, in the relations of individuality, of race, of family, and of nationality, and is therefore sufficient for all, however situated as to these conditions of life.[1] He realized the ideal in all the essential relations of life, especially in those which are attended with most difficulty and temptation; and has thus shown not only *that*, but *how*, good may be preserved intact, and come off victorious in all circumstances. He exemplified it not only in single and prominent virtues, not in a partial and fragmentary manner, but in the entirety of life, as a single and perfect

[1] Compare what is said, pp. 51-55, with regard to the universality of the moral character of Jesus.

work, resulting from complete harmoniousness of mind. He consequently stands before us as a true and universal example,—not as a model of which we are to copy the separate parts, but as a type the true spirit of which we are to appropriate as a whole. Nor is it less a characteristic that it is *intelligible*. It is deep and rich enough to furnish a subject which human comprehension and delineation can never exhaust; and, at the same time, it is placed before mankind in features so grand and mighty, yet so direct and affecting, that the simplest soul, yea, the mind of a child, can understand it, and even those who would resist, are impressed by it. We may consequently affirm of the moral example of Christ, that it is one *universally binding*; and in this sense also may we apply to it the words of the apostle, 'In Christ Jesus there is neither Jew nor Greek, bond nor free, male nor female.'[1] This example is destined alike for all, that all may make it their own; and all alike are destined for it, that it may live in them for ever. But that which thus stands in its all-embracing greatness *above* humanity, although it is at the same time truly human, which has not proceeded from, and is, notwithstanding, destined ever to enter into humanity, is stamped with the seal of a Divine revelation.

Sec. 2.—The Sinless Jesus as the Mediator between God and Sinful Man.

Although the revelation of the nature and will of God form an essential part of the scheme of salvation, yet it is evident that by it alone man cannot be saved. The relation of man to God is not merely one of intellect to intellect,—it is a relation of person to person, and embraces the whole life. And the more so, since the matter here in question concerns the position which the creature occupies with reference to

[1] Gal. iii. 28.

his Creator, and thus to Him who is in all respects the source and support of his whole being. Hence nothing will suffice but perfect communion of life and of love. But this communion is opposed by sin, whose very nature is antagonism to God; and sin, which, as well as the guilt it implies, and the consequences that flow from it, is a *real* power in human life, cannot be done away with merely by means of knowledge, though this were the purest and most complete which can be conceived. In order to break its might, and destroy it, there must be opposed to it another equally real but higher power. But this power cannot come from man,— it must come from God. For it is only God who can forgive men their sins, and take away their guilt; from God alone can the scheme of reconciliation go forth; God alone can, by the actual communication of His grace, set up a new power in the soul, which shall be mightier than sin and all its consequences. And yet, since it is for *men* that the reconciliation is designed, it is only by a corresponding *human* medium that it can be consummated. Moreover, this human mediator must be capable of imparting to the soul a principle of life and goodness, in the place of the principle of sin, which is now subjugated. Just such a medium do we find in the sinless Jesus, as we shall now proceed to show.

In Him, the Son of God, who is one with the Father, we recognise not merely a typical and symbolical representation, but an actual realization and communication of the holy love and saving grace of God. All that He was, all that He did and suffered, had the joint purpose of bringing back sinful man into fellowship with God, of bestowing upon him Divine grace, and of bringing about a true reconciliation between him and the holy God. His sufferings and His death, which form the consummation of His whole life of self-sacrifice, occupy so special a position in this respect, that our attention must be more particularly directed to them.

And, first, Jesus Himself attributes to His death and sufferings the utmost importance in this respect. In His view, His death was an essential element of the Divine counsel, and an indispensable part of that work of redemption which He came to accomplish.[1] And in what sense it was so, is obvious from His own words. He calls Himself the Good Shepherd, who, while the hireling flees from the invading wolf, lays down His life for the sheep, that they may have life, and have it more abundantly.[2] He designates Himself as the corn of wheat, which, if it is not to abide alone, but to bring forth much fruit, must fall into the earth and die.[3] He compares Himself—the Son of Man—with the serpent which Moses lifted up in the wilderness for the healing of the people,[4]— thus alluding to His own lifting up on the cross,[5] the effect of which will be, that all who believe on Him shall not perish, but have everlasting life. He will give His life a ransom for many,[6] as the price for the redemption of those souls whom guilt has exposed to punishment. His blood is to be shed for the remission of sin,[7] and to become, by being shed, the blood of the new covenant;[8] that is, *the* blood through which the covenant of perfect union, of true reconciliation between God and man, receives its formal ratification and consecration. On the other hand, He would equally have His death regarded as the alone means by which true life is begotten in man; His flesh is meat indeed, His blood is drink indeed; and they who feed on Him, who by faith receive Him into their souls, are united to Him, and made partakers of everlasting life.[9]

It is thus that He who offers a sinless life as a pledge of the truth of His word, expresses Himself concerning the sig-

---

[1] Luke xxiv. 26, 46, 47. [2] John x. 11–16. [3] John xii. 24.
[4] John iii. 14, 15. [5] John viii. 28. [6] Matt. xx. 28.
[7] Matt. xxvi. 28. [8] Mark xiv. 24; Luke xxii. 20.
[9] John vi. 51–58.

nificance of His life and death. In His own eyes, His death was undoubtedly the chief means of expiation, reconciliation, and communication of new life; and if He does not call it in so many words *an atoning sacrifice*, He plainly implies that it is so, while His apostles afterwards decidedly express the fact. In directing our attention to the death of Jesus in this point of view, it cannot, however, enter into our purpose to discuss the act of redemption and atonement thereby accomplished in its full extent.[1] On the contrary, we would, in conformity with the course of our argument, bring forward only that which stands in unmistakeable connection with the sinless perfection of Jesus, and the conclusions involved in the very nature of this doctrine. Our subject thus leading us to the significance of the death of Christ, especially as an atoning sacrifice, we shall endeavour, on the one hand, briefly to show that such a significance cannot be conceded to His death unless He is indeed sinless; and, on the other hand, that if He is so, this significance is but the natural consequence of His sinlessness.

Atonement, generally speaking, turns upon the fact that the pure, the innocent, the unpolluted, is given up, is offered to God, in the place of the sinful, guilty, and vile, in order to bring about the deliverance of the latter. It has for its object to restore that relation of man to God which sin had disturbed, and to reconcile the sinner to God; and it takes place where there is a knowledge of sin and of the holiness of God, as well as of the antagonism existing between them, and consequently a felt need of pardon and grace. An approximation to this idea of atonement existed even in some

---

[1] An excellent and full dissertation upon the point which we are now to consider may be found in the Essays of Schöberlein: *Ueber die Christliche Versöhnungslehre, Stud. u. Krit.* 1845, 2; and *Ueber das Verhältniss der persönlichen Gemeinschaft mit Christo zur Erleuchtung, Rechtfertigung, und Heiligung*, ditto, 1847, 1; and in a recent and comprehensive article on the doctrine of Redemption in Herzog's *Real Encyclopädie*, B. 17, pp. 87–143.

heathen religions. But it was in the religion of the Old Covenant that it was first fully apprehended, because here, first, we find a full consciousness of God's holiness, and of the penal character of sin, as opposed to the Divine law. Here sacrifice had a twofold object: on the one hand, it sought to deepen in the mind of him who offered it the feeling of sin and guilt, and to give a strong expression to that feeling; and, on the other, it furnished a means whereby the offerer might receive an assurance of Divine grace, and be replaced in a right position towards God. In both respects, the fundamental idea is that of *substitution*. The sacrifice of the animal, in which the worshipper gave up something of his own,—something belonging, as it were, to his own person, placing himself in direct connection with it by laying his hand upon it, and generally slaughtering it himself,—shadowed forth the self-sacrifice of him who offered it; while the death which the animal suffered, represented the death which his sin deserved. Then, as the consequence of his penitence, and by virtue of the promise which was attached to the sacrificial offering, he received the assurance that God accepted the ransom, and now looked upon the sinner with favour.

Now this service of sacrifices, although it unquestionably arose out of a deep religious want, although in itself highly significant and full of meaning, and well adapted to that particular stage of religious development, had, nevertheless, something inadequate about it, and could never thoroughly accomplish that real *abolition of sin* and *implantation of holiness* which the nature of the case required. All was symbolic representation, and there was no actual moral transaction. In general, sin was acknowledged to be sinful, but the full extent of its guilt was unperceived. Divine grace was prefigured, but not actually communicated. The relation in which the offerer of the sacrifice stood to the animal he sacrificed, was a voluntary, not a necessary relation; the rite was to him an outward event, the sacrifice was not received into his very soul. As the sacrifice offered was an animal which had indeed, as a thing consecrated to God, a sacred character ascribed to it, but which of course could not be really holy, there could go forth from it no sanctifying power. Hence, although these sacrifices might for a time calm the sense of guilt, they could not take away sin, and establish in its place a true fellowship with God and a new life. Hence sacrifices of this kind, as has been already shown, could neither powerfully affect the heart, nor continue efficient in all time, but needed to be constantly repeated. They could effect a temporary relaxation of the variance between God and the sinner, but could obtain no eternal redemption.[1] Now, what could not thus be accomplished—viz. the restoration of a life which should be inwardly reconciled to God, and really free from sin—was performed by Christ. But it was not merely by the abolition of sacrificial worship that Christ accomplished this; it was by realizing *in Himself* all that had been striven after, but never attained, in sacrifices. The perfect self-surrender of Him, the All-holy, for sinful men, which was the only real and sanctifying sacrifice, whose efficacy should last for ever, came in the place of those merely typical sacrifices which were now to cease, having found their true fulfilment in that great sacrifice.

A free self-sacrifice of this kind necessarily presupposes and is based upon the sinless purity of him who offers it. The very idea of such an offering could have been justifiably conceived only by one who knew himself to be pure and spotless in the sight of God; and such an offering, if made by a really sinless being, could not fail of effecting the purpose contemplated. The sacrifice of Jesus is distinguished from all previous sacrifices chiefly by this, that it was not a representation and foreshadowing, but a real

[1] Heb. ix. 12.

moral transaction; it was a free action, of a purely ethical character. Jesus, in whose Person the sacrifice and the priest are one, offered Himself, as the Epistle to the Hebrews expresses it, through the eternal Spirit unto God.[1] And in this offering of Himself, He preserved the most perfect liberty of action. For however we may regard His death to have been brought about by circumstances, still we must acknowledge that it was by a free decision of His own will that He took it upon Him. Now this act, thus freely determined on, can only be regarded as the result of a will thoroughly pure and unenslaved by sinful love of self; and we must regard this sublime resolve as the culminating action of a life which was itself, from first to last, a perfect sacrifice. But this free self-determination to death can only be viewed as a purely moral action, and free from all tincture of fanaticism, if based upon a full consciousness that this death was necessary to the carrying out of the Divine plan of salvation, and an indispensable condition of the redemption of man, and the establishment of a kingdom of God upon earth. This consciousness could be possessed only by One who, in virtue of His holiness and His oneness with God, had a clear insight into the whole purpose of God in salvation. Again, Jesus could desire to offer Himself as a sacrifice for sinners, only if He felt that He was pure and stainless; and might therefore regard His offering as a sacrifice well-pleasing to God. It was, in truth, an indispensable condition of the sacrifice that the victim was immaculate, for only such a one could be worthy of God. The *physical* immaculateness of the animal sacrificed, rises in this personal self-sacrifice of Jesus into *moral* stainlessness. That He who sought to give Himself as a sacrifice to free the world from sin should have been conscious of being Himself a sinner, or felt Himself to be in any one respect unclean before God,

[1] Heb. ix. 14.

would have been not merely a contradiction, it would have been a gross impiety: if, on the other hand, He did not make upon all the impression that He was perfectly sinless, then one might suppose that it was for His own sin, for His own guilt, that He suffered. Only in the case of One who was perfectly free from sin can we feel confident that the suffering which He underwent, however much it may have conduced to His Divine perfecting, was endured not on account of His own guilt, but for the guilt of others.[1]

The principal thing, however, is that the *sinless holiness* of Jesus was an essential reason why His free act of self-sacrifice *really attained* the ends which previous sacrifices had but aimed at: that is, it became the means of imparting a full knowledge of sin, and was itself an actual communication of Divine grace, a substitution in the truest and deepest sense, a real destroying of sin, and a real implanting in its place of a new life of sanctification.

In the first place, it is in the contemplation of the self-immolation of the Holy One, that we come to understand what *sin* is, in its absolute antagonism to holiness. For in the fact that both love, unreservedly sacrificing itself, and sin, in all its power and malignity, are here exhibited in utmost distinctness and placed in juxtaposition, the true nature of each becomes clearer to us, and even the dullest understanding can appreciate to some extent the vast difference between them. But further, we cannot fail to observe, that the sin which is here brought before us is not sin in its isolated phenomena, but that it is the dominant sin of the race,—that sin which operates as a universal power in humanity, and of which we may trace the workings in ourselves. The Holy One dies, 'not in a conflict with sin in any special manifestation, but with sin itself,'[2] in order to break its

[1] Heb. vii. 26, 27.
[2] De Wette, *Wesen des christlichen Glaubens*, § 57, S. 297.

entire power; and in His death both the power of sin and its opposition to God are exhibited with incomparable distinctness. There is, as has already been shown, no more effectual means of awakening the heart to a knowledge of sin, and a true sorrow for sin, than the life-picture of the Holy One, as it is presented to us in the gospel; but, above all, it is from the contemplation of the Crucified offering Himself for the sins of the world that this benign influence proceeds; and assuredly no one can deny that the consciousness of sin is called forth in a manner infinitely more clear and more intense by the sacrifice of the sinless Christ, than it ever was by former sacrifices. These contained, at most, a general monition against sin; they did not hold up to the soul the mirror of a love freely giving itself up for the sinner to suffering and to death.

But here, too, the *positive* side is much stronger. All that the sacrifices of the earlier dispensation could accomplish, was to typify and symbolize the Divine *grace:* but the sacrifice of Jesus actually *communicates* that grace. For if the sinless One is so united to God that His love is to us a real manifestation of the love of God Himself, and that we must recognise Him to be an impersonation of the Divine love, all this must be most forcibly expressed in that highest act of His life, His free surrender of Himself to death from love to man. In this act we see two things: we see One who has established His claim to be regarded as the Son of God, freely giving Himself up to die; and we see God not sparing His own Son, that He may give Him up to death for the salvation of man. In the sacrificial death of the Holy One we see *immediately* the reconciled and gracious God, because therein the eternal love of God—that love whose very nature it is to be a sin-forgiving, a saving, a helping love—is not only manifested, but so offered that it may be directly accepted by the sinner. Nor does this love offer itself at the expense of the holiness of God: on the contrary, it does so in a manner which alone truly satisfies the claims of that holiness; for the sacrifice of the sinless One possesses, in a very different way from the earlier sacrifices, a vicarious significance and a sanctifying efficacy.[1]

Against sin itself there can exist in God only a righteous displeasure, fully bent upon its extirpation. To the sinner, *as such*, He must not be a gracious, but an angry, because a holy God; and such does the sinner know Him to be when conscience awakes within him. If God is to bestow His favour upon him, this can only be done on condition that the partition wall of guilt shall be done away with, and the foundation of the sinner's sanctification at the same time laid. On the other hand, the sinner, too, needs a pledge and assurance of the Divine favour, if he is to have that delight in goodness, and that power to perform it, which lie at the very root of holiness. Thus on both sides a mediation is requisite; and here it is that the holy and sinless One comes in, and is seen living, suffering, and dying, as the sinner's *Substitute*. By His unconditional surrender of Himself to God and to mankind, He renders the forgiveness of sin and the bestowal of grace, the restoration and renewal of the sinner, really possible.

There is an essential difference between the one great sacrifice and the previous typical sacrifices. In these, sin was borne, and that but externally, by an unconscious animal, which was itself without the sphere of religion and morality. Jesus, however, moved by compassionate love, consciously and unreservedly entered into the world of sinners, and though Himself untouched by sin, took upon Himself, as an actual member of the same, the sins of all. Then, voluntarily appearing before God with these sins upon Him, He suffered their fearful consequences to fall upon Himself, as though

[1] Compare on this whole subject Rothe's *Ethik* (vol. ii. pp. 279-312): *Der Erlöser und sein Erlösungswerk.*

He had been the most flagrant of sinners and evil-doers. Thus He fully satisfied the claims of Divine justice against mankind; and by surrendering Himself to death, made an atonement for the sin of all, which sinners themselves were unable to furnish. In this manner was the wall of partition between the holy God and sinful man broken down, and the destroyed relation between them so restored, that the love of God may now be unreservedly bestowed upon man. In the Son, in whom He is well pleased, God looks upon mankind, and beholds first a race restored, and then individuals under a process of restoration. In the holy Son of God, who shed His blood for the forgiveness of sin, the sinner beholds One in whom he possesses the assurance that God is, of a truth, a reconciled and gracious God.

That this is possible, depends again on the nature of the fellowship which is perfectly realized in Christ, and which takes so important a place in His whole work. For as, on the one hand, Christ is so absolutely one with God, that His whole manifestation, especially His death, must be regarded as an actual living manifestation of God Himself, as a God of love; so, on the other hand, He becomes equally one with men, enters into the fullest life-fellowship with them; gives Himself entirely to them, in His love; lives, suffers, and dies, not for Himself, but for them,—not in order to procure some one special benefit, but that He may purchase the salvation of the whole race. And in virtue of this self-devotion, which truly unites Him with humanity, He is no longer to be regarded as a separately existing individual, but as the universal man, as comprehending the whole of humanity in Himself, as its *Substitute and Head.* In this way, Christ being one with humanity, communicates to it everything which He Himself possesses. A holy and happy exchange takes place between Christ and man, by which

He who took upon Him our sin and guilt, and suffered our death, imparts to us His righteousness, His peace, His happiness, and bestows upon us that which He obtained for them.

Doubtless this presupposes something *on our side:* we must enter into *His* fellowship, we must by faith lay hold of the salvation offered to us, and thereby become partakers of the reconciling power of His life and death. And here, again, we trace the difference that exists between the old sacrifices, and the one all-efficacious propitiation of Christ. The ante-Christian sacrifices remained *without* the offerers; and although they doubtless made some impression upon their minds, they were still external to those for whom they were to make an atonement, and could not penetrate into their hearts with quickening and renewing power. The sacrifice of Christ, on the contrary, is from its very nature such, that it *cannot* remain a merely external, strange, and accidental circumstance, where there is any susceptibility for its reception, but must enter into the soul, and place him who by faith appropriates it, in a living relation to the object sacrificed. And this is the case, because this object is a person, and the sacrifice itself the voluntary act of holy love. Hence it is that a stream of love and life goes forth therefrom, that a tie is formed between Him who offers Himself as a sacrifice, and him who appropriates this sacrifice. By this inward personal union it is that strength is imparted to the latter, in virtue of which there is begotten in him, together with an assurance of pardon and reconciliation, the actual beginnings of a *new life* and of victory over sin.

Viewed thus, the idea of substitution—which, if understood merely in an external and formal sense, is indeed to be rejected as dead and false—becomes something living and true. The connection between Christ and His believing followers is expressed by St. Paul in words of profound significance, as 'being in Christ.' So close is the living union between the Head and the members, that they form parts of one whole. His fellowship with Christ, from which the Spirit and the life of Christ pass into his soul, makes the believer a partaker in all that Christ Himself is. In this fellowship he learns to know God as a God of grace. In this fellowship, even when it exists only in its early dawnings, he does not stand alone in the sight of God, but is in His sight as one who has been grafted into Christ, and is united by faith with Him. On this account, God can in His love impart to him His grace, even although sin still exists within him, because in his oneness with the sinless Christ the dominion of sin is destroyed, its power is broken, and a hope and a pledge of its ultimate total overthrow are bestowed.

Hence, when it is said that in Christ God is gracious to the sinner, this does not mean that He is so by reason of an arbitrary act of grace, but that He is gracious to the sinner in Christ, because, as soon as a sinner becomes united to Christ, God beholds in him one in whom there is given, not in virtue of his own strength, but in virtue of the operation of Christ in him, a pledge that he will attain to actual freedom from sin.[1] Now if this importance attaches to the sacrifice of Christ, it is apparent how His sacrifice must be regarded as the only sacrifice, offered *once for all*.[2] It possesses entirely and for ever the power to communicate Divine grace, and to impart the new life. And therefore it is not possible objectively to renew His sacrifice: the only way in which it can be offered again is a subjective one; that is, by such an inward following of the example of Jesus by each believer, that, being thus himself a priest, he may also offer himself to God as a spiritual sacrifice in Christ.

In this sense it is that we recognise in the sinless One the

---

[1] Schleiermacher, *der christliche Glaube*, ii. 145, § 104.
[2] Heb. vii. 27, ix. 12, 26–28.

only true Mediator between God and man. In Jesus we see Him in whom God is well pleased with man, and turns to him in grace,—Him in whom man may behold with unveiled face, and believingly appropriate this grace, and thus be transfigured into the Divine image. But this naturally involves a further consequence. If Jesus, by His sinless holiness, thus restores the vital fellowship between sinful man and God, He thereby becomes at the same time the author of *the true fellowship between man and man*, the founder of a kingdom of God, a kingdom of faith, extending far beyond the limits of those circumstances which have hitherto exercised a separating power over mankind; and it is as occupying this no less fundamental position, that we have now to consider Him more closely.

Sec. 3.—*The Holy Jesus as the Founder of the True Fellowship of Men.*

Men being by their very nature disposed to associate one with another, we find that all the chief activities of human life, as well as its fundamental arrangements, are calculated to bring about such association. Everywhere we meet with a reciprocal giving and taking, an acting and producing on the part of some, a being acted upon and a receiving on the part of others, a drawing together of the congenial, and an excluding of the uncongenial; and they who would entirely withdraw from the mutual interaction thus arising, cannot but be regarded as individuals of unsound and incomplete development. Hence there necessarily arises upon the foundation of the family, as the primitive and typical association, civil, political, and national associations; and those associations for the purposes of art, of science, and of intercourse in the various spheres of intellectual pursuits, which are partly restricted to the former, and partly of far greater relative extent. But all these fellowships, great and important as they are, have yet their strict and definite limits. They are either confined within certain local boundaries, or are inseparably connected with some special kind of nationality or endowment, and often even with a certain degree of culture or social position. Hence, by their very nature, they involve, to a certain extent, a principle of separation, as well as of association. They do not unite men *as such*, but only men of certain definite peculiarities, and thus exclude all those who are not thus distinguished.

There is, however, a task allotted to all men, without exception, and for which all, as beings made in God's image, possess the requisite endowments: and this is the recovery of the right relation to the holy and living God, and to every human being. This task, besides being universal, is absolutely the highest that can be engaged in; and if co-operation and association are requisite for the accomplishment of any human undertaking, they are so in this instance. For it is only upon the soil of society that piety and morality can display a healthy and vital energy, only from such a soil that they can derive the nutriment necessary to their growth and perfection. In their case isolation would be synonymous with deformity, degeneracy, annihilation. If in these respects that which is true and excellent is to be obtained, there must of necessity exist a fellowship which, transcending all existing limitations, is by its very nature calculated *to embrace all men without distinction*, and to promote the attainment of that eternal destination which is alike set before all. Not till such a fellowship exists will the true foundation be laid for every other kind of association among mankind. Not before, will a possibility exist of preventing those distinctions which naturally divide men, from effecting a hostile separation. Not before, will communities and individuals, nay, different nations, recognise the fact that they are made, not for themselves alone, but for each other,—that they are destined mutually to aid and supplement each other,—that thus, by the reciprocal action and reaction of the better gifts of all, humanity may be fashioned into a true and living unity.

Now, a fellowship of this supreme and universal kind can be founded only upon that union between man and God which is effected by faith or religion. Hence its very existence is an impossibility so long as religion cannot be found in a state of purity and independence, but only in combination with other and particular elements, by which it also is placed in a position of specialty and particularity. This was the case in the præ-Christian world, and is still so in nations beyond the pale of Christianity. In these we everywhere find a religion so indissolubly connected with the special constitution of a country, with peculiarities of nationality, with the degrees of culture and political institutions of certain nations, that it cannot be separated therefrom. We find religions in which nature, religions in which art, is deified,—state religions, and religious states; but we do not find a religion free from all admixture with foreign elements, and keeping within its own proper territory,—a religion which is entirely itself, and will be nothing else but itself, which makes that, and that only, which is its special province — even the eternal salvation of its professors—its chief concern. Such a religion is not found previously to the appearance of Christianity, and is found in Christianity alone. Here religion is brought back entirely to its own special province, and thus offers that firm and self-supporting point whence the whole circle of human life may be worked upon, and gathered into one harmonious whole.

But this could be effected only by a person whose whole and sole task it should be to exhibit in perfect purity the Divine image in man, and to make that image comprehensible to all,—by One who actually did accomplish this task, and that in such wise, that none who were susceptible of such an emotion could fail of being touched thereby. The sinless Jesus was such a Person. By manifesting religion not only in its perfection, but also in its unmingled purity and entire independence, He at the same time laid the foundation of a fellowship which, being restricted by no kind of external condition, was capable of including the whole human race,— a fellowship which, while remaining faithful to its original purpose, may exercise a free and real influence upon every department of social life, upon art and science, upon legislation and politics, without intermeddling directly with these things, much less putting itself in their place.

In the foundation of such a community, Jesus Himself recognised an essential element of His mission. He invites all who need redemption; that is, all men.[1] He wills that all should be one in Him, as He is one with the Father; and it is by this very union through Him, and in Him, that the world is to know that the Father has sent Him.[2] He proclaims the kingdom of God as at hand, as having already come,[3] as His kingdom. It is not, however, to be a kingdom of this world, but a kingdom of heaven,[4] to be developed indeed in the world, but to be pervaded by heavenly powers, and to attain maturity in a future and heavenly period. For its earthly development—during the course of which He particularly distinguishes between what is God's and what is Cæsar's, and thus points out the propriety of separating the spiritual from the secular[5]—He would have a Church, to be gathered from all nations, from the whole human race.[6] To effect this, He sent forth His apostles, and endowed them with His Spirit. For the regular continuance of the Church which they were to found, and which, consequently, was to be a manifest and visible one, He made special preparations,

[1] Matt. xi. 28.   [2] John xvii. 21.   [3] Luke x. 9, xvii. 21.
[4] John xiii. 36.   [5] Matt. xxii. 21.   [6] Matt. xxviii. 19.

by instituting holy Baptism and the Lord's Supper, and by laying down rules as to how those who were disobedient in the Church were to be treated.[1] And in all this He was so sure of success, that He not only promised to the Church which He called His an imperishable existence, against which no power should prevail,[2] but He already beheld with a glance which surveyed and comprised the whole process of the world's development, the whole redeemed human race as *one* flock, under Himself, the *one* Shepherd.[3]

Jesus, however, not merely purposed to institute such a community, He not merely announced such a purpose, but possessed in Himself the power to form and to maintain it. An all-embracing fellowship of personal spirits, united by a common faith and a common love, presupposes a personal head. And He, the holy Son of God and Son of Man, who lived entirely for men, and gave Himself a sacrifice for them, was, from His very nature, this Head. For the Head must be so constituted, that the Spirit by which the community is to be pervaded and governed, may continually flow forth therefrom in pure and inexhaustible fulness. And this is the qualification which is offered in Him in most abundant measure.

Men, sinful and limited as they are, do not possess, in and of themselves, the power of forming themselves into a lasting fellowship of the highest kind. They must find the living point of union for such a purpose in a holy Being exalted above themselves, and capable of lifting them up above self, in One who, by uniting them to Himself, at the same time brings them into vital union with each other. But when One thus holy and thus exalted has once really laid hold of the hearts of men, this union will be the inevitable result. For there is in the Divine, when vividly presented in life, a

[1] Matt. xviii. 15-18.   [2] Matt. xvi. 18.   [3] John x. 16.

magnetic power which draws minds out of their isolation, and unites them with an unseen but powerful bond. This life-magnet, this infinite force of attraction, is introduced among mankind, in the Person of that Divine and Holy One who sacrificed Himself in holy love for the sinful race. By Him must every one who is susceptible of its influence be drawn out of his own narrow self. But it is not only out of self that those who feel the powers of Christ are attracted, through that faith which He calls forth within them. They are also drawn into His life, made one with Him, and thus made one among themselves. This kind of union is at once the most perfect and the most lasting, for it is the work of the Highest: through it, man is raised above himself; and by it, that selfishness which otherwise obstructs all true fellowship, is, in its very essence, destroyed.[1]

It is true that all this applies immediately to those only who have actually laid hold of Christ by faith. But then these are the salt of the earth, the leaven which is destined gradually to leaven the mass. They are to introduce an ever-extending, and at length an *all*-comprehending union. The moving spring of this union is love,—*that* pitying, seeking, saving love which was brought into the world by the holy Jesus of the gospel. This love sees in every one who needs its aid, not only the possessor of a common nature, but rather *Him* who said, ' Inasmuch as ye have done it unto one of the least of these my brethren, ye have done it unto me.'[2] This love sees in the sinner, not merely a guilty and condemned man; in one sitting in the darkness of

---

[1] It may be said that, in this respect also, Jesus has a *substitutionary* significance. The higher kind of fellowship of which we have been speaking is as much an ethical requirement, as those more limited associations which we designate as civil and political. But though a participation in such a fellowship is at once the duty and the need of all, none would have been able to found one, unless Christ, with His personal power and authority, had done this for all men.

[2] Matt. xxv. 40.

spiritual death, not an uninteresting, or perhaps a repulsive object;—it sees in both, one made for redemption and adoption into God's family, one who is to be brought by it into the kingdom of God. This love, flowing forth in boundless fulness from Christ, has not a human but a Divine source. It therefore contains in it a guarantee that the kingdom of God will come forth victorious from all its conflicts, and will in the end succeed in effecting a union of the whole race.

Thus we see that there dwells in the Person of the holy Christ, a power of uniting men, which effects its purpose from an inward necessity,—a power which first, indeed, brings together those who are His by faith, but which afterwards impels these to spread on all sides that salvation which they have themselves experienced, that all may be saved by Christ, and all brought into the same fellowship. It is a fellowship which exists only for the sake of satisfying the deepest, the universal needs of men: it is the kingdom of God, for it is even this which is visibly manifested in the Church of the Redeemed, so far as it is ordered according to His will and word. And where else do we find anything *equal* or even *similar* to this? The very idea of forming a society which should embrace the whole human family, never entered the mind of the greatest sages, or lawgivers, or founders of empires, before Christ.[1] And if the thought had occurred to any of these, *which of them* could have realized it? The Holy One of God, and He alone, could do this, because in Him alone was the true uniting power, and because the kingdom of God was contained in Him, and had only to develope itself from Him. Regarded in this light, Christ is presented to us as the *centre* of the *world's history*.

---

[1] This idea is enlarged upon by Reinhard in his celebrated work, *Ueber den Plan welchen der Stifter der christlichen Religion zum Besten der Menschen-entwarf*, fifth edition, with additions by Heubner, Wittenburg 1830.

He is this, not merely in that more ideal sense, according to which the whole spiritual life of mankind before His appearance was one continual aspiration and longing after Him, while all the spiritual life which has been found among men since His coming exhibits decided marks that He is its author; but in that far more real aspect in which He is beheld as the true point of union for the race, the life of humanity, the pulsating heart and quickening spirit, by means of which humanity is formed into an organic whole, into a body animated by the power of God, and consisting of many members. And it is a fact of very deep significance, that Christ makes it a ground of faith in His Divine mission,[1] that by union with Himself and with God He brings men into union among themselves; because a work such as this, the most noble which the human mind can conceive, could have proceeded from none but God.

Sec. 4.—The Sinless Jesus as the Pledge of Eternal Life.

The fellowship founded by Christ, however,—and this is the last point to be considered,—is not destined merely for this earthly existence, but has the promise of eternal life and perfect victory in a future and heavenly state. This promise holds good to every living member of Christ in particular, as well as to the community, formed of such members, in general. And the pledge for its performance is found in the sinless perfection of. Him who, through what He was and what He did, became the sole foundation and all-comprising head of this fellowship.

This promise is, in the first place, expressed with the utmost assurance by Jesus Himself. He testifies of Himself that the Father has given Him to have life in Himself;[2] that no one takes His life from Him, but that He lays it down of

[1] John xvii. 21.   [2] John v. 26.

Himself; that He has power to lay it down, and power to take it again.[1] He feels certain also, that through sufferings and death He shall but enter into the glory which He had with the Father before the world was.[2] In like manner He represents Himself as giving life to the world, and calls Himself, in this very sense, 'the Resurrection and the Life.'[3] His people especially are to be sharers of His eternal life and glory. 'Because I live,' He says, 'ye shall live also;'[4] 'Where I am, there also shall my servant be;'[5] and, 'Father, I will that they also whom Thou hast given me be with me where I am; that they may behold my glory, which Thou hast given me.'[6] They are to attain to true life, to be received into everlasting habitations[7] in the Father's house of many mansions, where a place is prepared for them,[8] where a day shall come in which 'they shall ask nothing,' and a joy shall be bestowed upon them which no man shall take away from them.[9] He speaks of Himself as one having life in Himself, and imparting it to His followers, both individually and collectively, as to those who are with Him, and through Him, partakers of an eternal life. And this implies that the same may be predicated of the fellowship of His followers, of the Church united in Him, and founded according to His institution. In this sense He also very decidedly announces, though in the figurative manner which is in this case alone appropriate, a future perfect realization of the kingdom of God,[10] which, after the final exclusion—by means of a Divine interposition—of all who persevere in opposing it, is to enter upon an entirely new condition.[11] At the same time, however, He promises also to His believing people, who, until this consummation takes place, are still in

---

[1] John x. 18.
[2] John xvii. 5.
[3] John vi. 33, xi. 5.
[4] John xiv. 19.
[5] John xii. 26.
[6] John xvii. 24.
[7] Luke xvi. 9.
[8] John xiv. 2, 3.
[9] John xvi. 22, 23.
[10] Luke xiii. 21-30, and other places.
[11] Matt. xix. 28, xxvi. 29.

a state of warfare upon earth, that He will be with them always, even unto the end.[1]

We now proceed to inquire whether that which is thus testified and promised by the Lord Jesus, is not likewise the necessary result of this sinless holiness,—in other words, what is the relation borne by this doctrine to the subject now under consideration?

It is certain that not a few so-called Christians see in Christ nothing more than a historical personage, who lived more than eighteen centuries ago, who taught certain doctrines, and perhaps performed also certain unusual acts, but who—beyond what has been handed down to us concerning Him in this respect—does not stand in any very close and immediate relation to the present generation. In such a merely historical Christ, they who are really in earnest in their belief in His words, and sincerely His followers, do assuredly possess certain benefits. To them, however, may well be applied the saying, 'Why seek ye the living among the dead?' And if they will but observe somewhat more closely the Christ presented to us in the Gospels, they will be constrained to admit that He declares Himself to be—and that, if but the chief features of His character are correctly *drawn*, He *must* actually be—something very different from a past historical phenomenon. For the actual historical Christ, and especially the Being who proved Himself to be sinlessly holy, necessarily implies the *living* Christ, the ever *living*, ever *acting* Christ; and it is only when we admit this, that we really receive even the historical Christ, in the full completeness of all that is testified concerning Him.

If Jesus is sinless, and consequently the holy Son of God and Son of Man, as He declares Himself to be, He is one whose very existence is a pledge of *indestructible life* and

[1] Matt. xxviii. 20.

supreme *glory*. Even if He had not declared this, it is the necessary and direct result of His whole life. All that He said or did pointed to a heavenly order of things, and was pervaded by the powers of eternity. The wall of partition which conceals from us the invisible world had no existence for Him. On the contrary, as His life was one continuous intercourse with God, so did He constantly behold the eternal and imperishable, and live and act therein as in His proper element. Thus true life was not revealed by Him as something to come, but as something already present. And this life is, moreover, of such a nature, that not only is the thought of annihilation through death irreconcilably opposed thereto, but it can only be conceived of as, by virtue of its inherent power, eternal and victorious over death. The resurrection, too, and exaltation of Jesus, when viewed in their rightful connection with His character, cannot be regarded as events happening to Him merely through an external and miraculous interposition of God, but must also be looked upon as proceeding from His own intrinsic nature, as the normal development of that Divine and eternal life which was ever present in Him, as consequences which, when once the limitations of His earthly life were removed, were simply inevitable.

But He who is thus exalted by the power of that Divine life which dwells in Him, cannot be otherwise conceived of than as the *acting*. And if even during His earthly course His agency related to the whole human race, the sphere of its influence cannot be a more circumscribed one, now that the restrictions of His earthly existence are done away with. We must not picture it to ourselves as similar only to that exercised by all whose lives have produced powerful effects upon history. Such persons do indeed exercise a lasting influence by means either of their deeds or of their intellectual productions. This, however, is not a direct, a living, a personal influence, but an after effect, brought about by historical tradition, and separate from all present connection with their persons,—an effect which generally becomes weaker and weaker in proportion to the remoteness of the ages in which they lived. We cannot stop at such an influence as this when we contemplate the Lord Jesus. For although, with respect even to this kind of influence, whether its depth, its extent, or its duration be considered, He occupies the highest place, He yet, by virtue both of His Person and of the work He effected, lays claim also to one of an entirely different kind. Through His absolute self-surrender for the good of mankind, His perfect obedience, and His atoning death, He has become the royal *Head* of the human race, and that not merely in a figurative, but in a real and living sense; and we cannot conceive of a living Head which does not exercise a continual influence upon its members. But besides this, He is also the Son of God and Son of Man— proved to be such in all the conflicts of life—who was perfected through sufferings, and who has entered through death into glory. The fulness of the Divine life and nature which was in Him on earth, though restricted by human limitation, can now freely and perfectly develope itself; and in virtue of the exalted position which alone becomes Him, we are constrained to assume that His agency is also of a Divine kind, and therefore not limited by time or space, nor confined to ordinary means, but direct, personal, and everywhere present. It is only in this sense that Christ can be said to be ever living, and at the same time exercising a living agency; and that this is actually the case, is the necessary consequence of that perfect and uninterrupted communion with God, which, by means of His sinless holiness, He ever maintained.

But, again, we cannot conceive of the eternal life and continuous agency of the Head, unless the *members* also are partakers of eternal life, and susceptible of the influence of their Head. The very idea of a personal God, a Creator who is love, involves the admission that the personalities whom He has created, upon whom He has impressed His image, and whom He has invited to fellowship with Himself, are also designed for an eternal and perfect existence, and cannot be destined to be merely resolved into their natural elements by corporeal death. But the matter assumes an entirely different aspect when such personalities are also members of Christ, and have become intrinsically one with Him; and when, therefore, that life, the design and foundation of which was already within them, has actually begun to be realized. For if Christ has by His very nature eternal life in Himself, and if faith is that which, according to its primitive sense, it ought to be,—viz. the complete appropriation of the life of Christ by a perfect surrender to Him, so that He becomes the proper vital principle of every believer, —it then naturally follows that they who have entered into real fellowship with Him, are through Him made partakers of the same imperishable existence.

But least of all can we conceive of an exalted and eternally living Christ, really the Head of His believing people, but unpossessed of the power of bringing them into His glory, and continually losing them through death. It would be but a very poor compensation to say: He can continually be taking new members to Himself as the old ones die away. This would be to commit the folly of conceiving not only of a heavenly Head with merely earthly members, but also of an eternally living Head, with members in a continual state of coming and going, in a condition of perpetual change. It is quite as impossible to combine faith in an actually living Christ with the supposition of the continual dying off of His members, as it is to supplement the idea of a living and personal God with the notion of the annihilation of the human personalities whom He has called into existence. In the latter case, together with a belief in personal existence after death, we are compelled to surrender also our belief in a personal God, who is love, and to abandon ourselves, if not to atheism and materialism, yet to the pantheistic doctrine of a universal life, ever ceaselessly changing between birth and death. So likewise in the former case, the eternally living Christ must be transformed into one who had a merely past existence, the after effects of which have now entirely disappeared, and who is therefore a historical Christ only in a very limited sense, before it can be maintained that His followers are destined to perish. Either we must say, that as believers fall a prey to annihilation, this must also have been the case with Christ Himself, or that because He lives and reigns, they shall also live and reign with Him. He has made them partakers of the Divine nature. He has impressed upon them the image of His life, and thereby imparted to them eternal life also. For how could that be said to be a Divine nature which was absolutely perishable? And how could Christ be Himself the truly living One, if the highest effects which have proceeded from Him in forming personal beings were ever and again to be dissolved into nothingness?

What is true of the individual members of Christ holds good also of His members viewed collectively, of the *kingdom of God*, and its manifestation in the *Church*, which is the body of Christ. From the very first, it was not as an isolated individual that Christ received each man into His fellowship, but as one who was also destined to form a member in His body. And this relation can never cease, but must ever become more real and true. As the life of the individual is perfected in a higher state of existence by his being made partaker in ever-increasing fulness of the life of Christ, even so, and in equal measure, must the life of the community of

Christians be perfected, until the body of Christ is presented in perfect symmetry and beauty. We can never imagine a moment when the body should be left without its Head, or the kingdom without its King; but neither can we conceive of the Head existing without the body, or the King without His kingdom. If the kingdom of Christ, in virtue of the creative power which dwells in its Founder, has in Him a sure pledge of its ultimate perfection, then it has also in Him the assurance of an endless duration; and we have no alternative but either to deny that Christ is the true King of a real kingdom, or to regard Him as the immortal, eternally reigning King of His eternally triumphant Church.

If what has been advanced in this last part rests upon sound reasoning, Jesus is thus proved to be, in virtue of His sinlessness, the *One Being* in our whole race in whom Godhead and manhood are personally united, and in whom a man well-pleasing to God, a typical man, has appeared. And if by this very fact He has also perfectly revealed the nature and the will of God in so far as this was needed by the world of sinners, and effected a true reconciliation between them and the holy God; if He has at the same time established upon this foundation a kingdom of God among men, as the highest human community, and as the guardian of His saving benefits, and has assured to this community, and to every living member thereof, a life of eternal happiness and glory,—then has He also fulfilled all the conditions under which alone it was possible for man, separated as he was from God by sin, to be readmitted to blissful fellowship with Him, and has done this in that form in which alone it could be done, in a truly vital and really efficacious manner, in the form of personality, of personal example and personal intervention. A more exalted Being than one in whom Godhead and manhood were united is necessarily inconceivable. He is, and ever will be, supreme in matters of religion,

—'Jesus Christ, the same yesterday, to-day, and for ever.'[1] His mediatorial work cannot be surpassed, since the restoration of man to fellowship with God was actually effected thereby. Nor can it possibly be regarded as needing completion. It is a perfected and finished salvation continually offered, that it may be appropriated and lived upon by all who need it.

We have now arrived at that point which we at first designated as the end we had in view, and which we may now describe as the result of what has hitherto been stated. And this was to show that Christianity, of which Jesus Christ is the inalienable vital centre, and all whose essential elements are comprised in Him, is not merely *a* religion, which may have its own special advantages beside or above other religions, but that it is *the* religion in a supreme sense,—the perfect and exclusively Divine means and revelation of salvation; and that a supreme and satisfactory, though not the sole pledge that it is so, is offered by the sinless holiness of its Founder.

[1] Heb. xiii. 8.

CONCLUSION.

THE results at which we have now arrived are not only important in a theoretical, but also in a *practical*, point of view; and it is on this latter aspect of our subject that we now propose to add a few remarks.

When the Apostle Peter declares to the Gentile Cornelius [1] that, in every nation, he that feareth God and worketh righteousness is accepted of Him, this assertion implies, as the context plainly shows, not that every kind of worship and righteousness can in themselves render a man acceptable in the sight of God, but that it pleases God to receive into His kingdom, and into the fellowship of Christ, without respect to their former faith—whether they are Jews or Gentiles—all men in whom are found the necessary religious and moral conditions. St. Peter, like the other apostles, makes salvation depend, not on anything that man can offer by way of worship or righteousness, but upon Christ alone. This is unanswerably shown by his immediately following discourse, as well as by his other most express declaration, that 'there is salvation in none other, and none other name under heaven given among men, whereby we must be saved.' [2] In these very words is given the summary of all that our previous arguments are designed to prove.

If, then, the Person of Christ has this all-deciding importance with respect to the salvation both of the individual

[1] Acts x. 36.   [2] Acts iv. 12.

and the whole race, it is obvious that everything will depend upon the *position* occupied with respect to His Person. Evidently this position cannot be merely a matter of knowledge; it must, on the contrary, be a matter of the heart, the will, and the conscience, because that which concerns our supreme relation, our relation to God, claims not only our intellect, but our entire personality, and especially its moral centre.

To occupy no position at all with respect to the Person of Jesus, when once we have become acquainted with it, is simply impossible; for there is in the holy a power which can never be utterly inoperative; and man, even in his present sinful condition, is a moral being possessing an ineradicable tendency towards the Divine. As such, he is so constituted that he is incapable of remaining absolutely indifferent to that which is holy when he actually meets with it, or when it is powerfully brought to his knowledge. He can avert, or forcibly close, his spiritual eye; yet if but a ray of holy light penetrates his soul, he cannot possibly conduct himself as if there were no such thing in existence, but must necessarily take up some position with respect thereto.

And this position cannot, at least for a continuance, be a neutral or an undecided one. The Lord, indeed, when He says, 'He that is not against us, is on our side,'[1] seems to assert the opposite, viz. that conduct which just stops short of being inimical, deserves a certain amount of approbation. This saying, however, refers solely to the external following of Christ in combination with His disciples,—to the relation maintained to Christianity viewed in its corporate aspect. Where, however, the far more important and internal relation of the individual to the Person of Christ is concerned, that testing and severing saying, 'He that is not with me is against me, and he that gathereth not

[1] Matt. ix. 40.

with me scattereth abroad,'[1] applies. The very nature of the case makes it impossible that it should be otherwise. In presence of the holy and the Divine, the human soul has no other alternative than for or against, affection or dislike; a joyful acceptance of the benefits therein offered, or a repellent withdrawal into itself, followed by an ever-increasing aversion, which at last becomes open enmity. Thus did the manifestation of Jesus, even during His earthly career, act with a dividing effect upon all hearts and minds, and reveal their inmost thoughts and dispositions; thus, to this very day, does it, wherever it is faithfully testified to, irresistibly compel a decision. This decision may indeed be delayed or postponed; the soul of man may hesitate between the Holy One of God and the world; but a decision must at last take place; and if it is not made by an express resolution of the will, a continuance of not being *with* Christ is in itself a being *against* Him, and must inevitably manifest itself to be such with more and more distinctness.

But in what does being *with* and *for* Him really consist? Not in a merely æsthetic approbation of His character, but in a hearty love of His Person. If this is indeed in us, we shall be willing, first of all, to allow ourselves to be convinced of, and thoroughly humbled for, our sins by Him, the Holy One, and shall then surrender ourselves in perfect confidence to Him who is also the Son, full of grace and truth, and willingly and thankfully accept at His hands the gifts of forgiveness, life, and salvation, which He offers without our merits or deservings. But this is nothing else than what is called *believing in Him*. And thus the only rightful position which we can occupy towards Christ, the position all-decisive with respect to our own salvation, is that of

---

[1] Matt. xii. 30; Luke xi. 23. On the mutual relation of these seemingly contradictory sayings, see my article in the *deutschen Zeitschrift*, 1851, Nos. III. and IV., especially p. 29, etc.

faith. But faith thus understood can be none other than a living faith, fruitful in all good works. For when a man thus wholly surrenders himself to Christ, Christ really imparts Himself to him: such a one receives the life of Christ into himself, and lets himself be ruled by Christ's Spirit. And where the Spirit of Christ is, His love is shed abroad in the heart; and the works of this love naturally follow. From such a faith there is no need to require good works: 'Neither does it inquire whether good works are to be done; but before they are asked for, it has done, and is ever doing them.'[1]

Let him who refuses this faith clearly understand what such refusal involves. There is, as we have seen, no neutral ground to which he can retire. In his, as in every case, there will at last arise the necessity of deciding for or against. He, too, will be compelled either to open his heart, by trustful self-surrender and humility, to the Holy One of God, or to close it against Him; and having turned away from Him, to seek salvation—if indeed he still feels himself in need of it —in ways of his own devising. If, however, he decides for the latter, he should do so with a clear knowledge of the full significance of his choice. Perhaps he may think it possible to give up Christ, the Son of God and Redeemer of the world, and to retain the pure and holy Son of Man as an example. This, however, is not possible; for it is the pure and perfect Son of Man who testifies of Himself that He is the Son of God, the Mediator, the alone source of salvation. Besides, it is precisely His pure and perfect manhood which leads, by an inward necessity, to His Divine dignity, and to the truth and reality of His redeeming work, and which involves and furnishes the surest guarantee of both. In short, we cannot have the one without the other. For

[1] The well-known words of Luther, in the excellent passage on faith, in his Preface to the Epistle to the Romans.

when we have set aside the Son of God and the Redeemer of the world, there is no longer a place for the holy Son of Man. Then the only perfectly pure specimen of humanity is taken out of its midst, and its whole process of development lacks that central point after which it is ever striving, and from which, when it is once obtained, it receives its deepest, its creative impulse. Then all previous hopes and aspirations that a true man, a man as God had willed him, would one day really appear, have been but an empty delusion; all faith that such a one has really appeared—a faith which has made men strong in life, and joyful in death—has been childish folly. Then the heart of man may look in vain in the midst of its sorrows for a Divine, a holy, but also a truly human heart, which it can entirely trust, to which it can unreservedly surrender itself, and from which it may receive full comfort and perfect peace, in life and in death.

Of him who, on the contrary, inclines to this faith, it demands that he should embrace it with his whole heart, and in the full extent of its requirements. The Redeemer will not be satisfied with a divided heart. He who gave Himself wholly to us, desires that we also should give ourselves wholly to Him. He who receives Him, must do so in a manner suited to His sacred dignity,—must accept from Him that which He is willing to bestow. For He is not here to be fashioned and formed according to the desires and fancies of those who need His salvation, but they must let themselves be formed and fashioned, or rather transformed and refashioned, in their inmost nature and being, by Him, and thus become recipients of the true basis of all true and exalted human progress. Neither is it His will that faith should be timidly concealed in the inner sanctuary of the heart. He would have it gladly confessed before men, and shining forth like a bright light from the whole walk and conversation.¹ He, moreover, who is with Christ, must also 'gather' with Him; that is, he must diligently promote the interests of His kingdom, and lend his aid to propagate more and more widely the saving and cleansing virtue which proceeds from Christ. Not one special class alone is called to this work. All believers must, after the example of the one High Priest, offer spiritual sacrifices, both in their actions and persons, and show forth the praises of Him who hath called them out of darkness into His marvellous light.² Only in proportion as this general Christian duty is fulfilled, in addition to the regular agency of those who are officially called to spread the knowledge of Christ, will the whole fellowship continue to grow up into *Him* who is the Head; only thus will be laid the foundation of a faith realized and perfected in Him, and the life of the sinless and Holy One be, by means of this faith, increasingly imparted to mankind.

[1] Matt. x. 32, and v. 16. [2] 1 Pet. ii. 5, 9.

SUPPLEMENTS.

I.

THE HISTORY AND LITERATURE OF THE SUBJECT.

THE great importance of the sinlessness of Jesus, with regard both to Christian faith and to that impression thereof which we designate doctrine, has at no time been ignored. The attention paid to it, however, by Christian teachers and theologians, has been by no means uniform. The importance of the fact, and its manifold consequences, have not been at all times equally perceived, while its relation to other elements of Christianity has been variously estimated, and its treatment has been undertaken with different purposes and in different manners.

A complete statement of the various ways and modes in which the dogma of the sinlessness of Jesus has in different ages been viewed, proved, and applied, carried out with relation to the whole course of development which doctrine and practice have gone through in the Church, might well form the subject of a separate treatise of no slight interest. Such an undertaking would far transcend our limits. We feel, however, that it is due to our subject to follow up the allusions given in the Introduction by a few general outlines, and especially to make the notice there given of its literature more complete.

History and Literature of the Subject. 255

To the Christians of the *apostolic* age, and to the most distinguished of the apostles, the sinless perfection of their Master was an inalienable element, nay, a fundamental factor, of their faith in Him as the Messiah sent by God, the Son of God and Son of Man, the Reconciler and Redeemer of mankind. With them it was not a subject of reflection. They merely reproduced in very decided and pregnant statements the impression which Jesus had in this respect made upon themselves, and plainly indicated the inseparable connection existing in their eyes between His sinlessness and other elements of Christianity, especially the atoning and priestly agency of Christ.

In the further development of the doctrine of Christ within the Church, this apostolic view of the subject continued to prevail. A more explicit reference to the doctrine of the sinlessness of Jesus, especially in its historical bearings, was nowhere attempted; because it was regarded as an absolutely self-evident fact, and as an article of belief essentially interwoven with the whole organism of the Christian religion. But as soon as the doctrine of the Person of Christ began to be more fully elaborated, this article of belief was most prominently brought forward.[1] We find this already in the writings of Irenæus and Tertullian, of Clement and Origen.[2] But they give the subject a different form and position.

---

[1] The first writer who uses the technical expression ἀναμάρτητος with reference to Christ is Hippolytus (*Galandii Biblioth.* ii. 466). Then we find the term repeatedly employed by Clement of Alexandria; still he uses also the word ἀνεπιθύμητος (*Stromat.* vii. 12),—a word which, more than the other, has reference to the inward state.

[2] It would lead us too much into detail were we to give all the passages of the fathers referred to. The reader may consult Duncker's *Christologie des Irenæus*, S. 219 ff.; Hagenbach, *Dogmen-geschichte*, B. i. § 67; and Baumgarten-Crusius' *Dogmen-geschichte*, vol. ii. p. 162. Suicer also, in his *Thesaurus Ecclesiasticus*, gives a tolerably complete collection of passages from the fathers under the words ἀναμαρτησία, ἀναμάρτητος — vol. i. pp. 287–289.

Generally the difference is this: either the sinlessness of Christ is inferred from His Divinity, as by Tertullian; or it is regarded, as by Origen, as a peculiar property of the human soul of Jesus,—a property resulting from a free undisturbed love of all that was Divine and good, and making that soul capable and worthy of perfect union with the Divine, eternal Logos.

In the *Christology* of Apollinaris this doctrine has a peculiar import attached to it. He proceeded from the belief that along with human nature there is always mutability and change in the moral life, gradual development, conflict, and therefore sin: in his view, it is impossible to conceive of a complete man without sin. But as, according to his own belief, the Redeemer of men must Himself be free from all sin, nay, elevated above all conflict therewith, he was thus led to form the opinion, that in Christ the Divine and eternal Logos had taken the place of the necessarily vacillating and sinful human soul. This Logos being in itself immutable and self-determined, is thus supposed to have imparted to every action and emotion of Christ an irresistible tendency towards the holy and the Divine, and to have raised Him above all conflict with sin. Now even if by the adoption of this view the doctrine of the sinlessness of Christ seems to be placed upon a firmer basis, an evident injury is thereby done to another most vital doctrine, namely, that of the perfect humanity of Christ, and the truth of His typical character as a real man; because both these truths rest upon the assumption of a rational human soul in Christ.

Hence the importance of holding fast the doctrine of Christ's sinlessness along with that of His true human nature. Both were fully recognised by Athanasius, who directed attention to the fact that sin, although found by experience to be really present in all mankind, yet belongs not to human nature in itself considered, whose original state was, on the contrary, a state of sinlessness. Hence it was possible for Christ to take upon Him the whole nature of man, without thereby becoming subject to sin; nay, He must have done so, in order that He might thus show that it was possible for one who is entirely human to preserve himself free from sin. Since His time, both truths have continued to be recognised in the Church—the perfect manhood of Christ, and His absolute sinlessness. In the creed of Chalcedon (451) this doctrine first found expression as an article of faith. In this creed, while testimony is at the same time borne to His proper Divinity, Christ is spoken of as 'truly man, with a rational soul and body, of like essence with us as to His manhood, and in all things like us, *sin excepted.*'

This settled the doctrine, at least within the domain of the Church; and no important change of opinion with respect to it afterwards took place. It now became more a subject of *theological* discussion, although it was not treated in a comprehensive spirit until modern times.

In the *Middle Ages*, theologians were content to abide by the decisions of the Church; but at the same time they fully recognised the importance of the subject. The Schoolmen indeed allowed, that if the human soul of Jesus were viewed independently, and its union with the Divine Logos left out of the question, the *possibility* of His sinning could not be denied.[1] On the other hand, however, the fact of His perfect sinlessness was most expressly acknowledged. This feature was prominently brought forward as a thoroughly essential one in the character of Jesus from the most opposite quarters,[2] and we may regard it as not improbable that, in

[1] Peter Lombard says, *Lib. sent.* iii. 12: *Non est ambiguum, animam illam entem unitam verbo peccare non posse, et eandem, si esset et non unita verbo, posse peccare.*

[2] This was to be expected in the case of theologians. I will here name only two poets: Otfried von Weissenburg, who, in his *Poetical Version of the Gospels*, iii. 21, 4, uses the expression, ther *suntiloso* man, concerning

the well-known controversy of the Thomists and the Scotists about the immaculate conception of the Virgin, one chief point of interest for the defenders of that tenet was, by proving the perfect original purity of the mother of our Lord, to establish that also of the Saviour Himself. But this dogma was damaging to the position of Christ in another aspect. For hitherto Christ alone, according to apostolic testimony, had been regarded as free from all sin, hereditary sin included. Now, however, this quality began to be attributed to His mother; and thus not only was the uniqueness of Christ in this respect done away with, but His dignity as the world's Redeemer was impugned, together with the indissoluble connection between the work of redemption and absolute sinlessness. For if there really existed a human being besides, nay, before Him, entirely unaffected by sin, the necessity of being redeemed and sanctified by Christ would be no longer absolute and universal. Consequently His position as Redeemer would be lowered; and though this took place *in fact* only at a single point, yet in principle the whole doctrine would be affected. That this was the case was immediately felt and expressed. At the very first appearance even of the dogma of the immaculate conception, St. Bernhard despatched an epistle to the Canonist of Lyon, who had about the year 1400 introduced a new festival in honour of this doctrine, in which, among other things, he says: 'If it is given to some few of the sons of men to be *born* in holiness, it is not given them to be thus *conceived*, that thus this pre-eminence of holy conception might continue to be His *alone* who was to sanctify all, and who *alone coming into the world with-*

Christ; and Dante, in whose view Christ is like Himself alone, and who on this account never makes his name rhyme with any word but itself, nor permits it to be uttered in hell on account of its supreme dignity, says, *Inferno*, xxxiv. 114, 15, 'Where the man who was born and lived without sin, perished.'

out sin, was to effect the purification of sinners.' In a similar manner do several other excellent authorities express themselves; among whom we may specially name the Dominican John of Montesono, who, in 1367, published at Paris several theses on this controversy.[1] The movement, however, continued, and an increasingly idolatrous honouring of the Virgin prevailed, until at last, in our own days, though not without a partial protest by the more pious and enlightened of Romish theologians, the dogma of the immaculate conception was formally promulgated by the Roman see.

While the theology of the Middle Ages continued in theory unwaveringly faithful to the decisions of the apostolic, and the ancient Church concerning the Person of Christ, a corruption of another kind set in; not, in the first instance, within the sphere of theology, but in that of the Church and of Christian life generally. Christ, while strictly adhered to doctrinally, began to disappear from Christian consciousness as a living, directly operating personality, and as the only medium of salvation. The Church, with its mediation of priests, put Him more and more into the background, while His pretended earthly representative usurped His place. The chief merit of the *Reformers* consisted in restoring the Divine and human Person of Christ to its central position as the one only ground of salvation, and re-establishing the direct character of the relation of believers to Him, and, through Him, to God the Father. They did this, because they felt Christ present to their inmost soul in His Divine

---

[1] These may be found in Dupin's edition of the works of Gerson, vol. i. p. 693. In thesis x. it is said, 'It is expressly contrary to our faith to hold that *any* except Christ has been born free from original sin;' and in thesis xii., 'It is as contrary to Holy Scripture to say that *one* human being besides Christ is excepted from original sin, as to say that ten are.' In thesis ix., moreover, it is laid down as a general axiom, that, 'to declare anything true which is contrary to Scripture, is most expressly contrary to our faith.'

and human dignity, in His redeeming and saving power; and they sought for no further proof of that which was to them a second nature, and which was confirmed and sealed by the word of God and the testimony of His Spirit. They received the doctrine concerning Christ as set forth by the Church,—the Church universally Christian and truly catholic; and since the sinlessness of Christ formed an essential part of that doctrine, we find it also enunciated in their writings.[1] A minute discussion of it would, however, have been at variance with their spirit; to them it was not a matter requiring proof, but an immediate certainty, far removed above all controversy. As soon, however, as evangelical doctrine was formed into a systematic whole, this dogma had to undergo a more thorough discussion. This is first found in the writings of the dogmaticians of the second generation after the Reformation;[2] and not less so in those of subsequent systematizers, particularly in works on doctrinal and on moral theology. But it is in modern times that the subject has been most prominently brought forward, owing to the growing consciousness of the extreme importance of the doctrine of sinlessness in treating of Christology, and indeed of Christianity in general.[3]

[1] *E.g.* by Luther in the Larger Catechism.

[2] See Schmid, *Dogmatik der ev. luth. Kirche*, pp. 231, 236; and Hase, *Hutt. rediv.* § 96, p. 226, 7th ed.

Among the works of the older Protestant theologians the following may be specially noticed:—Gerhard, *Loc. theol.* Pt. iii. p. 237; and Buddeus, *Compend. theol. dogm.* § 497. Among modern writings in which the doctrine is briefly or extensively treated, may be mentioned:—Doederlein, *Institut.* ii. pp. 206, etc.; Zacharias, *bibl. Theologie*, Pt. iii. pp. 38–46; Töllner's *theolog. Untersuchungen*, vol. i. Pt. ii.; Reinhard's *Dogmatik*, § 91; Bretschneider's *Dogmat.* vol. ii. §§ 135, 138; Wegscheider, *Institut.* § 122, pp. 446, 447, 7th ed.; Knapp's *Vorlesungen*, Pt. ii. § 93, p. 151; Schleiermacher's *christl. Glaube*, Pt. ii., in the whole section concerning Christ, especially pp. 39 and 86 of the 2d ed.; De Wette's *christl. Sittenlehre*, Pt. i. pp. 173–193, and *Wesen des christl. Glaubens*, § 53; Nitzsch, *System der christlichen Lehre*, § 129; Rothe, *Theolog. Ethik.* vol. i. § iii. p. 279, etc.— Remarks on the subject will also be found in Daub's *Judas Iscarioth*, No. I.

And nothing has done more to awaken this conviction than the *doubts* which have arisen in recent times upon this subject, even within the domain of Christian belief and of theology. Indeed the development of the doctrine which we have sketched above had not been carried far enough for the sinlessness of Christ to be at once recognised by all men, at all times, as a perfectly unquestionable fact. As early as the ages of ancient Christianity, we see suspicions arising and limitations adduced in isolated instances.[1] But it is in modern times that we first find the doctrine an object of decided and detailed attack. And here we have not so much in view the application—made with greater or less directness against the sinlessness of Christ—of the position, that Christ did actually share our sinful flesh;[2] we rather refer to the direct calling in question of sinlessness as a possibility and as a fact, as it has been called in question by rationalism, both deistic and pantheistic.[3]

pp. 55, 64, 73; and Steudel's *Grundzügen einer Apologetik*, pp. 56, etc. It is also discussed in Steudel's *Glaubenslehre der evangelisch-protestant-Kirche*, Tüb. 1834, pp. 233–245; in Sack's *christl. Apologetik*, 2d ed. p. 201, etc.; Hase's *Leben Jesu*, pp. 23, 32; and Jul. Müller's *christl. Lehre von der Sünde*, 3d ed., in various places. Among the latest works, compare the doctrinal writings of Grimm, Schweizer, Lange, Schoeberlein, Liebner, and Martensen; *die biblische Dogm.* of Lutz, pp. 293–299; Dorner's *Entwickelungsgeschichte der Lehre von der Person Christi*; and Schumann's *Christus*, vol. i. pp. 284–297.

[1] Basilides, the Gnostic, appears to have been the first who entertained doubts concerning this doctrine. He even applied to Christ, as man, the maxim that every one who suffers, does so as an expiation for his *own* sins. Yet he shrinks from charging Jesus with actual sin, and places Him, in this respect, on a level with children, who suffer indeed, not on account of sins committed, but because of the inclination to sin existing in them,— because of the ἁμαρτητικόν. Clemens, *Strom.* iv. 12; Neander, *gnost. Syst.* pp. 49–53. Arius and Theodore of Mopsveste admit only the moral perfection of Christ in a more limited sense. See Baumgarten-Crusius, *Dogmengeschichte*, ii. p. 164, note 1.

[2] See on this subject the note on p. 125.

[3] The Wolfenbüttel Fragmentist is, with respect to our subject, the advocate of the former; Strauss, in his *Glaubenslehre*, vol. ii. pp. 190, etc., of the latter. Pécaut, whose still more recent work has been already so

These doubts, based as they were, not only upon historical and critical, but upon very decided and utterly negative doctrinal prepossessions, assailed the very heart of Christianity; and there could not fail to be a reaction against them from the Christian side. If, in former times, the moral character of Christ had often been the subject of special discussion, this was now of necessity much more the case; and we find a whole series of single works upon this subject, with direct reference to the question of sinlessness.[1] But not only were more numerous works thus called forth,

frequently alluded to, may also be mentioned as belonging to the deistic side.

[1] Among works entirely devoted to this subject are the following:— Walther, *Dissert. theol. de Christi hominis ἀναμαρτησίᾳ*, Viteb. 1690, and *Dissert. de dissimilit. ortus nostri et Christi hom.*, in his *Dissertatt. theol.* ed. Hoffmann, Viteb. 1753, pp. 207-244; Hoevel, *de ἀναμαρτησίᾳ Christi ejusque necessitate*, Hal. 1741, *recusa* 1749, 37, p. 4—(this treatise, whose author, Carl Ludwig Hoevel, is a pupil of Baumgarten, is strictly orthodox, and written with much scholastic acuteness. It follows Wolf's method of demonstration, and bases the sinlessness of Jesus upon the *unio personalis* of the Divine and human natures. In the first part the necessity of this doctrine is laid down; in the second it is defended against objections);— Erbstein, *Gedanken über die Frage ob der Erlöser sündigen konnte?* Meissen 1787—(this work denies the possibility, in opposition to Doederlein, *Instit.* § 234);—*Ueber die Anamartesie Jesu*, in Grimm's and Muzel's *Stromata*, Pt. ii. pp. 113, etc.; Ph. A. Stapfer, *Versuch eines Beweises der göttlichen Sendung und Würde Jesu aus seinem Charakter*, Berne 1797; and in French in the collection of Stapfer's writings recently published at Paris—(it contains a very spirited and eloquent description of the moral manifestation of Jesus, and such inferences therefrom of His Divine dignity as were not easily drawn in that period of rationalism);—J. L. Ewald, *über die Grösse Jesu und ihrem Einfluss auf seine Sittenlehre*, Hanover 1798; also his *erste Forts. Beantwort. verschied. Einwürfe*, Gera 1799; M. Weber, *Progr. Virtutis Jesu integritatem neque ex ipsius professionibus neque ex actionibus doceri posse*, Viteb. 1796; and in his *Opusc. Acad.* pp. 179-192—(Weber, while firmly adhering to the sinlessness of Jesus, insists upon grounding this doctrine solely on the inspired testimony of the apostles, and thus of God Himself, who, as knowing the heart, can alone pronounce authoritatively in this case);—Fr. von Meyer, *war Jesus Christus der Sünde fähig?* in the *Blättern für höhere Wahrheit*, new series, 2d collection, Berlin 1831, pp. 198-208; J. G. Rätze, *die Heiligkeit und die Wunderthaten als die höchsten und genügenden Beglaubigungsgründe der Gottheit des Welterlösers*, Zittau and

History and Literature of the Subject. 263

—there was also a more acute apprehension of the idea of sinlessness, and a more profound investigation of the questions involved in it. Nevertheless, two distinct modes of treatment were followed; some theologians dealing with the subject in a manner purely doctrinal, while others, taking it up chiefly in its historical aspect, used it also in the interest of apologetic aims. In the former aspect, the influence of Schleiermacher in itself marks a fresh era. He, as is well known, defines Christianity as fundamentally a

Leipsic 1834—(it is possible that miracles, inasmuch as they differ from the ordinary phenomena of nature, may be doubted both on historical and philosophic grounds; but such doubts are extinguished by the holiness of Christ's Person and life. A holiness manifested by precept and example, and in accordance with the religious and moral ideals of reason, is its own best credential; and they who deny it, would at the same time deny the consciousness of the Divine existence and the moral law);—Al. Schweizer, *über die Dignität des Religionstifters*, in the *theol. Stud. und Kritik*. 1834, No. III. pp. 521-571; No. IV. pp. 813-849—(Schweizer here endeavours to prove, in a speculative way, the necessity of the absolute religious perfection, the infallibility and sinlessness of Christ, from the notion and nature of the Founder of *that* religion which is to be the religion of the whole human race);—Christ. Frid. Fritzsche, *de ἀναμαρτησίᾳ Jesu Christi Commentationis*, iv., Hal. 1835-37—(the author criticises the treatises on the Sinlessness of Jesus by three theologians of Halle, viz. Hoevel, Weber, and myself, and makes objections against those of the first and last. An answer will be found in the *theol. Stud. und Kritik*. 1842-3);—Hase, *Streitschriften*, No. III. 1837, pp. 105-114—(an excellent and acute refutation of rationalistic objections);—Guil. Naumann, *Dissert. de Jesu Christo ab animi affectibus non immuni*, Lips. 1840; Gotth. Ferd. Doehner, *de dictis aliquot Jesu Christi quæ ἀναμαρτησίαν ejus infringere videantur*, Zwiccau 1840—(the contents of these two works are cited and condemned in an article by Theile, *Litt. Blatt. der allgem. K. Zeitung*, Feb. 1841, Nos. XIX. XX. XXI.);—Theile, *über die sittliche Erhabenheit Jesu allg. K. Zeitung*, June 1841, Nos. XCII. XCIII. XCIV.—(a good description of the typical nature of the character of Christ, and of its significance for Christianity).—Remarks referring to our subject will also be found in Käuffer's *Jesus Christus unser Vorbild*, Dresden 1845, especially p. 98, etc. An article in Swedish against my views, by Prof. Thomander of Lund, in the quarterly paper edited by himself and Reuterdahl, unfortunately did not come to my notice till it was out of print. I am, however, able to refer to a more detailed review by Prof. Van Oordt, in the Gröningen journal, *Waarheid in Liefde*, 1838, No. I. pp. 117-224, especially pp. 218 sq.

system of redemption, and makes redemption consist essentially in the communication of the sinlessness of the Redeemer. In doing this, however, he not only specially vindicated, for the doctrine of Christ's sinlessness, a position which, however modified, will still retain its importance; but he gave to the discussion of this doctrine an impulse which has caused the feature of sinlessness in the character of Jesus to be regarded, in general, in a manner totally different from that in which it had hitherto been viewed, and has placed this essential trait in a point of view more particularly apologetic. The manner in which it has been treated in more modern times, in this latter aspect, need not, after what has been stated in the Introduction and notes, be further alluded to here.

II.

THE DIFFERENT VIEWS HELD WITH RESPECT TO THE TEMPTATION.

THE object of the brief notice given in the Treatise, of the history of the temptation, was principally to point out the relation between the fact of our Saviour being tempted and His sinlessness. We endeavoured to show what aspect this relation bears, as seen from the various points of view occupied by those who have discussed the two subjects; and with this purpose we referred even to those opinions which present the greatest difficulty. But what was there said would be insufficient and unsatisfactory without a further investigation of the whole subject. We subjoin, accordingly, an examination of the various expositions of this passage,[1] and

[1] The most recent literature on the subject of the temptation has been given above, p. 130, to which may be added Riggenbach's *Lectures on the*

supply a fuller vindication of the view which, in our opinion, deserves the preference.

Everywhere in the Bible the exposition of the details, and the view to be taken of the whole, reciprocally modify each other; and this is especially the case with reference to the passage before us. But while, as is evident, the details can be fully understood only by a correct appreciation of the whole, there is a great danger of allowing one's self to be influenced in fixing the meaning of the separate histories by a predetermined conclusion on the import of the whole narrative. That we may avoid this danger, and pursue the safest course, we shall first state what can with certainty be determined with regard to the details, and then proceed to the general history, that thus justice may be done to both, by a due consideration of their mutual relation.

CHAPTER I.

EXPLANATION OF THE DETAILS.

In the first place, there arises the question as to the *meaning of the several temptations*. This has, as is well known, been made the theme of frequent discussion. And yet the opinions even of the most recent commentators differ so widely, that it may well repay our trouble if we submit this point to a more minute investigation.

The temptation which both Matthew and Luke agree in giving as the *first*, consists in the call addressed to Jesus to

---

Life of Christ, pp. 271-286. More information may be found in Hase's *Life of Jesus*, and De Wette's *Exegetical Handbook*. Specially rich in literary notices is a treatise in the (Catholic) Tübinger *Quartalschrift*, 1828, 1 and 2.

change stones into bread. Now it is self-evident that such a temptation, if it were to have any meaning, could only be made under certain conditions. Manifestly the person to whom it was addressed must, on the one hand, have been so constituted that he could feel a want of food, which at that moment could not be gratified in any ordinary way; and again, he must have been one who was supposed to possess the power of satisfying that want in an extraordinary and miraculous manner. Now, to the former of these conditions, the intimation of the evangelist, that Jesus was then an hungered, and that He was in the desert, where the ordinary means of support were wanting, exactly corresponds; the latter, again, we find in the opening words of the temptation, 'If Thou be the Son of God,' which at once bespeak a personality possessed of supernatural powers. Hence this temptation may be represented as follows: it was an attempt to persuade a person endowed with miraculous power, to use that power for the purpose of satisfying his bodily wants; and the point against which this attempt was directed, was the urgent physical need which he was at the time suffering. It is obvious that the need which the miraculous power was to supply was that of *the person tempted;* for though it has been remarked[1] that this is not expressly stated, yet this omission is of no importance,—a matter so self-evident requiring no mention, and being sufficiently implied by the previous allusion to the fact that Jesus was an hungered. For whose wants could even Jesus have wrought a miracle at this juncture but *for His own?* Is it replied, For those of the members of His kingdom, or of the needy multitude in general? There were as yet no members of His kingdom, and neither a smaller or greater number of people were just now at hand. Besides, if the temptation had related to such

[1] Pfeiffer, *die Versuchung des Herrn* in the *Deutschen Zeitschrift*, 1851, No. XXII. p. 177.

a supply, our Lord did not remain faithful to the principle with which He repelled it, for the Gospel history narrates several instances in which He relieved the temporal necessities of the people in a miraculous manner.

We now proceed to a closer inquiry as to the manner in which Jesus met the proposal. We may anticipate that His answer will throw some light upon the nature of the temptation itself. But here we are met by several conflicting opinions. The retort of Jesus is expressed in words taken from Deut. viii. 3: 'Man doth not live by bread alone, but by every word that proceedeth out of the mouth of the Lord doth man live.' The majority of commentators understand the meaning of these words to be this: The preservation of the life of man is not necessarily connected with the ordinary means of subsistence, but it can be sustained without bread by the word, *i.e.* commandment, that proceeds from the mouth of God, in an extraordinary way, as the Israelites were sustained by manna in the wilderness.[1] This explanation does certainly correspond with the meaning of the words as they occur in Deuteronomy, taken along with their context. Yet we have good ground for asking whether we are restricted to this meaning alone when the words are reproduced by Jesus Christ. There can be no doubt that Jesus and His apostles often made use of passages of the Old Testament in a freer and a spiritual sense,—that they frequently gave them a more general application, and raised them altogether into a higher sphere. And there is reason enough to suppose that this is the case in the passage before us.

In the explanation usually given, a special import is attached to the fact that Jesus was requested to make in a miraculous manner, not any kind of food, but only *bread*, for the satisfaction of His hunger. But this is clearly incor-

See Neander in his *Life of Christ*, fifth ed. p. 115.

rect. The question is not as to His appeasing His hunger by means of *bread* in particular, but as to His doing so by *any means*, and as to His employing miraculous agency for that purpose. Among the various kinds of food by which this might have been effected, bread is mentioned, partly as being the most general and symbolical of all other nourishment, and partly on account of the resemblance of loaves to the stones which were to be transformed into bread. The antithesis is certainly not between bread and any other means of supporting life, but between it and the word of God; in other words, between the means of *bodily* nourishment (actual bread) and the means of *spiritual* nourishment (every word that proceedeth out of the mouth of God; in other words, the bread of life). Again, the words, 'not by bread alone,' in that higher application of them as used by our Lord to repel the temptation now presented to Him, are not to be understood of bread merely as bread, but of bodily nourishment, as that to which man is not to be exclusively referred for the maintenance of life, in opposition to that which imparts spiritual life. Thus, when Jesus is asked by the tempter to make His power to do miracles available for supplying His physical wants, to use the higher, God-given faculty in the service of mere human self-gratification, He replies, in a spirit of freedom and self-denial which triumphs over the merely sensible want: No; for there is a higher life which is not upheld by any outward nourishment, but which lives by all that comes from the mouth of God. In these words He says essentially the same thing which He afterwards expressed thus: 'My meat is to do the will of Him that sent me, and to finish His work.'[1]

The temptation which in St. Luke occupies the third place, is—more correctly, as there can be no doubt—placed *second* in St. Matthew. This, as well as the former, has been

[1] John iv. 34.

variously explained. This temptation consisted in a summons addressed to Christ to cast Himself from the pinnacle of the temple, and, like the first, is based upon the assumption of a peculiar personality in Jesus; in other words, it presupposes that the Tempted was, as the 'Son of God,'—the Sent of God,—under the special care and protection of Jehovah. Many have supposed that Jesus was here asked to perform an *epideiktical miracle,—a show miracle*. In favour of this view there is adduced not only the character of the miracle demanded, which is something quite exorbitant, but the fact that the contemporaries of Jesus did actually require from Him, in corroboration of His Divine mission, signs from Heaven. We must, however, decidedly reject this interpretation, although we formerly held it to be the correct one.[1] In the first place, it is clear that, in order to an epideiktical miracle, spectators who should be sensibly overpowered by the manifestation were indispensable, whereas throughout the whole scene we do not read of any one being present. There is, also, another consideration to be borne in mind: when the tempter calls upon Jesus to throw Himself down from the temple because God would protect Him by His angels, it is not so much to the wonder-working power of Jesus Himself that he appeals, as to the miraculous help of God. His proposition is not that Jesus should perform some unheard-of miracle, but that He should expose Himself to an evident danger. If in this temptation also the chief stress is placed upon the employment of miraculous power, there would, since this formed the turning-point of the first temptation, be nothing really new in it, but a mere repetition, though in an aggravated form. But this view of the temptation is best refuted by the passages from Scripture employed on the occasion, whether that by which the tempter supported

[1] Compare on this subject Kohlschütter in the *bibl. Studien der sächs. Geistlichkeit*, ii. 75, 76.

his demand,[1] or that by which the Saviour repelled it.[2] The former contains not a trace of allusion to any popular approbation to be gained by the performance of a miracle, but solely to the Divine protection, under which the Beloved of Jehovah stood. The latter gives not even a remote hint of the impropriety of a miracle for such a purpose, but only points out how impious it would be to tempt God by throwing one's self needlessly in the way of danger.

The enticing element in this temptation was the idea of *calling forth the Divine protection*,—of proving whether God would preserve His anointed Son in circumstances of most imminent danger, and that a danger which did not come in the simple, God-appointed path of duty, but was arbitrarily and vaingloriously incurred.[3] There can be no doubt that a temptation like this has a certain charm for men who feel penetrated with a consciousness that they have a special mission to perform; and many a one whom an idea like this has blinded, has precipitated himself from very exalted pinnacles into the abyss of perdition. Thus the attempt might well be made with Jesus,—who, though pre-eminently the Sent of God, was yet truly man,—to test whether the thought of putting the Divine protection to the utmost proof had any attraction for Him; and this attempt constitutes the second temptation. In it we have vividly brought before us the contrast between a true and sound confidence in God, by virtue of which even one who is conscious of a Divine mission will walk in none but ways of God's appointment, and that rash presumption, by which a man is misled, while invoking the Divine protection, to rush into self-chosen danger.

We have now to speak of the *third* temptation. This is

---

[1] Ps. xci. 11, 12.   [2] Deut. vi. 16.
[3] This is essentially the view of Neander; but he mingles with it, in what seems to me an unfitting manner, the notion of an epideiktical miracle. *Leben Jesu*, pp. 116, 117.

rightly put last by St. Matthew, for it obviously forms the climax of the whole, and in it the tempter appears in an undisguised form. The devil calls upon the Saviour to worship him, and promises that, if He does so, he will give Him all the kingdoms of the world. The temptation here has been generally held to consist in the invitation to found an *earthly* kingdom,—an external theocracy, instead of the true inner kingdom of God which Christ had come to establish. But another view has also been maintained. It has been said that the question whether the kingdom to be founded should be an earthly and external, or a heavenly and spiritual one, is not introduced into the temptation; that, on the contrary, the seductive element really lay in the fact that, for the acquirement of a sway which might in itself be good, a bad means, a submission to Satan, a doing homage to him, was to be employed.[1] This exposition is correct, if we are to confine our view to the words spoken by Satan. But this we cannot do: we must contemplate these words in the connection in which they stand, and under the supposition from which they are spoken. Immediately before, we read that Satan had shown our Lord the kingdoms of the world and their glory. Now, to go no further than this expression, the 'glory' of the kingdoms of the world which he showed, of itself points to a kingdom, not of self-denying love, but of splendid dominion, and thus to a mere outward kingdom. Besides, Satan appears here as the prince of the world,[2] and offers to transfer to Christ his sovereignty over it. Now such a kingdom as *he* could possess[3] and offer, must from its very nature have been a merely earthly, external, *ungodly* kingdom. A sovereignty received from Satan could only be one opposed

---

[1] Bleek in a MS. communication.
[2] Κοσμοκράτως. See John viii. 44, xii. 31; Eph. ii. 2, 6, 12; and other passages.
[3] Luke iv. 6.

to the dominion of the true kingdom of God; and he who could desire such a sovereignty must have been willing to enter into a league with the devil, and render him homage. In the idea of worshipping the devil, viewed in itself, there could be nothing alluring, nothing tempting; and if the evangelical record brings prominently forward the proposed homage of our Lord to Satan, it can only be because there was something to be obtained by this homage which might prove attractive and ensnaring; and this was the world-dominion which was in this way to be attained.

The dominion of the world is thus the great object here presented by the devil, but at the same time he states what is the only way whereby it could be gained. And the way is unquestionably bad, for it is by subjection to the prince of the world. And in rejecting it, which He does by a reference to the great truth, that to God alone, the LORD of all, are homage and worship due, Jesus at the same time renounces the object which could only thus be arrived at. We see, then, that in this temptation a kingdom of outward glory is offered to Jesus, as to One, who must in the fullest sense be regarded as destined to be a king. And the whole turns upon the antagonism between a kingdom of the world which could be set up only by the use of worldly means, and the kingdom of God which could be founded only by the total rejection of such means, by the pure worship of God alone.

If we now briefly sum up what has been said, we shall find that in the three temptations the following alternatives were presented. In the first, the use of supernatural gifts for the purposes of sensuous self-love; or a complete entrance upon a life of self-denial, which expects support and strength from God alone. In the second, a presumptuous reliance upon Divine assistance, which, in the consciousness of a special mission, enters upon self-chosen paths of danger; or a pious confiding in God, which shuns all devious, God-tempting courses, and meekly follows in the prescribed paths of duty. In the third, the acquisition of worldly might and glory by means of the world and its prince; or contempt both of this end and the means by which it must be won, for the sake of living only for the service of God, and the establishment of His kingdom.

Having thus determined the meaning of the three temptations, the question now arises as to whom they concern. It may be thought that this is quite a superfluous question, as it is so clearly and emphatically stated that it was Jesus who was the object of the devil's assaults. Yet some have thought otherwise. Some have taken exception to the possibility of Jesus being tempted at all, others to the particular form of temptation recorded in the Gospel. Consequently they have regarded the alternatives expressed above, as intended to form merely a symbolical representation of the fundamental principles of His kingdom,[1] or of certain maxims essential to the usefulness of its members in general, and of the apostles in particular. Now there is a certain amount of truth in this view, inasmuch as whatever belongs to the Founder of the kingdom of God has a typical character, and intimately concerns all its members. But the principal validity and import of the temptation was in reference to Him who was its Founder. If in our treatment of the temptation we pass Him by, and apply the whole immediately to His kingdom and its members, we manifestly put a forced interpretation upon the narrative, and violate the natural sense, not only of this portion of the history of Christ, but also of the whole apostolic Christology.

[1] Pfeiffer especially refers the temptation to the kingdom of the Lord, and the mode of its establishment (*Deutschen Zeitschrift*, 1851, No. XXII.). He makes the three temptations to be: (1) The temptation to satisfy the sensible wants of men, and thus to obtain authority and dominion among them; (2) To set up a kingdom of caprice, of lawlessness and licence; (3) To establish a sovereignty of merely external power.

It being thus apparent that it was Jesus Himself who was the subject of the temptation, the next question that arises is: Was it chiefly as the Messiah, or as a man, that He was tempted? And here, too, opinions are divided. There are still, in the present day, writers who think that the proposals made to Jesus were temptations of a general human character.[1] But it is manifest that these temptations presuppose in the Person tempted a very peculiar character and destiny,—a Person destined and endowed to be the Founder of the kingdom of God. But if there can remain no doubt in the minds of the unprejudiced that the temptation of Jesus was the testing of the Messiah, it is quite as certain—as we have already shown[2]—that there could have been no real and actual temptation, unless addressed at the same time to His human nature. Both sides of His nature must be regarded as concerned in it, if we are to reach a full view of the truth.[3]

Although it was to Jesus Himself that the temptation

---

[1] So Rink, *Deutsche Zeitschrift*, 1851, No. XXXVI. p. 293. He thinks that the more *generally* the temptations are viewed, the more truly and deeply will the idea involved therein be manifested; and in fact he regards them, in the most general way possible, as the temptations of 'the lust of the flesh,' 'the pride of life, and the lust of the eye.'

[2] See above, pp. 134 and 135.

[3] While Rink insists upon receiving the temptation in this general manner, Laufs, on the other hand (in the *Stud. und Kritik*. 1853, 2, pp. 355-386), brings forward too exclusively its Messianic aspect. Giving in this sense an original view of the several temptations, he finds in the first (the changing of stones into bread) the false Messianic notions which obtained among the Jews; in the second (the sway of the world), the false idea of a Messiah in the heathen sense, which was based on the expected alliance of the Messiah with the Roman power; in the third (casting Himself from the temple), the notion entertained that the Messiah's work must begin, in spite of all dangers, at the temple, the theocratic centre of the nation,—and therefore in the midst of the scribes, Pharisees, and priestly officials,—that the capital being thus subjugated, the whole land might be conquered with *one* blow. This view, in spite of its ingenuity, is too far removed from the literal interpretation of the Gospel narrative (especially the answers of our Lord), and by far too artificial, to be entertained.

immediately and chiefly referred, its bearings are not confined to Him. For He is not an isolated individual, but the type of His kingdom and its members: hence this narrative has a more general and typical significance. Considered as a testing of the Messiah, the temptation must be of importance for the kingdom of Messiah, and typical for its members. The principles which the Founder of the kingdom of God opposed to the assaults of the devil, are also the principles of His kingdom, and maxims for the guidance of its members. And these we have seen to be self-denial and devotion to the service of God, and a life sustained by the word of His mouth; a confidence in God which renounces all arbitrary self-will and presumption, and walks in ways appointed by Him; and an unconditional devotion to the service of God, labouring in His strength for the interests of His true kingdom,—a kingdom which is to unfold itself from within.

But since Christ could be tempted as Messiah only in so far as He could be tempted as a man, we must own that this history of His temptation has in it something also of a more general character, and that it must be regarded as typical of the temptations by which men are commonly assailed. Only, there is a distinction to be drawn here. In the case of Jesus, the temptations addressed to Him presuppose certain peculiar personal qualities: the first is based upon His power of working miracles; the second, upon His Divine mission; the third, upon His destination to supremacy. Now these are no common human qualities. Still the first temptation can only be regarded as a common, a universal human temptation, if for the power to do miracles we substitute those God-given faculties which every man possesses, and which every man may either turn to purposes of selfishness and self-love, or use in the service of a higher life. The second temptation can apply more particularly, only to that smaller circle to whom, by reason of great mental endowments or a high position in life, a peculiar mission has been assigned. The third temptation also has a special application only to the very small number who are called to a position of sovereignty. And yet even these two last temptations have a more general application, inasmuch as the sinful inclinations of every man offer—though in other forms—some point assailable to their attack, by means of which he may be led into the sin of tempting God, or cherishing a lust of earthly rule. With regard to the principles put forth by Jesus in opposition to the tempter, it is evident that *these* are of universal application.

We have thus, by an examination of the several temptations in detail, obtained a starting-point for the exposition of the narrative regarded as a whole. Let us, then, proceed to this latter consideration.

CHAPTER II.

GENERAL VIEW OF THE HISTORY OF THE TEMPTATION.

IF commentators have been divided in their opinions concerning the details of this history, we shall find that they differ far more widely in the views which they take of the whole narrative. Here we meet with a graduating scale of expositions, embracing all conceivable diversities, from the spiritualism which regards the history as nothing more than a figurative mode of inculcating doctrine, to the realism which receives every word in its most literal acceptation. We may, however, make a general division of the various explanations into two principal classes: the first consisting of those according to which the whole narrative is a mere product of thought, having no basis in actual facts; and the second, of those in which an actual historical substratum is recognised, which allow this passage to be the record of a real temptation to which Jesus was actually subjected. For the reasons adduced in our treatise, we take up a decided position on the latter side of the question. We must, however, consider somewhat particularly the explanations of the former class, in order, by a brief refutation of these, to prepare the way for that view which appears to us the true one.

Sec. 1.—Explanations which represent the whole Narrative as a mere Product of Thought.

If that portion of the Gospel history which we are now considering is to be regarded as nothing more than a mental creation without any objective historical foundation, two suppositions are conceivable with regard to its authorship: it may have originated with Jesus Himself, or it may be the production of others. In the *former* case it would be a figurative doctrinal discourse delivered by Jesus,—a parable, having for its object to bring vividly before the mind of His disciples certain principles of His kingdom, and certain fundamental maxims to guide them in their work of establishing that kingdom. On the *latter* supposition it is to be regarded simply as a myth,—a tradition, which arose from the tendency to glorify Christ as the conqueror of evil and the evil one. Let us test these opinions.

The view which regards the passage as a parable, has, as is well known, been supported in modern times by names of no small importance.[1] It is however worthy of note, that

---

[1] Schleiermacher, *Kritischer Versuch über die Schriften des Lucas*, p. 24 ff.; Baumgarten-Crusius, *Bibl. Theol.* § 40, p. 303; Usteri, *Theol. Stud. u. Kritiken*, 1829, No. III. pp. 456–461; Hase, *Leben Jesu*, § 48, pp. 85, 86. Hase, however, admits an actual temptation of Christ; only he holds that

the theologian who has most explicitly and fully defended this view, has himself seen cause to renounce it, and has adduced against it most important considerations.[1] Regarded in itself, there is nothing objectionable in the notion that Jesus should have prescribed to His disciples, at the beginning of His course, fundamental maxims for the guidance of their labours on behalf of the kingdom of God,—namely, that they were to work no miracles for their own personal advantage; that they were not to tempt God, or (according to another view) that they were to do nothing for the sake of mere ostentation; and, finally, that they were not to found the kingdom of God on external power and glory.[2]

But it is difficult to see why Jesus should have chosen the form of parables to convey to the minds of His disciples these simple rules; and it is altogether inconceivable how these parables should from the first have been so misunderstood by the disciples, that they have come down to us as *history*, and that we cannot discover the slightest trace of a parabolic character about them. This narrative, as it lies before us at the present day, appears as an important event in the life of Jesus; and there can be no doubt that, in the apostolical tradition concerning Him, it occupied a most conspicuous, and even an essential place. Everything in the story relates immediately to Jesus Himself. Nowhere do we find any direct reference to the apostles; and indeed it is difficult to

---

the inner temptation is presented as a parable, and, moreover, that the representation is of a mythical character, because there are unhistorical features in it.

[1] Usteri, *Theol. Stud. u. Kritiken*, 1832, Heft 4, p. 729 ff.

[2] The maxims and dispositions reproved by Christ have been variously stated. Hase views them quite generally, viz. as worldliness, covetousness, and ambition; Karsten (*Mecklenb. Kirchenblatt*, 1837, 1), as selfishness indolently craving miracles, vanity boastfully tempting God, and idolatrous love of the world; Theile (*Theol. Lit. Bl.* 1841, Feb. No. XX.), as abuse of miraculous power, partly for selfish purposes, partly to excite attention, and assumption of political Messianic power.

see what the point of such a reference would have been.[1] Then, surely, if this had been a direct instruction to the apostles, it would have come in more appropriately in the passage devoted to this special subject, viz. among the rules which Jesus gave them to guide them in their ministry.

Besides, the apostles themselves, when this communication was made to them, could not at first have avoided referring it to Jesus, and not to themselves. But so radical and general a misunderstanding would cast a reproach upon the teaching of Jesus Himself; for He must then have presented the thing to them in so unintelligible a way, that they took what He meant to be a parable for actual history. This idea is entirely contradicted by the whole character of His teaching on other occasions. The origin of such a misunderstanding could be no otherwise explained than by supposing that Jesus made Himself the subject of the parable; but this would have introduced from the very first an inappropriate and unintelligible element. For either the introduction of the Person of Jesus had, or it had not, a definite purpose. If the former,—*i.e.* if Christ therein represented Himself as the Messiah who rejected every false principle of conduct,—then the disciples were necessitated to think of some actual occurrence, some real temptation which He had undergone, and then the parable would pass into history. If the latter,— if the Person of Jesus was introduced without any definite purpose,—then it was manifestly unsuitable so to introduce it. For then the parable, being neither wholly history nor wholly allegory, would have produced a vague, unsatisfactory impression of something that was partly the one and partly the

---

[1] De Wette, *exeget. Handb.* 1, 42. All the temptations, together with the maxims expressed by their rejection, lose their full meaning, unless referred to the *Messiah*. This applies more especially to the third, the offered supremacy over the world, and to its refusal, which cannot be applied to the apostles without doing the greatest violence to the narrative.

other,—would have thus been in fact a failure; and this we cannot attribute to the greatest Master of this method of instruction.[1]

The *mythical* interpretation comes next to the parabolic. This has, in modern times, been variously represented. It was first defended by Usteri,[2] who sought to establish it in the following way: The myth is a poetical production, the substance of which is a religious or philosophical idea clothed in a historical garb. The idea thus presented is something eternal, something which existed before all history. In the myth, history, poetry, and philosophy combine to form a truth, which may be merely an ideal truth, without there being any historical reality for it to rest upon. The deeper truth of the temptation consists in the idea that Christ and the devil are in absolute antagonism to each other, are absolutely apart from each other; so that although the devil may assail Christ and seek to tempt Him, Christ lets him have no advantage over Him, and will not yield to his temptations. This idea is presented to us historically as a threefold attempt of the devil to make Christ do evil, on the occasion when Christ, previous to His public appearing, had prepared Himself—after the example of His great models, Moses and Elias—by prayer and fasting for His public ministry. Thus argues Usteri.

His view, however, involves difficulties by no means insignificant. If we allow a præhistoric time in the life of Jesus—though the expression is anything but happily chosen, when its meaning with regard to the heathen myths is considered—still it must be acknowledged that this period ended with His baptism; while the temptation succeeds the baptism,—and this not merely by accident, but of necessity. We

---

[1] Against the parabolic interpretation, compare Hasort, *Stud. u. Kritiken*, 1830, 1, p. 74 ff.; and Strauss, *Leben Jesu*, vol. i. § 51, p. 416.

[2] Usteri in *Theol. Studien u. Kritiken*, 1832, 4, pp. 781–791.

should thus be obliged to own the existence of mythical elements in the history of Christ's public life; and this, apart from other difficulties, would quite destroy the alleged distinction between historical and præhistorical. The Old Testament analogy, which is here adduced, furnishes not a trace of the mythical; for why may not Jesus, as well as Moses and Elias, have *really* retired into seclusion before entering upon His ministry? But the principal consideration is this: It is difficult, on the given explanation, to find any germ of reality in this myth, and to point to any satisfactory connection between substance and form. The idea to be clothed in a historical garb must surely be itself true; otherwise we have no myth, we have a mere fabric of the imagination. Now, what is the idea supposed to be represented here? It is this, that Christ and the tempter are absolutely apart from each other; that although the devil seeks to tempt Christ, Christ will not let Himself be tempted, because to be tempted in a human sense, is contrary to the nature of the Redeemer. But can it be believed that the idea of the absolute impossibility of Christ being liable to temptation should have been clothed in a historical form narrating an actual temptation? Such an idea would certainly lead us to expect an entirely different outward representation, *e.g.* that of an open assault, a violent onset upon Christ on the part of Satan. Further, if the temptation as a fact is contrary to the idea of the Redeemer, it must also as a myth be contrary to that idea. If Christ could not in any wise be really tempted, then the idea of His temptation ought never to have once entered the minds of those who best knew Him. Thus, even in the mythical form, there would be here an error on the part of the apostles,—an error, too, affecting the cardinal point of the Christian religion, the knowledge of the Person of Christ. Finally, although we must say of the supposed fabricator or fabricators of the myth, that for them the devil existed as a real personality, this cannot be said of its present expositor. Hence he is found to give up another considerable portion of the actual myth, and there remain, from his standpoint, only a few meagre and incomprehensible fragments. Nay, the myth is as good as deprived of all meaning; for a tempter who has no existence, and a person tempted who could not really be tempted, do truly furnish the strangest materials for a myth on the subject of temptation! As for the truth that Christ and evil were in a state of absolute opposition to each other, this did not need the illustration of a myth, both because it was self-evident, and because it could be much better illustrated in many other ways.

The mythical view is presented in a more natural form by two other scholars, Strauss and De Wette. From the general point of view taken by the former,[1] he could not have done otherwise than assign a mythical character to this portion of the evangelical history, as well as the rest: besides, this passage seemed to hold out to him certain points, of which he was eager to avail himself, in favour of the correctness of mythical interpretation in general, because here several parallels might be brought forward from the Old Testament. According to Strauss, the essential purport of the myth of the temptation is to show that the Messiah, as the Head of all just men, and the Representative of the people of God, must of necessity have been tempted in like manner as the principal men of God in Old Testament antiquity, *e.g.* like Abraham, and like the people of God, especially during the march through the wilderness. De Wette,[2] while at the same time attending to various points of detail, expresses himself similarly with regard to the general import of the myth. He deduces therefrom, that 'Satan is the enemy of

---

[1] Strauss, *Leben Jesu*, vol. ii. § 52, pp. 417–428, 1st ed.
[2] De Wette, *Exegetisches Handbuch*, i. 42, 43.

the Messiah and of His kingdom; and that the former, being subjected to the moral conflict,[1] had necessarily to contend with him, not only during the whole course of His agency,[2] and at the close of His life,[3] but also at His entrance upon His ministry; that as the accuser of men had proved Job, so did he prove the Messiah also; and that he did this at the first by the pleasures of the world, and at last by its terrors.'

These expositors have this advantage over Usteri, that the temptation of Christ, being in their view not absolutely inadmissible as a fact, may naturally be allowable as an idea. Hence they far more simply make the purport of the myth to be, the tempting of the Messiah by Satan, not a conflict with Satan. Moreover, the story takes a much more natural form in their hands, from their method of defining the conception of the myth, and of applying it to the evangelic record. But hence arises, it must be confessed, another and a greater difficulty, affecting the general view of the evangelical history, especially in so far as that is taken up with the public and Messianic life of Jesus. If this be entirely mythical, with the exception of a scarcely definable minimum of fact, if it be even in most instances interfused with mythical elements, then undoubtedly the temptation is one of those parts which offer the least resistance to a mythical interpretation. It is unnecessary, however, after the elaborate discussions to which this mythical view of the Gospel narrative in general has been subjected, to show here the difficulties to which this theory is exposed, and how it leaves the existence, not only of the Christian Church, but even of the Christian faith, an utterly unexplained enigma; nay, is utterly at variance with these undeniable facts. If, on the contrary, we find that the evangelical record rests in the main upon a historical foundation, the necessity then arises of establishing the historical basis also of the separate parts of that

---

[1] Heb. iv. 15.   [2] Matt. xiii. 39.   [3] John xiv. 30.

record, even those which are surrounded by most difficulties. And so long as this can be done for the narrative of the temptation in a satisfactory way, we, who firmly maintain the fundamentally historical character of the Gospel history in general, shall not see ourselves necessitated to have recourse, in this instance, to the mythical explanation.

Sec. 2.—*Explanations which recognise a Historical Basis of the Narrative.*

The explanations according to which our narrative records an actual occurrence may be divided into two classes. First, there are those which regard the event related as something which took place inwardly in the soul of Jesus; and those which regard it as something external, as an actual transaction between the Lord Jesus and the tempter. Now, certain as it is, that if a real temptation took place, we shall be constrained to suppose also an actual agitation in the soul of Jesus; yet the idea of a *purely* internal occurrence by no means comes up to the meaning of the evangelists. We shall thus be necessitated to acknowledge that there was something really objective in the transaction. But before proceeding to make this more evident, we will briefly test the opinion that the temptation was only of a spiritual and internal character.

This view appears in three different forms. The event internally experienced may be regarded either as a vision or as a dream, or it may be viewed as the sum-total of certain seductive thoughts which came before the mind of Jesus when in a state of perfect consciousness. Each of these different possibilities has been adopted; but with so little success, that we need not devote much space to their discussion.

The idea of a *vision* or *ecstasy* introduces an element of fancifulness and extravagance entirely opposed to all that we read elsewhere of the clearness and self-possession which characterized the enthusiasm of Jesus, subjects Him to an alien and evil power, and is entirely without analogy in the rest of the Gospel history. Besides, this view makes the evil and seducing images arise from the soul of Jesus, and thus represents that soul itself as defiled. This applies also to the *dream* hypothesis.[1] It is true that analogies for this may easily be found in Bible history, though such significant dreams as may be adduced will be found to present an entirely different character, and always to be decidedly defined and limited as dreams, while in the present narrative there is nothing to indicate where the supposed dream begins and where it breaks off. Besides, a temptation in a dream is virtually no temptation; for consciousness and self-control enter into the very notion of the testing and proving of any man. If the conflict was dreamt, so was the victory; and thus the narrative loses all its meaning.

Among the interpretations which belong to this category, the one which appears most plausible is that which represents the whole occurrence as a *mental* one, experienced, however, neither in a state of dream or ecstasy, but undergone in a condition of *full consciousness.* According to this view, the whole stress must be laid upon the testing of the Messianic character of Jesus, and it must be supposed that He, before entering upon His public ministry, vividly realized the false and carnal idea of the Messiah which was prevalent in the world around Him; and yet, notwithstanding the attractions it presented, both sensible and spiritual, entirely rejected it, and decided upon a life of activity in the way appointed by God. This inward experience Jesus is supposed to have afterwards communicated to the disciples

---

[1] See Meyer, *die Versuchung Christi als bedeutungsvoller Traum; Theol. Stud. u. Krit.* 1831-32, pp. 319-329.

in the more intelligible form of an outward objective and personal temptation, in which He holds up to their view the process of thought through which He passed. In this form His communication forms a component part of the evangelistic record of Jesus as the Messiah.[1]

In support of this view, there may be quoted from Scripture objective representations, whose character is, in like manner if not in equal degree, symbolical; and reference may be made to the fact, that inward experiences have always and everywhere been presented in a figurative form as outward facts. It must also be admitted that this explanation allows of a higher degree of actual temptation than do those above referred to. And yet it has great defects, and cannot be regarded as in any way exhaustive of the meaning of the text. It is not enough to confine the trial to the Messianic character of Jesus. We must, if the temptation is to be a real one, keep in view also His general human nature. Besides, without destroying the Gospel image of Jesus, we cannot concede that the temptation arose only from His own soul. It must have come to Him from without,—from a real, objective source. Thus only can the meaning of the Gospel narrative be preserved, for this would never have intended to symbolize, by the person of Satan, thoughts which arose from the soul of Jesus; and in our explanation of the whole, we must not do violence to this intention of the evangelists.

If, then, we accept the narrative of the evangelists simply as it lies before us, it will appear indisputably evident that what we have to do with here is an external event, which, however, from its very nature, powerfully affected the soul of Jesus. Further, the idea of the evangelists is evidently that of a *personal* tempter acting upon Jesus from without, in order to seduce Him from the path which was pleasing to God, and especially from that way which, as Messiah, God

[1] Compare Hocheisen, *Tübinger Zeitschrift*, 1833, 2, p. 124.

had ordained for Him to walk in. Some who have acknowledged this, but who at the same time have disliked the idea of the tempter having been the devil, have endeavoured to substitute for him some *human tempter*,[1] whether an individual or a body of men, and have imagined that it was by a priest or a Pharisee, or by a deputation from the Sanhedrim, that the seductive propositions were made to Jesus.[2] But the simple words and meaning of Scripture preclude such an idea. Occurring without the article, the word διάβολος might mean a *tempter* generally, whether human or otherwise, but with the article it can only be understood of the chief of evil spirits; and the same is true of πειράζων with the article. Besides, in the mouth of a *man* these temptations would be strange, preposterous, inadmissible, especially the demand to be worshipped, and the promise of dominion conjoined therewith. In a word, this explanation is so little

[1] This opinion is supported at length in the above-cited article of the *Tubingen Quartalschrift*.

[2] Lange has attempted a very peculiar combination in his *Leben Jesu* (Pt. i. vol. ii. § 7, p. 205), a book in which so many ingenious theories are advocated. On the one hand, he agrees with those who view the transaction as an internal temptation of Jesus, resulting from the national and secular spirit, especially the prevalent and false Messianic notions of the age. At the same time, he insists that this influence was brought to bear upon Him by means of certain external temptations. It is in the deputation of the Sanhedrim to John the Baptist (John i. 24) to demand an explanation of His nature and office, that he finds the connecting link between the external and the internal. This deputation, having their attention directed to Jesus by the Baptist, he supposes to have sought Him in the wilderness, and to have made the attempt of gaining Him over to their own hierarchical aims. Thus this hierarchy, with their seductive proposals, form only the prominent historical feature of the occurrence, and are the outward instruments of a temptation which, in its deeper source and its whole contrivance, we cannot but regard as satanic (see note on p. 219). This combination gives just prominence to the fact that the transaction must not be regarded as a *merely* external one, because if there was to be a real temptation, there must be an entrance of the seductive ideas into the soul of Jesus. But if we maintain an objective seducing power, this entrance of ideas must be called the *subjective* aspect of the temptation, and not be distinguished as an internal from an external

in accordance with the view of antiquity and the spirit of Scripture, that it ought to be entirely dismissed as the heterogeneous production of modern opinion.

Accordingly, nothing remains to us but to understand the tempter to be Satan, as the evangelists represent. And then we have the following alternative presented to us: either we must deny the historical credibility of the Gospel account, and regard the whole as a myth; or, admitting its trustworthiness, we must take the record as it is given us, and endeavour to render it intelligible. When we reflect upon the entire character of the Gospels and their contents, as well as upon those expressions which on other occasions fell from the lips of our Lord Himself, we have no hesitation in deciding upon the latter alternative, and shall accordingly, without any pretension to exhaustive argument, make a few remarks on this view of the subject.[1]

temptation. Besides, there is no actual ground for supposing with Lange, that the external element was furnished by the Pharisaic deputation to John, for we are left without the slightest allusion to any intercourse between Jesus and the Pharisees in this respect; while if the interview in question had really taken place, it would have been of so far greater importance than that with the Baptist, that it could scarcely have been passed by unnoticed in the Gospel history. And, lastly, such a view of the narrative of the temptation is anything but in keeping with the whole tenor of the narrative; the notion especially of a plurality of tempters is entirely at variance with the representation of the single agency of Satan.

[1] The view of the whole as a temptation by Satan in person is defended by Olshausen, *Biblical Commentary*, vol. i. p. 169 (Clark's For. Theol. Lib.). His explanation, however, can scarcely be considered a strictly literal one, since he admits only an internal influence of the devil, and that only upon the soul of Christ, while His spirit remains unaffected thereby. The supposition that Jesus was during this occurrence deserted by the Divine Spirit, must be rejected as being contrary to Matt. iv. 1. Another advocate of the literal interpretation, though in a somewhat extraordinary position, is D. Paul Ewald (*die Versuchung Christi*, Bayreuth 1838), answered in the *Theol. Lit. Blatt.* Feb. 1841, No. XX. Finally, we may also mention Ebrard, in the *Wissenschaftl. Kritik.* p. 298, who maintains without further explanation the visible appearance of Satan; and Briggenbach (*Leben Jesu*, pp. 275, etc.), who treats this very question at greater length.

Against the personal appearance of Satan the following objections have been urged—not to mention the general scruples entertained against admitting his existence at all, which have unmistakeably influenced those who have advanced them. The bodily appearance, or speaking of Satan, it is said, is never elsewhere mentioned in the New Testament. His personal appearance, even if disguised in a human form (to which the text makes no allusion), must at once have taken from the temptation all its attractions; for the Son of God must have recognised him at a glance.[1] Besides, if we are to take the narrative in its strictly literal sense, many other difficulties arise which it is by no means easy to set aside. If Jesus followed the devil willingly to the mountain and to the pinnacle of the temple, then the will of the devil determined His will; if against His will, then was He in the power of the devil, in a manner which we cannot possibly admit. Again, are not the temptations of too gross a nature to have been suggested by the subtlest of spirits? And how is the showing Him all the kingdoms of the world to be understood? Here at least we must depart from the literal interpretation; and if here, where are we to stop?

These and similar questions might be raised in goodly number; and in truth they cannot all be so answered as to remove every difficulty. We must not forget that we have here to do with a subject about which, from its very nature, there must ever hang a certain amount of obscurity. Our general answer is as follows:—Without entering at present upon inner and weighty reasons whose discussion would lead us too far from our more immediate object, we cannot but admit that a belief in a kingdom of evil spirits, and a ruler thereof, as well as of the influence of both upon mankind, is an important part of the teaching of our Lord and His apostles. This is too expressly laid down to allow us to

[1] De Wette, *Exeget. Handbuch*, i. 87.

suppose that the expressions of the New Testament on this subject are used merely in deference to contemporary notions and expressions, or that they are to be regarded as, in any sense of the word, a mere accommodation. Whoever, then, receives the doctrine not merely of the apostles, but especially of Jesus Himself, must receive this portion of it along with the rest. Now, if the existence of the devil and the possibility of his influence over men be admitted, the fact that he actually tempted our Lord also, far from presenting insuperable difficulties, will rather possess a peculiar significance. And its significance consists not merely in what has been already referred to,—viz. that Jesus, in conquering Satan, proved Himself victorious over the principle and the power of evil in general,—but further, in the consideration, whose full meaning is first fully brought out by this narrative, that 'it was a *personal will* which Jesus repelled and conquered.'[1] Undoubtedly there are temptations which come from things or from persons, without their conscious will. But where, as in the case before us, there is temptation in a pre-eminent degree, we shall find ourselves obliged to admit that the seductive influence does not proceed from an unconscious agent, but from a determined *purpose* to lead astray,—from the will of the tempter. And to this the evangelical narrative makes express allusion.

Now, if we admit this, we shall have to understand the case as the narrative presents it to us. In other words, even though we maintain the historical character of the narrative, we yet distinguish very decidedly between a recognition of its *essential reality* and a *literal* interpretation of every detail. It is evident that the narrative *cannot* be taken in its strictly literal sense, as is indeed proved by the one fact that there is no mountain from which all the kingdoms of the world can be seen. There is undoubtedly *somewhat* of a symbolical

[1] Martensen's *Christliche Dogmatik*, § 105.

Different Views of the Temptation. 291

character in the manner in which the facts are represented.[1] Pictures are here held up to the imagination,—powerfully drawn and significant pictures,—in order to impress upon it as strongly as possible the fundamental truths of the history. Hence it happens that to modern taste the temptations appear coarse and unskilful. That they have, nevertheless, a very important meaning, and are in perfect keeping with the circumstances in which our Lord was then placed, has, we hope, been sufficiently shown by our previous exposition. The visible appearance of Satan, and the different situations in which Jesus is presented to us with regard to him in the different temptations, may, however, partly belong to the symbolical part of the history. At least, without doing any violence to its substantial truth, we may easily conceive that the agency employed was of a more spiritual nature than the letter of the narrative describes, and that those mental experiences, for which it was impossible to find any adequate expression in words, were delineated in that manner in which alone they could be generally understood, viz. in a series of powerful and striking pictures, which suggest even deeper truths than they exhibit.

[1] Comp. Neander's *Leben Jesu*, fifth ed. pp. 113 and 122 (Eng. Trans. in Bohn's Lib. 1852, pp. 74, 77).

INDEX.

I.—PASSAGES OF SCRIPTURE ILLUSTRATED OR EXPLAINED.

Genesis iii. 6,	Page 138	Luke xv. 15, 18,	Page 26
Deuteronomy vi. 16,	270	xvii. 21,	235
viii. 3,	267	xviii. 19,	153-156
1 Kings xix. 8-15,	50	xix. 41-44,	120
Isaiah ix. 6,	57	xix. 45-48,	148
liii. 2,	191	xxii. 39-47,	140
liii. 9,	46	xxiii. 46,	143
Psalms xxii. 1,	142	xxiii. 47,	42
xlv.	191	xxiv. 28,	156
xci. 11,	270	John i. 31-33,	67
Matt. iii. 13-17,	70	ii. 14-18,	148
iv. 1-10,	130-138, 265-291	iii. 11,	187
viii. 28-34,	148	iv. 34,	268
xi. 28,	235	vi. 15,	119
xi. 29,	59	vi. 64, 70,	151, 152
xv. 18,	20	vi. 68,	186
xix. 17,	153-156	vii. 8-10,	156
xix. 27-30,	120	viii. 46,	71-77, 209
xxi. 12-17,	148	x. 16,	236
xxi. 17-22,	146	x. 30,	80
xxii. 21,	235	xiii. 36,	235
xxiii. 19,	235	xiv. 6,	79
xxv. 40,	238	xiv. 9,	80
xxvi. 36-47,	140	xiv. 19,	198
xxvii. 19, 54,	42	xiv. 27,	51
Mark v. 1-20,	148	xvi. 9,	27
x. 18,	153-156	xvii. 3,	211
xi. 11-26,	146	xvii. 21,	239
xi. 15-19,	148	xvii. 24,	240
xiv. 32-43,	140	xviii. 37,	60
Luke i. 15, 32,	47	xx. 22, 23,	71
ii. 41, 42,	145	xxii. 21,	235
iv. 13,	139	Romans v. 19,	61
viii. 26-39,	148	vi. 23,	28
xi. 9,	235	viii. 3,	126

Romans viii. 7,	Page 26
xiv. 23,	27
2 Corinthians v. 17,	84-86
Galatians ii. 20,	86
v. 21,	126
Philippians ii. 8,	61
Hebrews iv. 15,	135, 144
v. 7,	144
v. 8, 9,	61
Hebrews vii. 26, 27,	Page 231
ix. 12, 26-28,	231
James i. 14,	128
i. 15,	21
ii. 8-10,	22
iv. 12,	25
2 Peter i. 4,	245
1 John i. 8,	72

II.—SUBJECTS AND AUTHORS.

Ackermann quoted, 217.
Action and suffering combined in Jesus, 57.
Adam, the second, 203, etc.
Agony of Jesus in Gethsemane, 140-142.
Ἁμαρτία, import of the word, investigated, 72, etc.
Ἀναμαρτησία and ἀναμάρτητος, the meaning of the words, examined, 99.
Apollinaris, his Christology, 256.
Apollonius of Tyana, and Jesus Christ, 98.
Apologetics, the aim of, 4, etc.
Appearance, the physical, of Jesus, 190, etc.
Athanasius holds both the true humanity and sinlessness of Jesus, 256; seems to assume the sinlessness of other human individuals besides Jesus, 201.
Atonement of Jesus by His sacrificial death, 222.
Autonomy repudiated, 23.

Baur quoted respecting Apollonius of Tyana, 98.
Bretschneider referred to respecting the *anamartesia* of Jesus, 66.

Calling of Jesus, the, 49.
Centurion, the, his testimony to Jesus, 42.

Character of Jesus, import of the idea of the, 63.
Christianity, its nature, 4; how to be vindicated, 3-7, etc.; its effects in the domain of morals and religion, 81; new life of, in its religious and moral aspects, 83-90; combines the elements of morality and religion, 90.
Christology of Apollinaris, 256.
Church, the Christian, founded by Christ, 232-239; His kingdom, 246.
Church of the Middle Ages pressed Christ into the background, 259.
Cicero quoted respecting Socrates, 54; respecting the impossibility of finding a wise man, 97.
Condescension, the, of Jesus, 48.
Consciousness of Jesus of His own sinlessness, 77-81.
Creative Divine influence in the origin of the personality of Jesus, 164.
Cross, the sufferings of Jesus on the, 142-144.
Cursing the fig-tree, Jesus, 146.

Daub's conception of Judas, 150.
Death of Jesus, the, a true sacrifice, 222.
Demosthenes, *De Corona*, quoted, 99.

Desertion by the Father, Jesus' sense of, 142.
Development of the Person of Jesus, 109, etc.; does not necessarily involve antagonism with sin, 110, etc.; of Jesus perfectly normal, 110, 111; opposed to everything unnatural and monstrous, 111, 112.
Devil, the, who tempted Jesus, 287.
De Wette quoted, 75, 76, 163, 279, 282, 289.
Διάβολος, 287.
Divine nature of Jesus viewed in relation to His sinlessness, 196.
Doing and suffering, their relation in the life of Jesus, 57.
Dream, the temptation of Christ not a, 285.
Duty not the principle which regulated the actions of Jesus, but love, 16.

Ego, the, becomes the centre of life to fallen man, 27, etc.
Epictetus asserts the impossibility of moral stainlessness, 99.
Error in knowledge and fault in life, their connection, 183.
Eternal life, the sinless Jesus the pledge of, 239, etc.
Example superior in power to law, 213, etc.
Example of goodness, why a belief in, is not universal, 216.
Example of Jesus, its significance for us not destroyed by holding the Divine formation of His personality, 165.
Experience, arguments drawn from, against the sinlessness of Jesus, examined, 160-169.
Evidence, moral, however strong, may be resisted, 37; this true in relation to the evidence for Christ's sinlessness, 37.

Faith in humanity and God, 161, etc.
Faith necessary on man's side to enter into fellowship with Jesus, 230, etc.
Faith and love due to Jesus, 250.
Fathers of the Church, the older, their views of the physical appearance of Jesus, 191.
Fellowship of men, a true, formed by Jesus, 232.
Fig-tree, Jesus cursing the, 146.
Finiteness of Jesus, the, involves no sin nor guilt, 167.
Founder of the Church, Jesus the, 232-239.
Freedom, moral, an indestructible attribute of human nature, 164.
Free-will resident in a moral personality, 16.
Fulfilling of the law, love the only real, 26.

Gethsemane, 140-142.
God the centre of life to man, 27.
'Good, none but One,' 153-156.
Goodness, the image of, in Jesus, 218.
Goodness, the example of, why not the object of universal belief, 216.
Gospel portraiture of Jesus, 47-69.
Greatness of Jesus, 47; serenity of, 50, etc.

Harmony of the life of Jesus, 50, etc.
Hase's *Life of Jesus*, as to the plan of Jesus, 115, note, 116, note; as to the supposed struggle of Jesus with error, 117, note; as to the infallibility of Jesus, 185; as to the temptation of Jesus, 278.
Hasert quoted, 141.
Heathen world, under the dominion of nature without a consciousness of sin, 85; viewed in relation to piety and morals, 92.
Hercules, parallel between Prodikus' story of, and the two

ways, and the temptation of Christ, 139.

Hippolytus first uses the word ἀναμάρτητος in reference to Christ, 255.

Hocheisen quoted as to the supposed parallel between the temptation of Jesus and that of Hercules, 139.

Holiness, innocence, and freedom from sin, how distinguished, 34, etc.; embraces morality and religion, 90-93; as a quality of man and an attribute of God, 91; viewed in relation to heathenism and Judaism, 92, etc.

Homer quoted, 48.

Human, the universally and the individual, united in Jesus, 52-55.

Human nature of Jesus, 182.

Humanity, the idea of, 174; realized in the sinless One, 176.

Humility and majesty of Jesus, 59, etc.

Humility, as an attribute of Jesus, does not imply sinfulness, 167.

Idea of the character of Jesus, its value, 63; not the idea of, but the fact, has influenced the world, 94-106.

Idea, the moral, arguments drawn from, against the sinlessness of Christ, examined, 169, etc.

Idea, the Divine, of humanity, 174.

Image of goodness in Jesus, all-comprehensive and intelligible, 218.

Impeccability and sinlessness, the difference between, 34.

'In Christ,' 231.

Individual, the, and the universally human, united and reconciled in Christ, 52-55.

Infallibility, the necessary result of moral perfection, 183, 184; this applied to Christ Jesus, 186, etc.

Inferences from the sinlessness of Jesus as to His human nature, 182, etc.; in respect to His Divine nature, 196, etc.; in regard to His relation to mankind, 207, etc.

Jesus, personally viewed, the idea whence the vindication of Christianity must proceed, 7; the influence of His image on the heart, 12; possibility of sin in, 34; His sinlessness may be denied, yet believable, 37; testimonies borne to His sinlessness by men of different characters—Pilate, Pilate's wife, 42,—the centurion, 42,—Judas, 43, — apostles and apostolic men, 45; His moral greatness, 47, etc.; condescension, 48; a religious and moral personality, 49; harmony of His life, 50, etc.; relation of the individual to the human in the person of, as to family, nation, and humanity, 52-55; His self-reliance, 56, etc.; union of doing and suffering, 57; humility and majesty, 59, etc.; obedience to the Father's will, 61, etc.; love to man, 61, etc.; beauty of the portrait of, 63, etc.; impossibility of inventing such a character, 64, etc.; His sadness—its cause, 121; His temptation, 123, etc. (see Temptation); His agony in Gethsemane, 140, etc.; His sufferings on the cross, 142, etc.; His relation to Judas, 149, etc.; His physical appearance, 191, etc.; as a teacher, 186, etc.; as a worker of miracles, 194, etc.

Jesus, the Gospel portraiture of, 47, etc.

Jesus, His self-testimony to His sinlessness, 69-81.

Jesus, His relation to mankind,

207; as the personal revelation of the nature and will of God, 209; as the Mediator between God and sinful man, 219-232; as the founder of the true fellowship of men, 232-239; as the pledge of eternal life, 239-247.

Judaism, the consciousness of sin in, 85; character of its conception of holiness, 92.

Judas, his testimony to Jesus, 42; relation of Jesus to, 149-153.

Josephus' testimony to Jesus referred to, 41.

Kingdom of Jesus ever set forth by Him as spiritual, 118; not of this world, 235.

Lauf's view of the temptation of Jesus, 274.

Law, the moral, its nature and origin, 21-25; fulfilled by love, 26; inefficacious in comparison with example, 213.

Life, eternal, the sinless Jesus the pledge of, 239.

Love the fulfilling of the law, 26.

Love to God and man the regulating power of the life of Jesus, 61, 62.

Lücke quoted respecting the sinlessness of Jesus, 76.

Luther quoted, 251.

Majesty and humility of Jesus, 59.

Mediation, its necessity, 228.

Middle Age theologians, their adhesion to the sinlessness of Christ, 257.

Miracles, their apologetic value, 10.

Miracles of Jesus, the mode of their performance, 194, etc.

Mission of Jesus, the, 114; its object, 235.

Mohammed laid no claim to sinlessness, 100.

Monotheistic religions without the idea of sinless holiness in man, 99-101.

Moral idea, the argument drawn from the, against the sinlessness of Christ, examined, 169, etc.

Moral life, the new, in Christianity, 83-90.

Morality and religion united in holiness, 90-93.

Morals and religion, influence of Christianity in the domain of, 81; distinguished, 82.

Müller, Dr. Julius, his *Doctrine of Sin* quoted, 34; on the nature of personal development, 110; on the moral idea, 176.

Mythical view of the temptation of Christ examined, 280, etc.

Nationality of Jesus blended with the universal spirit of humanity, 53-55.

Nature, subjection of the heathen to the dominion of, 85, 92.

Nestorius and Nestorianism falsely reproached with Pelagian views, 201.

Nitzsch quoted as to the ἀσθίνεια of Christ, 126.

Obedience of love, the great principle of the life of Jesus, 61.

Objections to the apostles' testimony to the sinlessness of Jesus examined, 65, etc.

Objections to the sinlessness of Jesus examined — first, His mental and moral development, 109-114; secondly, the development of the Messianic plan, 114-123; thirdly, His temptations, 123, etc.,—temptation viewed as allurement to sin, 135-137,—temptation from sufferings, 139-144; fourthly, New Testament facts, viz.—His apparent disobedience, 145,—His cursing the fig-tree, 146,—permitting the demons to destroy the swine, 147,—driving the buyers and sellers out of the temple, 148,—His relation to Judas, 149, etc.;—fifthly, experience, 160.

Œtinger's *Contributions to the Theology of the Koran* quoted, 100.

Old Testament sacrifices, their nature and design, 223, etc.

Olshausen's *Biblical Commentary* quoted on the human development of the Messiah, 112, etc.; on the call of Judas, 150; on the temptation of Jesus, 288.

Order of the world in the domain of nature, 16; in the ethical kingdom, 17-19.

Osiander quoted respecting the joyousness and sadness of Jesus, 121.

Parable, the temptation of Christ not a, 277.

Πειράζων, the, 287.

Pelagianism, its relation to the Person of Jesus, 200.

Person of Jesus, the, not His doctrine, the source of His influence, 83-84; the centre of our religion, 248.

Personality of Jesus, the religious, 49; formed by Divine creative influence, 164.

Pfeiffer's view of the temptation of Jesus, 266.

Pilate, his testimony to Jesus, 42.

Plan of Jesus, objection to the phrase, 115; not altered, *ibid.*; but ever the same, 115-118.

Plato, his portrait of a righteous man, 96.

Plenipotentiary of God, Jesus the, 147.

Portrait, the Gospel, of Jesus, 47-69; not the creation of the fancy of the early Christians, 64, etc.

Possibility of sin in Jesus, a truth, when rightly understood, 33.

Proof, moral, however strong, may be rejected, 37.

Reconciliation and redemption through Christ, 88-90.

Reformers, the Protestant, their principal merit, 259.

Religion, its basis and nature, 5, 6; and morality distinguished, 82; combined in holiness, 90, etc.

Religious life, the new, created by Jesus, 86; consisting in reconciliation and redemption, 88.

Religious personality of Jesus, the, 49.

Revelation, the sinless Jesus, the personal, of the will of God, 209.

Righteous man, the, Plato's portrait of, 96.

Sacrifice of Jesus, a sacrifice of atonement, 222; the condition of, 224; reveals sin, 226, etc.; awakens sorrow, 227; communicates grace, *ibid.*

Sacrifices of the Old Testament, their nature and design, 223.

Sadness of Jesus, its cause, 121.

Salvation only in Christ, 248.

Σάρξ ascribed to Christ in a good sense, 125.

Satan, who tempted Jesus, how to be viewed, 137.

Schleiermacher quoted, 112.

Selfishness the real essence of sin, 27, 28.

Self-reliance of Jesus, 56, etc.

Self-surrender to God's holy will, man's right relation, 26.

Self-testimony of Jesus respecting His sinlessness—negative, 69-71; positive, 71-81.

Sensuous element, the, in the virtue of Jesus, involved nothing sinful, 166.

Sin, its nature, 14, etc.; a violation of order, 17, etc.; a coming short of the true destination of man, 18, etc.; a violation of moral law which has its root in the Divine personality, 23, etc.; a forsaking of God, 26; selfishness, 27, 28, etc.; its effects—moral blindness, 29, etc.,—destruction of unity, 29,—alienation from men, 30,—destruction of moral fellowship, 30, etc.; the possibility of, in Jesus, when rightly understood, 33.

Sinfulness, and the possibility of sinning, distinguished, 163.

Sinlessness, both negative and positive, 1, 33; influence of the thought, 1; importance of, in relation to apologetics, 3-9; a moral perfection, 35, 36; perfect obedience, 35; perfect union with God, 36; distinguished from impeccability, 34; believable of Jesus, 37; testimony of Jesus to His own sinlessness, 69-81; effects of the belief of, 81, etc.; these effects not produced by an idea, but by a fact, 94, etc.; not invented by the apostles, 102.

Sinless perfection, a tradition of an actual life of, 2; the impression caused by such an appearance, 2, 3.

Sinners, all men are, 202.

Socrates and Jesus, 54, 65, 66, 97, 98.

Sophocles, the pictures of virtue which he presents, 95.

Spiritualism, 94.

Stapfer quoted, 181.

Steudel quoted on the possibility of sin in Jesus, 34.

Strauss, his mythical view of the temptation of Jesus, 282.

Substitute for sinners, Jesus the, 228.

Suffering and doing, the relation between, in Jesus, 57.

Sufferings of Christ, the, in Gethsemane, 140-142; on the cross, 142-144.

Swine, the destruction of the herd of, its bearing on the character of Jesus, 148, etc.

Teacher, Jesus viewed as a, 186, etc.

Temple, the expulsion of the buyers and sellers from the, by Jesus, 148.

Temptation, its relation to evil, 127-129.

Temptation of Jesus, its reality, 124; ground of its possibility, 126; the narrative of, considered in relation to the sinlessness of Jesus, 129; historical character of the narrative of, 131, 132; threefold, 133, 134; its reference to His Messianic character, 134; its reference to Him as man, 134-136; may be viewed as an outward or inward transaction, 136; His moral purity unsullied thereby, 137; exercised no determining influence over His inward life, 138; examination of details of the narrative of, 265-276; explanations which represent the narrative as a mere product of thought, 277-286; explanations which recognise in it a historical basis, 284-291.

Tempter, the, 287.

Testimony of Jesus to His own sinlessness, 69-81.

Union with Christ, 231.

Unity, the, of mankind, secured in Christ, 232-239.

Usteri's view of the narrative of the agony of Jesus in Gethsemane, 140; mythical view of the temptation of Jesus, 280, etc.

Vision, the temptation of Christ not a, 285.

Wandsbecker Messenger, the, quoted on the value of the idea of the character of Christ, 63.

Weber quoted respecting the sinlessness of Jesus, 66.

Weisse quoted on the moral sinlessness of Jesus, 190.

Will of God, the, concerning us, a will of holy love, 26, etc.; the sinless Jesus, the personal revelation of the, 209, etc.

Xenophon's testimony to Socrates, compared with the apostles' testimony to Jesus, 65, 66; quoted, 97.

Young man, the rich, 153-156.

Zeal of Jesus, the, 148.

THE END.

MURRAY AND GIBB, EDINBURGH
PRINTERS TO HER MAJESTY'S STATIONERY OFFICE.

www.ingramcontent.com/pod-product-compliance
Lightning Source LLC
Chambersburg PA
CBHW022050230426
43672CB00008B/1125